THE LEAGUE OF ARAB STATES

A STUDY IN THE DYNAMICS OF

REGIONAL ORGANIZATION

THE LEAGUE OF ARAB STATES

A STUDY IN THE DYNAMICS OF

REGIONAL ORGANIZATION

BY ROBERT W. MACDONALD

PRINCETON, NEW JERSEY

PRINCETON UNIVERSITY PRESS

1965

PREFACE

A GREAT deal of effort has been expended on critical evaluations of the organization and functions of the United Nations, the paragon of contemporary international organization, but similar studies of regional organizations are few. This book, a description and analysis of the League of Arab States, is designed both to contribute to the sparse literature in the field of regional organization and to treat critically a subject that has not received the attention it deserves.

The analytical approach selected for this study emphasizes the structural and operational aspects of the League of Arab States or, as it is generally called, the Arab League. The study is not intended to be a detailed history of the Arab League, and the history of the Arab Middle East since 1945 is considered only insofar as historical detail contributes to the analysis. It is my hope, therefore, that the study will be read and evaluated against a background of general knowledge of the contemporary Arab world. Those who wish to augment their knowledge of the area will find helpful such works as George Lenczowski's *The Middle East in World Affairs* (Cornell), and Hisham B. Sharabi's concise and penetrating *Governments and Politics of the Middle East in the Twentieth Century* (Van Nostrand), among other recent general surveys. A provocative and highly personalized account of regional tensions is available in George Kirk's *Contemporary Arab Politics* (Praeger). However, it is certainly not my intention to extract the discussion of the Arab League from its regional political context. Rather, within the scope of the study, I have tried to analyze and describe its activities in terms of the dynamics of the region.

A regional organization, after all, is something more than the sum of its parts. To insist, as do some casual observers of the Arab League, that national particularisms and intra-regional rivalries destroy the validity of the Arab League's claim to be a regional organization is to misunderstand the problem. The same line of reasoning would result in the dissolution of the United Nations and the Organization of American States. The fundamental approach of this study is that the Arab League—like other regional organizations and the universalist United Nations—exists to provide a means of accommodating these rivalries and national particularisms to a generally accepted urge toward greater peace and security, economic well-being, and social justice. It is a measure of the success of the organization that March 1965 marks the twentieth anniversary of the Arab League.

The purpose of this study, therefore, is to arrive at some sort of judgment of the degree of efficiency with which the organization is approaching its self-described goals of regional functional and political integration. The analysis is carried out by reference to an empirical model of regional organization and a brief review of the background of the Arab League, developed in Part I. The analytical and descriptive portions of the study, Part II (Policy Formulation and Execution) and Part III (The Operational Context), are based on a six-year study of the organization and the functions of the Arab League, including a consideration of the political environment which has at times threatened to destroy the organization. There are, inevitably, limitations inherent in studying the Arab League from the outside, but I hope that this initial effort will at least open the way to other studies of the many facets of the organization and of other regional organizations.

Appreciation and thanks are due many persons for

assistance in preparing this study. Dr. Hisham B. Sharabi, Department of History, and Dr. Roman Debicki, Department of Government, Georgetown University, provided comment and suggestions that materially assisted in the preparation of the final study. Valuable comment on the early stages of the League's development was provided by Dr. Majid Khadduri, School of Advanced International Studies, The Johns Hopkins University.

Dr. Hussein Kamal Selim, the late Director of the Arab Information Center, Washington, D. C., Dr. Jamal Sa'd, the current Director, and Dr. Mohammed Fathallah Khatib, former Director of Research, Arab States Delegation, New York, provided encouragement and material assistance and helped arrange for my visit to the Arab League Secretariat, Cairo, in November-December, 1960. Among the many officials seen at the Secretariat, special thanks are owed Mr. Ibrahim Shukrallah and the late Dr. Mostafa Hosni, then members of the Information and Press Department; to Mr. Waheed ad-Dali, Director, Political Department; and to Dr. Abdel Wahab el-Ashmowy, Deputy Director, Department of Social Affairs.

The documents included as Appendices A, B, and C are used with the kind permission of the Arab League. Three other documents, Appendices D, E, and F, are included with the permission of Muhammad Khalil and first appeared in his *The Arab States and the Arab League: A Documentary Record*, Vol. II (Beirut: Khayat's, 1962).

It is hardly necessary to emphasize, finally, that the development and orientation of the study are entirely my own. The research and most of the writing were completed before I became associated with the government, although the manuscript has been carefully revised to take into account developments within the Arab League through the second Arab summit conference in September 1964.

ROBERT W. MACDONALD

Arlington, Virginia

CONTENTS

CONTENTS

xi

CONTENTS

TABLES AND FIGURES

xiii

PART I INTRODUCTION

CHAPTER 1 THE FRAME OF REFERENCE

THE growth of regional international organizations has been one of the major developments in the field of international organization since the end of World War II. Yet, with the contemporary scene cluttered with "regional organizations" ranging from NATO and the Warsaw Pact to the Organization of American States (OAS) and the League of Arab States, little agreement exists on the organization, objectives, and dynamics of regional organization in the abstract. One purpose of this study is to provide some insight into these matters by a detailed study of one regional organization: The League of Arab States, or Arab League, an international agency established in the early months of 1945 which in 1962 added the thirteenth independent Arab state to its membership roster.

The problem of describing and analyzing the Arab League as a regional organization really becomes two problems simply because there are few authoritative standards against which to judge the operations of any regional organization. The first task, then, is to define a useable set of standards. The problem could be split into three parts, moreover, because some would deny the claim of the Arab League to be a regional organization at all. Let it suffice, however, to declare that the Arab League is a regional organization for reasons which will soon become clear. The problem still remains, nevertheless, of defining and describing—if only in the broadest terms—*regional organization.*

REGIONALISM AND UNIVERSALISM

Before World War II, in Woodrow Wilson's view, at least, the operating principle in international organization seemed to be expressed in the dictum that "there can be no leagues or alliances or special covenants or understandings within the general and common family of the League of Nations." Disastrous experience with regional ententes in Europe certainly seemed to confirm the wisdom of Wilson's precept. Such regional groupings as had appeared were restrictive in nature and aggressive by design. "Regionalism" to many close students of international politics, particularly American, was a synonym for "balance of power." When, in the early stages of World War II, men began to turn their thoughts ahead to the kind of world they wanted afterward, Wilson's dictum served as a sort of shibboleth, marking the difference between the "universalists" and a growing school of "regionalists" among international planning groups.

Practical experience within the League of Nations, on the other hand, had already revealed the problems of maintaining international peace under the aegis of a universal organization. The Draft Treaty of Mutual Assistance of 1923, prepared by the League's Committee on the Reduction of Armaments but never approved by the League's membership, embodied at least the germ of the regional concept, applied to international security. The major characteristic of this Draft Treaty was that the major power in each of several world "regions"—Asia, Europe, North America, Central America and the West Indies, South America, and Africa and Oceana—was to supervise the security of the region. While the Draft Treaty was never implemented, the idea that the major "regional power"—in most cases the European power— was to supervise regional security has persisted as a fundamental concept underlying such recent "regional se-

curity pacts" as SEATO, CENTO, the Warsaw Pact, and
—by an inversion of the power structure—NATO.

Immediately before World War II the League's "Committee of Twenty-Eight" reported that regional security pacts offered a good chance to deter aggression (from outside the region) by insuring that any such act would be met by prompt automatic counteraction from within the region. The working principle was said to be that successful use of a regional body required continuing and sincere efforts to resolve problems before a conflict could arise. This principle, in turn, argued for a permanent body of negotiators for each regional group: bilateral diplomacy would thereby give way to "collective diplomacy." In support of this body of negotiators, a permanent inter-national civil service of administrators and technical experts was to carry on the day-to-day business of each organization.

In a somewhat different context, the concept of regional action was advanced as a basis for "functional integration," or international cooperation in such fields as economics, social and cultural affairs, and science. While this idea seems to have no direct relation to the overriding political problem of regional security, the original advocates of functional integration based their proposals on the theory that war is caused by economic and social inequalities, among other things, and that regional cooperation in these spheres on a *non-political level* would contribute to regional peace—and, thus, to international security.[1] It was this latter concept of non-political functional integration which captured the imaginations of many of the regionalists of the World War II period.

Thus it was that prior to the advent of the Second

[1] For a balanced discussion of "functionalism," see Inis Claude, *Swords into Plowshares*, 2d edn. (New York: Random House, 1960), Chap. 16. The concept of "functionalism" was given its first systematic treatment by David Mitrany in *A Working Peace System*, published in 1937.

World War, the basic approaches to regional organization had been hammered out in draft treaties, committee reports, and scholarly studies. Two divergent approaches could be discerned: (1) regionalism as an approach to international security, by means of an implicit or explicit Great Power hegemony, and (2) regional functional integration by means of intra-regional cooperation in the fields of economics, cultural activities, and social affairs on a level presumed to transcend politics. Though both approaches were designed to limit international conflict, the assumption that "functional integration" transcends politics is demonstrably gratuitous. Nevertheless, the resulting dichotomy between regional security and functional integration carried over from the policy debates of postwar planners of the early 1940's and found its way into the United Nations Charter. Article 13 of the Charter, for example, explicitly divides the purview of the General Assembly between "international cooperation in the political field" (i.e., international security) and "international cooperation in the economic, social, cultural, educational, and health fields" (i.e., functional integration).

In the course of developing these two approaches to regional organization, considerable attention was given to mechanisms by which the universal body—the League of Nations or its successor—would maintain some form of supervision over the activities of the regional agencies. The motivations here were divergent, depending upon the approach to regionalism. Those who favored Great Power hegemony after World War II, including Winston Churchill, posed the problem of a resurgent balance of power complex which failed to satisfy the American planners, dominated by Cordell Hull.[2] The solution ad-

[2] For some details of the ensuing policy debate, see Cordell Hull, *Memoirs*, Vol. II (New York: MacMillan, 1948), pp. 1625-1713 and Sumner Welles, *Time for Decision* (New York: Harpers, 1944), Chap. 10. Walter Lippmann's wartime views on regionalism, which apparently influenced both Hull and Welles at various

vanced, therefore, was that of having the Security Council of the future United Nations supervise regional security activities. The mechanisms for this supervision, though only sketchily defined, were incorporated into Chapter VIII of the Dumbarton Oaks Proposals of 1944 and, subsequently, into the Charter of the United Nations as Articles 52 to 54.

Those who favored the "functional approach" to regionalism, however, sought a different type of relationship with the universal agency, a relationship which would be closer to mutual cooperation. The regionalists emphasized that the universal agency must provide the technological know-how and even financial assistance to support regional functional integration, in the interests of future international security. While the debates at the United Nations Conference on International Organization (UNCIO) clearly demonstrated these opposed points of view, the final version of the UN Charter deals specifically with the security functions of regional agencies and only by inference with the questions of regional functional integration.

The regionalist ideas developed during the prewar period have never been seriously challenged, though shifts in emphasis have been apparent. Regional organizations, therefore, appear to have two essential functions: (1) to contribute to international security, under the general supervision of the universal organization, and (2) to promote regional functional integration, in cooperation with the universal organization.

Perhaps because of the origins of the two concepts, the partisans of the security function have frequently thought in terms of an implicit role for the dominant Great Power. This is at least a partial explanation of

times, are summarized by Anwar Syed, *Walter Lippmann's Philosophy of International Politics* (Philadelphia: University of Pennsylvania Press, 1963), Chap. 5.

the emphasis on continuing control by the UN Security Council and for the later extra-UN "regional security pacts" such as NATO, CENTO, SEATO, and others. According to some of the wartime thinking, each of the five powers enjoying permanent status on the Security Council presumably was to have exercised supervision over regions of interest to it: the United States over Latin America, for example; the British over the Middle East and Africa, etc. But when the necessary harmony between the Powers failed to materialize after the Second World War, the Western Powers tended to act in the same manner but outside the Security Council and under the terms of Article 51—which, significantly, is outside the section of the UN Charter dealing with regionalism.

The attitude of American policy planners toward the role of regional organization in the postwar world was typified by Cordell Hull, who wrote in his *Memoirs*:

"In general, however, we did not oppose regional and other special arrangements supplementary to the general international organization so long as these did not infringe on the powers we thought should reside in the world-wide association of nations. We recognized the freedom of action of small nations to make such regional arrangements among themselves as might be to their mutual advantage. As an example, we viewed with sympathy the plans for an Arab union, particularly in the economic and social field. We had made clear our desire to see the Pan American system of cooperation continued and strengthened in the postwar period as part of the general plan for international cooperation."[3]

But as regarded regional security, Secretary Hull felt that regional arrangements patterned after the inter-American system could be useful in the over-all struggle to maintain world peace only under the aegis of the universal agency. Regional economic and social pro-

[3] Hull, *op.cit.*, p. 1644.

grams were to be encouraged, but only the Great Powers (who, Hull thought, would dominate the United Nations) were to be trusted with security matters. "When a house catches fire," he wrote, "the nearest neighbors hasten there with the common objective of putting out or preventing the spread of fire until the Fire Department, which has been instantly notified, can arrive on the scene."[4]

ARAB VIEWS ON THE FUNCTIONS OF REGIONAL ORGANIZATION AT SAN FRANCISCO

At San Francisco, in the wake of the heady springtime victories by the United Nations forces in Europe, the proceedings of UNCIO soon made it painfully obvious that the smaller nations—with their primary concern for regional arrangements—did not entirely subscribe to the views of the Great Powers. A half-conscious move was already afoot in non-European regions to cast off the remaining vestiges of 19th century colonial empires. Wary of the control of the Security Council by the major powers, the smaller nations sought to define "regional arrangements" as established by Chapter VIII of the Dumbarton Oaks Proposals in such a way that regional security became an *internal* matter and that prepared the path for full-scale functional integration at the regional level.

Among the delegations at San Francisco, two groups of small nations emphasized the importance of sound regional organizations—but always under the aegis of the United Nations: the Latin American states, members of the established Union of American Republics,[5]

---

[4] *Ibid.*, p. 1645.

[5] The Pan American Union is the popular but incorrect name often applied to this predecessor organization of the Organization of American States. The Union of American Republics was founded in 1890 and was represented in Washington by a Commercial Bureau; in 1910 this Commercial Bureau was renamed the Pan

and five Arab states, members of the newly formed Arab League. These delegations sought to formalize the principle of regional representation in the Security Council, a concept originally proposed by Sumner Welles. They tended to emphasize the importance of the proposed Economic and Social Council, the embodiment of the principle of functionalism, and recommended that it be given autonomous status. More significantly, perhaps, they cooperated in an effort to define the functions of the "regional arrangements" mentioned in the Dumbarton Oaks Proposals.

The five Arab League states, acting through the Egyptian delegation, proposed the following definition of regional arrangements for inclusion in the United Nations Charter:

"There shall be considered as regional arrangements organizations of a permanent nature grouping in a given geographical area several countries which, by reason of their proximity, community of interests or cultural, linguistic, historical or spiritual affinities, make themselves jointly responsible for the peaceful settlement of any disputes which may arise between them and for the maintenance of peace and security in their region, as well as for the safeguarding of their interests and the development of economic and cultural relations."[6]

The terms of reference of the definition summed up

American Union. Finally in 1948, a new Charter was adopted reorganizing the inter-American system and giving it the name Organization of American States, with the Pan American Union as its permanent secretariat.

[6] Document 553, II/4/A/9, May 23, 1945, p. 3, in *United Nations Conference on International Organization*, Vol. XII (New York: United Nations, 1946), p. 850. Hereafter cited as *UNCIO*. During UNCIO, the Egyptian delegates frequently acted as the official spokesman for the Arab League states present at the Conference: Egypt, Iraq, Lebanon, Saudi Arabia, and Syria.

the position of the regionalists. In the first place, the definition emphasized functional integration, in the interests of the regional states; regional security became a secondary issue. In the second place, peaceful settlement of disputes and regional security were made the concerns of the regional states. In other words, regional security is an *internal* matter. Such a concept was at variance with the Great Power idea of regional security which alternately prepared for and recoiled from potential conflict between regions. Subsequently, both the Arab states and the Latin American nations sought to revise the draft Charter to provide for UN approval of regional organizations and specific acknowledgment of the two existing regional arrangements: the Union of American Republics and the Arab League.

The major powers failed to support the definition of regional arrangements advanced by the Arab delegations. The attempts of both the Latin American states and the Arab states to win explicit acknowledgment of their existing regional arrangements under the terms of the new UN Charter also failed. In the final analysis, therefore, the Charter is anything but a reliable guide to the question of regional arrangements despite the inclusion of the subject in Chapter VIII (Articles 52 to 54).

Article 52/1 is permissive and emphasizes the role of regional arrangements in "dealing with such matters relating to the maintenance of international peace and security as are appropriate for regional action." The one concession to the regionalist point of view is the requirement that "such arrangements or agencies and their activities are consistent with the Purposes and Principles of the United Nations." By implication, therefore, regional arrangements should not only seek to maintain international peace and security. They should also seek to foster "international cooperation in solving international problems of an economic, social, cultural, or humanitarian character," as stated in Article 1/3, which lists the purposes of the United Nations.[7]

Despite the inability of the Arab states to secure approval of their definition of regional organization, the Arab League has always acted as if this were the true and proper definition. And this fact is of considerable significance in understanding the dynamics of the Arab League in action after 1945. It is also important to recognize the fact that the framers of the Pact of the League of Arab States, themselves all but unknown on the world scene before 1945, were keen students of the trends toward regional organization developed during the interwar era and debated during World War II. Both Egypt and Iraq, in a sense co-architects of the Arab League, had been members of the League of Nations in the last fateful years of that organization. Both countries were represented at the series of conferences in 1943 and 1944—UNRRA, Hot Springs, and Bretton Woods—when some of the framework of the postwar international community was being designed. The Dumbarton Oaks Proposals had been available to the Arab leaders in early 1945, before the League of Arab States had been formally constituted. Moreover, Egyptian political leaders who supported the formation of the Arab League are said to have studied reports on the organization, functions, and operations of the Union of American Republics. By April 1945 when UNCIO met in San Francisco, the Arab delegations were thoroughly familiar with the ideas and plans afoot for reconstituting a world peace organization.

In the years since UNCIO, the question of regional

[7] See Kamāl al-Ghāli, *Mīthāq Jāmi'at al-Duwal al-'Arabīyah* [The Charter of the League of Arab States] (Cairo: Dār al-Fikr al-'Arabī, 1948), pp. 162-163, where the argument is advanced that the *only* condition imposed on a regional organization is that it conform to the aims and principles of the United Nations, as stated by Article 52.

security has become of paramount interest in the context of the Cold War. Under the circumstances, however, the well-known "regional security pacts" like NATO, SEATO, and CENTO—composed of both regional and extra-regional powers—have frequently been hailed as regional arrangements under the UN Charter. That this view is erroneous is a major proposition of this study. A few remarks should serve to reveal the source of the error.

In the first place, all the so-called regional security pacts are based on Article 51 of the Charter, which is *outside* the chapter on "Regional Arrangements." Article 51 invokes the "inherent right of individual or collective self defense" and was clearly designed to permit local action to counteraggression without waiting for the Security Council to act. In point of fact, Article 51 was a concession to the Latin American states to insure them the right of defense against *external* attack, which at the time could only be expected from one of the five permanent members of the Security Council itself.[8] Article 51 is thus in contradiction of the basic premise of regional organization that regional security is oriented toward the pacific settlement of disputes originating *within* the region.

In the second place, Chapter VIII, Regional Arrangements, of the UN Charter, provides that "no enforcement action shall be taken under regional arrangements or by regional agencies without the authorization of the Security Council." And under terms of Article 52/2, the Security Council is to "encourage the development of pacific settlement of *local* disputes" through regional agencies. Only exceptionally is the Security Council to use regional agencies for enforcement action, and then only "under its authority."

[8] For background on this matter, consult Arthur H. Vandenberg, Jr., *The Private Papers of Senator Vandenberg* (Boston: Houghton Mifflin Company, 1952), pp. 190, *passim*.

Finally, Article 54 provides that the Security Council "shall at all times be kept fully informed of activities undertaken or in contemplation" by regional arrangements for the maintenance of regional security. Who in the West would be so foolish as to inform the UN Security Council of NATO contingency plans, for example, when the organization is oriented toward potential aggression from one of the Council's permanent members?

In the concise language of a noted commentator on the subject of regional security pacts, ". . . most of these are directed not to meeting common problems whose ambit is limited by the region, but to defense of the region against attacks from another region. Such arrangements may be justifiable, and indeed indispensable, but that does not make them 'regional arrangements' within Articles 52 to 54."[9] Nevertheless, the irony remains—overemphasis on Article 51 since UNCIO has served to subvert the basic control by the Security Council envisaged by Articles 52 and 54. Even bona fide regional organizations have been led to believe that they cannot qualify as "regional arrangements" under the Charter unless they demonstrate a capacity to protect themselves from external attack. Thus, both the Organization of American States and the League of Arab States have invoked Article 51 in their regional security pacts.

The opposing views of regional security were well understood by the Arab League states participating in the drafting of the UN Charter. The Egyptian delegation, for example, had proposed that the number of non-permanent members on the Security Council—to be elected on a regional basis—be increased. In the face of overwhelming opposition by the Allied Powers, Dr. Badawi, the Egyptian delegate and a noted international

[9] Julius Stone, *Legal Control of International Conflict*, rev. edn. (New York: Rinehart and Co., 1959), p. 249.

legal expert, withdrew the proposal with the biting comment: "The Egyptian delegation hopes that the great powers will, when suitable opportunity arises, revise their opinion and look upon the problem from the point of view of peace rather than from the point of view of war."[10] The regional powers were obviously greatly influenced by the functional approach to peace and just as obviously opposed to the perpetuation of Great Power hegemony over traditional spheres of interest in the postwar world. From the point of view of the Allies, close control over regional security activities by the United Nations was undesirable because it restricted "regional" freedom of action. From the point of the smaller regional powers, *regional cooperation* with the United Nations was both desirable and necessary.

This ready acceptance of close relations with the universal organization—usually combined with a disavowal of the need for regional security mechanisms—is characteristic of regional organizations. This phenomenon has both theoretical and practical foundations. During the interwar period, the League of Nations had provided a point of concentration for international activities of a "technical and non-political nature," thus promoting "the exchange of knowledge and the fruits of experience."[11] Regional agencies with limited resources could profitably draw on this reservoir of experience and knowledge. Theoretically, of course, the application of this experience to "functional problems" of an economic and social character serves to favor the less developed regions, where problems are similar, and permits optimum results

[10] Remarks of Badawi Pasha to the 4th meeting of Committee III (Security Council), June 20, 1945, in U.S. Department of State, *The United Nations Conference on International Organization: Selected Documents* (Washington: U.S. Government Printing Office, 1946), p. 798. Hereafter cited as *UNCIO/State.*

[11] Arthur Sweetser, "The Non-Political Achievements of the League," *Foreign Affairs,* XIX (October 1940), 190.

with minimum political action. The wartime proposals of non-European origin usually envisaged self-development, in concert with the future United Nations, and the eventual extinction of "colonialist" spheres of influence. And, finally, regional agreements and/or functional programs should be carried out "within the framework of a universal system" in the interests of efficiency and harmony.[12]

The urge toward functional integration was demonstrated with great force and clarity at UNCIO by the Arab delegation, often with the support of or in cooperation with the Latin American countries. In this regard, it is worth noting that most of the Great Power delegations to UNCIO were comprised of diplomats, military advisors, legal staffs, and economic advisors; the smaller Arab delegations, while frequently led by ministers of foreign affairs (and one prime minister) tended to be made up of experts from the functional fields and included few military advisors. The Egyptian delegation, for example, included the minister of health and the director general of the Department of Preventative Medicine; in addition to the advisor to the Ministry of Economy, the Iraqi delegation included the assistant director general of Education, the director of the State Agricultural Experiment Station, and an official of the Ministry of Supply; the delegation from Lebanon was headed by the minster of interior and education; the Syrian delegation included the minister of finance.[13]

It was no mere conference oratory, therefore, that prompted the Egyptian delegate to UNCIO to establish the Arab position as follows:

[12] See Wambaugh, "Universal *vs.* Regional System," in Institute on World Organization, *Regionalism and World Organization: Postwar Aspects of Europe's Global Relationships* (Washington: American Council on Public Affairs, 1944), p. 53.

[13] See list of delegations to UNCIO in *UNCIO/State.*

"I would term [organization for collective security] the negative side of the international problem. The positive side, in my judgment, consists in the development of international solidarity and cooperation. . . . [Peace and order] can be more easily attained by promoting cooperation in cultural understanding, by setting a better pattern for international trade and monetary problems and other economic systems, by assisting mankind to a higher standard of living based on the fact that the best conditions for maintaining a high standard in a country is to secure the highest standard possible in the other countries."[14]

The economic and social functions of the General Assembly and the proposals for an Economic and Social Council, Badawi observed, provided proof of this new conception of international affairs. A similar statement was presented by Charles Malik, UNCIO delegate from Lebanon and future president of the General Assembly, on the same day:

"In themselves peace and security are merely formal, derivative, and static. . . . Unless, then, the positive control of peace is determined on a foundation of real justice, there will be no real peace . . . educational and intellectual cooperation among the nations is of the utmost importance. A free exchange of ideas will train the mind in the ways of peace and will bring the nations together. The United Nations can save themselves many wars if they attend properly to the liberal arts of peace."[15]

Action followed the resounding phrases. The Arab states at UNCIO played a leading role, in concert with other small powers, in recommending that the Economic and Social Council (ECOSOC) be regarded as a major

[14] Speech of Badawi Pasha to Third Plenary Session, UNCIO, April 28, 1954, *ibid.*, pp. 287-88.
[15] *Ibid.*, p. 299.

organ of the United Nations.[16] They moved that the functions and powers of ECOSOC should include "the primary responsibility for determining the social and economic policy of the organization."[17] And they proposed that the Council's membership be based on regional interests: "The Economic and Social Council shall consist of twenty-four members. Representatives of the United States, the United Kingdom, the Soviet Union, China, and in due course, France, shall have permanent seats. The remaining seats shall be grouped into nine zones. The General Assembly shall elect two member states to represent each zone for a term of two years, nine retiring each year."[18] Except for the designation of ECOSOC as a principal organ of the United Nations, however, none of these recommendations was approved.

REGIONAL ORGANIZATIONS AND THE UNITED NATIONS

Whether on theoretical or practical grounds, it is apparent that true regional organizations must have a close relationship with any existing world organization. From the point of view of international security, regional organizations are primarily concerned with the maintenance of peace within their own regions. As an arm of the world organization they may thus perform the function of an enforcement agency. Conversely, however, since they are not particularly oriented toward defense from external attack, the regional organizations must depend to a large extent on the collective security machinery of the world organization in the larger context of security. From the point of view of functional integration, regional organizations look to the world organization for accumulated

[16] *Ibid.*, p. 114. Similar proposals were made by Australia, Cuba, Ecuador, Honduras, Venezuela, and New Zealand.

[17] *Ibid.*, p. 213.

[18] *Ibid.*, p. 208. The Philippine delegation proposed that membership in ECOSOC be based on 6 regional zones plus 6 major industrial powers, and 6 agricultural states (*ibid.*, p. 209).

ing with these agencies and the location of the articles in the Charter suggest that they are related primarily to international security and the settlement of regional disputes.

The Arab states, of course, were not alone in the fight for the recognition of a new type of regional organization. The Latin American states conspicuously used every effort to secure recognition of the regional principle, with particular reference to the inclusion of a reference to the inter-American system as one of the "regional arrangements" provided by Articles 52 to 54 of the Charter. One Latin American observer, incensed at the struggle between the regionalists and the "anti-regionalists" and universalists, wrote: "The Latin American nations presented a solid front and, with the cooperation of several statesmen from other regions of the world, achieved one of the most resounding collective victories since the advent of independence."[22]

In addition to the attempt to define the relations between the UN and the regional organizations, the regionalists sought to secure regional representation in the principal organs of the United Nations itself. Although it proved to be impossible to establish a designated system of regional representation in the Security Council, the principle of geographic representation was included in Article 23 of the Charter.[23] A similar attempt to estab-

[22] José Sanson-Teran, *Universalismo y Regionalismo en la Sociedad Interstatal Contemporanea* (Barcelona: Editorial Hispano Europea, 1960), p. 12.

[23] Egypt proposed that the Security Council be enlarged to 14 members including, in addition to the 5 permanent members, representatives of 9 regional zones to be elected for three year terms by the General Assembly. The Latin American states proposed various combinations, usually three, of Latin American members be added to the Security Council; Venezuela proposed the inclusion of three Latin American states and one each from the "Arab Confederation," the British Commonwealth, and Europe. The Philippine delegation proposed representation from 6 geo-

lish regional representation in the Economic and Social Council failed. An amendment proposed by Peru that the Military Staff Committee consult with regional organizations in any future establishment of regional subcommittees was, however, approved and included in Article 47/4. The reference in Article 33 to "resort to regional arrangements" was "part of a compromise worked out at the Conference with a view to integrating regional and global arrangements."[24] But an attempt by Syria to provide for the coordination of discussions on regional social and economic cooperation, as between Committee II/3 and Committee III/4 (Regional Organizations) was defeated by a special subcommittee.[25]

Despite the efforts of the regionalists at UNCIO to secure greater recognition, the final version of the Charter deals very cautiously with the question of regional organizations. Although only security functions are mentioned in Articles 52 to 54, other activities are not excluded. There is no provision for a formal relationship between the United Nations and regional organizations. Regional organizations, however, must be "consistent with the Purposes and Principles of the United Nations." In the case of regional security problems, the Security Council has supervisory authority—particularly when the regional organization is to be used for enforcement actions; otherwise, no provision is made for coordination

---

graphic zones: Europe, Africa, West Asia, the Western Pacific, South America, and Central and North America (*UNCIO/State*, pp. 139-42).

[24] L. M. Goodrich and E. Hambro, *The Charter of the United Nations* (Boston: World Peace Foundation, 1949), p. 242. See also Vandenberg, *op.cit.*, p. 193.

[25] Subcommittee III/4/A, May 15, 1945, found that regional forms of economic and social cooperation fell within the competence of Committee II/3 exclusively. The subcommittee, interestingly enough, was composed of representatives from Australia, Chile, Czechoslovakia, Egypt, France, Mexico, Norway, the USSR, the UK, and the USA. (*UNCIO*, Vol. XII, p. 833.)

of regional activities. Under the circumstances, interpreters of the Charter have resorted to exercises in exegesis to define the relationship between the UN and regional organizations.

About all that can be said with any certainty is that the Charter recognizes as appropriate for regional action: (1) pacific settlement of disputes, (2) enforcement action under the Security Council, and (3) measures against former enemy states.[26] As one authority noted, however, Article 53/1 "does not exclude other purposes suited to regional action," and Article 56, by which "all members pledge themselves to take joint and separate action in cooperation with the Organization" to advance economic and social conditions, can be construed to cover the activities of regional organizations in the functional field.[27] The requirement that regional organizations conform to the principles of the United Nations may be taken to mean that regional organizations are expected to be active in both security matters and functional activities.

Insofar as operational criteria are concerned, it appears that regional organizations must be (1) subordinate to the world organization, (2) in agreement with the principles and purposes of the Charter, and (3) capable of maintaining peace within their zones of interest. They must be made up of independent, sovereign states (Article 1), but members of regional organizations need not be members of the United Nations.[28]

The serious question of the continuing relationship

[26] Articles 52/3 and 53/1; the exception to Security Council control of actions by regional arrangements "directed against renewal of aggressive policy" on the part of former enemy states was inserted by the sponsoring powers over the objection of the regionalists, notably Egypt. (See *UNCIO,* Vol. xii, p. 864).

[27] Hans Kelsen, *The Law of United Nations* (New York: Frederick A. Praeger, 1951), p. 321.

[28] *Ibid.,* p. 85. Kelsen adds, "If a regional organization is considered to be an organ of the UN, non-member parties to regional organizations are indirectly members of the UN."

between the United Nations and regional organizations cannot be solved by exegesis, however, particularly in the field of functional integration which is of primary interest to these agencies. If regional organizations may from time to time come under the direct supervision of the Security Council as enforcement agencies, what is their status at other times? Hopefully, wrote one observer: "In practice . . . the world organization will undoubtedly maintain directly or through its various organs cooperative relations with regional agencies for the purpose of obtaining more effective results through coordinated efforts. Voluntary cooperation in all these [functional] fields between the regional agencies concerned and the appropriate organs of the world organization should be easily established because both will stand to gain from such a close relationship."[29] A stronger stand was taken by another observer in a discussion of regional organization in Southeast Asia who felt that a convention should be signed between the United Nations and the regional organization and that "UN organs should work through regional organizations in all matters within the jurisdiction of the latter." In return, the regional organization would submit regular reports to the United Nations.[30] Logical as this may seem, the Charter envisages no such relationship.

STRUCTURAL PATTERNS IN REGIONAL ORGANIZATION

Regional organizations must develop some sort of legal institutional framework adapted to the general considerations already discussed. As a minimum, the framework should provide for permanence, it should establish the relationships between sovereign states which are mem-

[29] M. S. Caynes, "The Inter-American System," in Panikkar, *Regionalism and Security* (London: Oxford University Press, 1948), p. 73.

[30] K. Santhanan, "Regional Authority for Southeast Asia," *ibid.*, p. 32.

bers of the organization, and it should include adequate machinery to permit effective operations consistent with the objectives of the organization.

The minimum essential condition for permanence is a treaty valid under international law. Beyond this point, permanent institutions may theoretically be provided by a simple alliance, a confederation of member states, or a limited purpose federation. Any further refinement, e.g., establishment of a full-fledged federation or union, would lead to the formation of a new sovereign state, not an international organization. And in practice, of course, a simple alliance implies a more or less transitory organization of specific power factors for a specific purpose, usually oriented toward externally motivated power factors, and therefore does not fulfill the essential condition of internal orientation required of regional organizations. Consequently, regional organizations tend to be either confederations or limited purpose federations.

In either case, states which form or become members of a regional organization must relinquish some of their sovereignty to the organization itself. The degree of sovereignty delegated to the central institutions of the regional organization may, however, vary in degree. The least loss of sovereignty occurs in the case of a confederation. This type of organization depends on voluntary cooperation, good will, and good faith for effective operations in limited fields where political problems are simple. Since coercive powers are denied the organization, in the interests of retaining the maximum sovereignty of each state, this type of organization is inherently ineffectual except in those cases where unanimity of views and purpose obtains. Furthermore, even when unanimity is assured, decisions may be carried out erratically or not at all by the members. Under the circumstances, confederations tend either to transform themselves into federations or to break up into their component parts.

The formation of a complete political federation obviously acts to destroy the regional organization rather than to perfect it. The effort to find a solution to this problem has led to the ideas of the "limited purpose" federation and the "supra-national organization." The basic idea here is that member states surrender certain aspects of their sovereignty almost completely, based on the limited purposes of the central organization. The European Coal and Steel Community, in which the Community derogates certain aspects of the police powers of member states, is an example of a limited purpose federation or a supra-national organization. There seems to be no cogent reason, however, why the same approach cannot be taken to a regional organization. The transfer of effective amounts of sovereignty to the central organization in several areas of mutual interest would not seem to undermine the concept.

The question of basic structure inevitably raises the question of the relations between member states of a regional organization. Since political entities other than confederations and limited purpose federations are more or less automatically excluded from consideration, it follows that the organization must comprise independent, sovereign states—no other political entity could participate effectively—in a treaty relationship. The degree to which sovereignty is surrendered to the treaty organization by each member state is a matter of definition under the terms of the treaty and a function of the purpose of the organization. In general terms, according to Arnold Brecht:

1. member states must limit their freedom of action in foreign policy matters to conform to the purposes of the organization;

2. member states pledge observance of minimum standards of conduct as regards justice, international

security, economic activities, and other technological matters;

3. member states remain free to form confederations among themselves provided the purposes of the organization are not violated.[31]

It must be emphasized that these are minimum conditions. Effective operations require deliberate delegation of sovereignty, if in limited amounts, to regional decision-making bodies. It is not inevitable, however, that the sovereignty of the member states be completely eroded if the transfer is properly controlled. The extent of delegation of sovereignty or, to put it another way, the extent to which normal government functions are "denationalized" is a matter for mutual agreement, starting with the original treaty and continuing throughout the life of the organization. Regional organizations must accept certain limitations and accommodate themselves to a certain amount of internal stress and operational inefficiency so long as they are based on mutual respect for the sovereignty of the members. For once sovereignty is completely transferred, the organization becomes a new sovereign state and ceases to function as a regional organization.

In their basic structures, however, regional organizations tend to be inherently unstable at any given time in proportion to the state of relations between member states and proportional to the balance struck between nationalism and internationalism. If it is true, as one writer has stated, that "regional systems tend to be built around the local great power and thus to take on the character of a solar system," those lesser states with well-defined national traditions will tend to increase or withhold the delegation of their sovereignty—despite the terms of the treaty—as their relations with the regional leader vary.[32] Ostensibly altruistic sacrifices of sovereignty by

[31] See Arnold Brecht, "Limited Purpose Federations," *Social Research*, x (1943), 149-50.
[32] Claude, *op.cit.*, p. 114.

member states of international organizations, particularly in the context of regional organization, may merely motivate the regional leader to embark on an imperialistic venture designed to maintain or influence the status quo in its favor.

Fortunately, however, the peculiar characteristics of regional organizations tend to balance the power factors. The insistence on genuine affinities between members, as illustrated by the Arab League's definition of regional arrangements at UNCIO, is not at all extraneous. One point of view maintains that the development of an appropriate psychological attitude is as important as any other prerequisite of regional organization. Perhaps more fundamental is the argument derived from the basis of natural law:

"Universal internal law exists common to all civilized communities, but alongside this law is particular law applicable exclusively to certain regions of the world. Put otherwise, the historical, geographical, psychological, political, and economic individuality of a region determines a complex of juridical principles unique to the states of this region which derogates in part from the universal law regardless of the extent to which all implicitly recognize the existence and validity of it."[33]

It is therefore possible to postulate that regional organizations are more stable than universal organizations to the extent that their members participate in a given regional culture. Mutual affinities should tend to unite them in cooperative efforts toward common objectives, while intra-regional differentiation tends to put them on guard against a suffocating regional imperialism. A further strengthening of the regional organization may, however, occur with the formation of intra-regional confedera-

[33] Sanson-Teran, *op.cit.*, p. 32 (my translation).

tions, or even federations, by members of the organization.[34]

A final consideration that affects relations between member states of a regional organization is the basis of membership itself. Acceptance of the principle of mutual affinities among members automatically serves to limit membership, regardless of geographical proximity. More to the point: "Regional arrangements . . . more often than not find their origin and justification in a desire for self preservation; it would be contrary to that urge and to reason to say a possible adversary should have the right to obtain partnership."[35] Membership in regional organizations, paradoxically, may therefore be restrictive under certain conditions without violating the principles of regionalism.

Permanent institutions must be established to exercise the delegated sovereignty of the regional organization's members and to execute joint programs determined by the organization's objectives. The operational word here is *permanent*. In general terms, the institutional organization is more or less dictated by the constitutional confederal nature of the organization itself. As a minimum, internal organization should provide for the continuous exercise, during peace and war, of the usual legislative, executive (and administrative), and judicial functions characteristic of the political process. It is, however, impossible to determine the ideal institutional configuration. This will vary, under given circumstances, with the objectives and requirements of the organization itself.

In practice, regional organizations tend to model themselves on the pattern of the League of Nations with a

[34] See Brecht, "Limited Purpose Federation," *loc.cit.* Such subgroups, of course, must be consistent with the objectives of the regional organization.

[35] E. N. Van Kleffens, "Regionalism and Political Pacts," *American Journal of International Law* 43 (October 1949), 669-70.

council of some form (usually incorporating both legislative and executive functions), a secretariat for continuity of administration, and a regional court or quasi-judicial organ for arbitration. After the collapse of the League, some students of regional problems proposed specialized functional agencies with specific executive roles: a defense organ, an economic organ, and/or an organ for intellectual cooperation, for example. At least one authority has suggested that direct access to regional officials should be available to individual citizens.[36] While this has interesting possibilities, the fact that the members of the regional organization are sovereign states would seem to militate against such a relationship except in specific instances. In the experience of the European Community, on the other hand, the selection of delegates to the European Parliamentary Assembly by parliaments of the member states preserves at least a semblance of popular choice. Moreover, the policy of seating members of this Assembly by political coloration rather than by country of origin helps to submerge particularistic nationalism. In the long run, however, the Assembly serves largely as a forum for discussion and exerts only a general guiding influence on the operations of the Community. In the final analysis, the Council of Ministers and the executive organs of the various component organizations exert the real controlling powers, under a system that has moved from unanimous voting to the use of qualified majorities.

On the other hand, as regional problems broaden in scope, it may be more important to provide for a judiciary body with the function both of judicial review of regional legislative and administrative decisions and of arbitration of disputes between members. The European Community has had such a court since 1958. Long-standing plans for regional courts by the Organization of American States

[36] See Brecht, "Limited Purpose Federations," *op.cit.*, p. 148.

and the Arab League have not been implemented, however.

The secretariat, by now an accepted organ of most international organizations, is indispensable in the case of regional organizations. While authorities differ on the role of the secretariat in carrying out executive as well as administrative functions, it is safe to say that the development of the secretariat in recent years has tended to be in the direction of the assumption of greater executive powers since it is normally the only agency in continuous operation. In practice, this trend has been opposed by the member states, which see a real threat to their own sovereignty and, especially, to their control over their own nationals.

Meanwhile the staff of the secretariat tends to become "system oriented," develops increasingly internationalist and functionalist approaches to problems of the organization, and chafes at the seemingly obstructionist tactics of member states—which continue to employ political tactics to gain their own ends within the framework of the organization. The conflict comes to a focus in the person of the Secretary General, who must be both a competent administrator and an astute statesman, since his tenure is determined by the member states themselves. A continual dialogue occurs between the member states and the Secretary General in an effort to maintain the equilibrium and the momentum of the organization.

It is indeed striking that the parameters of organization, function, and relations with the universal organization discussed in this introductory chapter were largely developed in a theoretical context prior to or during the early years of World War II, before any regional organization in the contemporary sense had been established. The close conformity of the Arab League, in principle and practice, to these parameters leads to the inescapable conclusion that influential Arab leaders—or their advisers—were thoroughly familiar with the literature on regionalism available in 1944 and 1945 when the League was organized. In a very real sense, then, as the following chapters demonstrate, the theoretical framework became a guide to action for the Arab League.

THE LEAGUE AND ARAB UNITY

THE chronicle of the formation of the Arab League has been reported too often to need detailed discussion. Nevertheless, a few significant points are worth reviewing, especially those concerned with the question of Arab unity *versus* regional organization since this question continues to obscure the issue.

Just as Arab nationalism had its origin in the dependent Ottoman Arab province of Syria before World War I, so the same area was the locus of a movement toward unity after the "balkanization" following World War I when Jordan, Palestine, and part of Lebanon were carved out of the province. During the early years of World War II, spurred by the abortive anti-British coup d'etat in Iraq in 1941, the British government determined to gain the support of the Arab leaders in Syria, Lebanon, and Iraq by lending its support to some form of regional amalgamation. Foreign Minister Anthony Eden announced the new policy on May 29, 1941, the day after the collapse of the Rashid 'Ali revolt in Iraq. As he spoke, Axis forces were at the Egyptian frontier, and Free French forces had yet to move into Vichy-French Syria and Lebanon. He said, in part:

"The Arab world has made great strides since the settlement reached at the end of the last War, and many Arab thinkers desire for the Arab peoples a greater degree of unity than they now enjoy. In reaching out toward this unity, they hope for our support. No such appeal from our friends should go unanswered. It seems to me both natural and right that the cultural and economic ties between the Arab countries, and the political ties too, should be strengthened. His Majesty's government for their part will give their full support to any scheme that commands general approval."[1]

Within a few days, the British were able to move to support the claims of the Lebanese and Syrians against the French that the former League of Nations' mandates were null and void and that the two countries should be considered independent. The genie was out of the bottle. When no overt moves toward a realization of the long-cherished dream of unity materialized, Mr. Eden repeated his pledge. In answer to a parliamentary interlocution on February 24, 1943, he stated that "so far as I am aware no such scheme, which would command general approval, has yet been worked out."

During the spring of 1943, however, Nuri as-Sa'id of Iraq came forward with a plan calling for immediate federation of Syria, Palestine, Lebanon, and Jordan under the sponsorship of the United Nations.[2] He also pro-

[1] Quoted in his account of the founding of the Arab League by George Kirk, *The Middle East in the War* (London: Oxford University Press, 1953), p. 334. A concise account of the establishment of the League is provided by Majid Khadduri, "Toward Arab Union," *American Political Science Review*, XL (February 1946), 90-100. Kirk gives perhaps too much credit to the influence of a wartime Allied organization for coordinating regional economic programs in the establishment of the League, but see Martin W. Wilmington, "The Middle East Supply Center: A Reappraisal," *Middle East Journal*, VI (Spring 1952), 144-66.

[2] The so-called Blue Book ("Arab Independence and Unity, a Note on Arab Independence and Unity with Particular Reference to Palestine and Suggestions for a Final Solution") published privately by Nuri as-Sa'id in Baghdad, 1943, for submission to Great Britain's Minister of State in Cairo, and circulated to Arab leaders. See Muhammad Khalil, *The Arab States and the Arab*

posed the establishment of an "Arab League," to be formed initially by Iraq and the new Syrian state but open to all other Arab states. In Nuri's plan, the "Arab League" was to have a permanent council nominated by member states and responsible for defense, foreign affairs, currency controls, communications, customs, education, and the protection of minority rights. The plan, circulated to other Arab leaders and made available to British authorities, was limited to what, in Arab views, amounted to political reconstitution of "geographical Syria." A special administrative regime, under international guarantee, was proposed for the Christian Maronites in Beirut. In Palestine, Jewish inhabitants were to be granted autonomous administrations where they formed a majority of the population; Jerusalem, however, was to become an international city. Nuri's plan was thus in general agreement with the long-standing goals of the Arab nationalist movement—i.e., "Fertile Crescent" unity—and with wartime Arab preoccupations with the "Palestine Problem." It is doubtful that Nuri meant any more by his term "Arab League" than a political confederation of Arab states that would eventually become a sovereign political entity.

Other Arab leaders by now had taken note of Eden's invitation. In Trans-Jordan, Emir Abdullah supported a plan for a "General Arab Federation" drawn up by "a number of Trans-Jordanian dignitaries" and submitted to Abdullah on March 6, 1963. In advancement of Abdullah's claims to suzerainty over "geographical Syria" growing from the Hashemite role in the 1916 Arab Revolt, the plan called for the formation of a "Syrian state" (Palestine, Trans-Jordan, Syria, and Lebanon), headed by Abdullah as a first step. The second step was to be

---

League: A Documentary Record, Vol. II (Beirut: Khayats, 1962), Document No. 4, pp. 9-12, for portions of the plan in English translation.

the formation of an "Arab Federation" (Syria, plus Iraq, and other Arab states) with coordinated foreign policies, defense establishments, economies, and educational institutions. The presidency of the Council of the Arab Federation was to be rotated among the member states.[3]

In Egypt, Nahhas Pasha, then Egyptian premier, declared in a speech read to the Chamber of Deputies on March 30, 1943 that he had studied Eden's speech and had "come to the conclusion that the Egyptian government should take up the matter officially and should discover the opinion of the various Arab governments and at what they aim."[4] He proposed to serve as a sort of mediator "to reconcile the differing contradictory views as far as possible" and to hold a meeting in Egypt to work out a program for the "Arab Union." Meetings were subsequently held during the summer of 1943 and the winter and early spring of 1943-44 between Nahhas Pasha and leaders of each of the Arab states in turn.

The complete record of the discussions is not available, but a memorandum dated August 24, 1943, from the Emir Abdullah to his prime minister—who was about to go to Cairo for talks with Nahhas Pasha—probably gives a fair picture of the scope of the discussions at that time.[5] Referring to talks on Arab unity between Nuri as-Sa'id (Iraq) and Mustafa an-Nahhas (Egypt), Abdullah strongly reaffirmed the need to "reunite Syria" as a counterbalance between Iraq and Egypt and dwelt on the

[3] See Document No. 5, in Khalil, *op.cit.*, pp. 14-15. The historical basis for the plan was the findings of the King-Crane Commission of 1919, the resolution of March 8, 1920 (regarding the unity of Syria) by the Syrian General Congress at Damascus, the wartime inability of the French government to carry out the League of Nations' mandate, and the British attempts to settle the Palestine problem.

[4] Quoted by Phillip Ireland, "The Pact of the League of Arab States," *American Journal of International Law*, 39 (October 1945), 798.

[5] See Khalil, *op.cit.*, Document No. 6, pp. 16-18.

necessity for an equitable solution to the Palestine problem. Then, broadening his view, Abdullah suggested that
Lebanon be allowed to join the proposed Arab union,
always safeguarding Syria's "rights" (to former Syrian
territories included in the Lebanese mandate by the
French); that an understanding was needed with the
Sultan of Morocco and the Bey of Tunis on the subject
of the Arab union; and that Egypt, "one of the leading
Arab countries," was welcome to join the union. Special
provisions were to be made for Saudi Arabia and Yemen,
on religious grounds, but these countries were to be kept
informed of the progress of the talks. Libya, still under
Allied military control, was expected to have "Arab"
status, but the question was open.

Following the extended series of bilateral discussions,
Nahhas Pasha announced in July 1944 that the Arab
states had been invited to a joint conference in Cairo to
consider actions to be taken. When the conference convened on September 25, 1944, at Alexandria instead of
Cairo, the participating delegations were from Lebanon,
Egypt, Iraq, Syria, and Trans-Jordan; observers were
present from Saudi Arabia, Yemen, Libya, Morocco, and
Palestine.

The primary problem of the conference was that of an
appropriate structural organization. According to participants in the conference, three forms of political organization were debated: (1) a unitary state with central
political authority, (2) a federated state with a central
parliament and executive committee with full political
power over federal issues, and (3) a loose confederation
with emphasis on coordination and cooperation.[6] For various reasons, the first two types of organization were un-
acceptable to all the conferees. The third form, the confederation, was thus selected by common agreement. The

[6] See Ezzeldin Foda, *The Projected Arab Court of Justice*
(The Hague: Martinius Nijhoff, 1957), pp. 6-7.

first article of the "Alexandria Protocol," the document developed by the conference (see Appendix A), emphasized that "a League [of Arab States] will be formed of the independent Arab States which consent to join the League. It will have a Council which will be known as the 'Council of the League of Arab States' in which all participating states will be represented on an equal footing."

The objectives of the League, by now far removed from the goal of Arab unity, were declared to be to supervise the execution of agreements made by member states, to strengthen the relations between the states, to supervise in a general way the interests of the Arab countries, to coordinate their political plans and to insure cooperation among them, and to protect their sovereignty and independence. Resolutions of the League's Council were to be binding only on those states which accepted them.

Once the choice of political organization had been made, the conference could move to a consideration of internal structure and functions. This work was done in six committees concerned, respectively, with political, social, economic, health, cultural, and communications problems. The subjects of joint defense and foreign policy proposed in Nuri's "Blue Book," were eliminated from consideration and one or two other categories were absorbed into other subject headings. The committee framework thus stressed technical or "functional" activities, including the provision of economic and cultural ties emphasized by Eden in 1941 and 1943 and endorsed by the United States.[7] About one-third of the completed Alex-

[7] The United States had also officially emphasized the importance of functional activities in notes circulated to the Arab countries in October 1943 and July 1944. The notes were prompted by a Saudi Arabian request for the official U.S. attitude on Arab union. The State Department expressed sympathy with Arab aspirations for independence and stated the desire to see economic and social conditions strengthened. While the U.S. viewed the

andria Protocol was devoted to the subject of "cooperation in economic, cultural, social, and other matters," while political coordination is mentioned in only the most general terms (e.g., coordination of foreign policies and agreement not to use force in the settlement of disputes between members).

The Alexandria Protocol was essentially a memorandum of understanding. It provided for further study of appropriate forms of cooperation in both the political and functional spheres in preparation for a general Arab conference to draw up a constitution for the proposed Arab League. The draft agreement was signed by delegates from Egypt, Iraq, Lebanon, Syria, and Trans-Jordan; the Saudi and Yemeni representatives referred the Protocol to their governments, which adhered in January and February, respectively, of the following year. Observers from Morocco and other Arab countries expressed their hope for eventual affiliation.

The decisions of the conference at Alexandria in the fall of 1944, therefore, were in favor of a cooperative association whose major role would be that of a coordinating agency in the field of common political and functional activities. The idealistic drive toward some form of Arab unity subsided in the face of practical politics. Although the conference delegates wrote into the Protocol the hope "that Arab States will be able in the future to consolidate that step [the formation of a loose league] by other steps," subsequent events seem to indicate that the words merely provided a means of rationalizing the ideal with the practical.[8]

---

move for unification with sympathy as long as any action conformed with the principles of the Atlantic Charter, it was felt that the first steps toward unity should emphasize strengthening "economic, social, and cultural domains." (Hull, *op.cit.*, p. 1546).

[8] A 1951 news bulletin published by the League Secretariat declared that, as a *regional organization,* the Arab League "is a

During the winter of 1944-45, the text of the Dumbarton Oaks Proposals were made available to the supporters of the Arab League movement, and the orientation toward a "regional organization" with ties to the future United Nations became increasingly stronger. The Egyptian Premier, Nahhas Pasha, is known to have studied reports on the organization and activities of the Union of American Republics during this period. And the strong support of regionalism at UNCIO by the Arabs would seem to indicate that the immediate objective of complete Arab unity had been abandoned, not merely deferred. The final draft of the "Pact of the League of Arab States," (see Appendix B) completed in March 1945, makes no allusion to eventual unity. On the contrary, the Pact emphasizes respect for the independence and sovereignty of the League's member states, though Article 9 permits "closer cooperation and stronger bonds" between member states which desire them in the future. It is, therefore, difficult to agree with those Arab critics of the League who maintain that the founders of the organization betrayed the drive toward Arab unity.

The Alexandria Protocol, read as a statement of policy by Arab leaders of the period, demonstrates that all-inclusive Arab unity was not considered a matter for practical politics.[9] And for those who thought it was, Article 9 of the League Charter provided an outlet. Arab leaders from the Fertile Crescent were understandably chagrined when the late-arriving Egyptians took over the unity

---

true reflection of a general Arab national consciousness . . . a continuation of the Arab struggle . . . a manifestation of orderly, organized, and total cooperation." ("The Arab National Consciousness Precedes the Establishment of the Charter of Collective Security," *Bulletin of the Secretariat,* 1 (June 1951), in Arabic.

[9] An Iraqi note of March 11, 1945, on the draft Charter, argued that no clear stand on the future of Arab unity was required since unification of two or more independent states was clearly within the right of each member state (see Khalil, *op.cit.,* Document No. 8, pp. 20-21.)

plans of 1943, but none of the innumerable grandiose unity projects since broached by Syrians and Iraqis has ever gone beyond the discussion stage. Moreover, the accretion of diverse independent Arab states to the Arab League since 1945 has decreased rather than increased the potential for the type of true political unification required by dogmatic Arab nationalists. By the soft light of history, it appears that the founders of the Arab League were on sound ground when they rejected political union in favor of regional organization. "Arab unity," nevertheless, remains the sacred cow of the League: it gives little nourishment, but no one dares kill it.

The Pact of the League of Arab states

In preparation for the General Arab Congress envisaged by the Alexandria Protocol, a committee of Arab foreign ministers and other experts met in Cairo during February and March 1945 to draft the constitution of the Arab League. The subject had been a matter for lively debate in the Arab capitals in the fall and early winter following the Alexandria conference. Two days after the approval of the Alexandria Protocol, Nahhas Pasha was relieved of his position as prime minister of Egypt; Egyptian political leaders denounced Nahhas and his followers as traitors and castigated the proposed Arab League as unworkable. The Syrian and Jordanian prime ministers, who had led their delegations to the conference, were also dismissed from their posts. Reaction was particularly violent in Beirut where the Christian Arab community, led by the Maronite patriarch and the Falangists, denounced the Alexandria Protocol as an attack on Lebanese sovereignty. The document which emerged from the preliminary drafting committees, however, generally confirmed the ideas of the Alexandria Protocol.

The General Arab Congress convened in Cairo on March 17th to review the draft pact, and the approved document was signed March 22nd by six of the seven founding members: Egypt, Iraq, Lebanon, Syria, Saudi Arabia, and Trans-Jordan. A copy of the Pact was sent to the Imam of Yemen, who signed it on May 10, 1945. Unofficial delegations from Algeria, Libya, Morocco, and Tunisia reportedly requested membership in the League of Arab States during the drafting of the pact, but the final agreement provided that membership was to be restricted to independent Arab states.[10]

The Pact of the League of Arab States is an international treaty signed by the heads of states or representatives of the founding members and duly ratified by the respective member states.[11] The Pact consists of a preamble, twenty numbered articles, and three annexes, all of which are reproduced in Appendix B. In its brevity, the Pact resembles the League of Nations Covenant more than anything else, and some of its phraseology and provisions seem to have been lifted from either the League Covenant or the draft United Nations Charter. A brief analysis of the principal provisions of the Pact will serve as background for the detailed discussion in later chapters. Reference points are: (1) purpose and functions, (2) membership and relations between members, and (3) institutional structure.

1. *Purpose and Functions*

Article 2 of the Pact of the League of Arab States, which amplifies the Preamble, establishes as the purposes of

[10] *al-Ahram* [Cairo], February 18, 1945, reported the foundation of a "Front for the Defense of the Maghreb" in Cairo, under the direction of Sheikh Mohammed el-Khadir Hussein of Tunisia, with the purpose of fostering the entry of the North African Arab countries into the League, *Oriente Moderno*, xxvii (1945), 17.

[11] Ratifications were as follows: Trans-Jordan, March 31, 1945; Iraq, April 1, 1945; Syria, April 3, 1945; Egypt, April 5, 1945; Lebanon, April 7, 1945; Saudi Arabia, April 7; Yemen, May 11. The Pact came into effect on May 11, 1945, fifteen days after Iraq had deposited its ratification with the League's Secretary General in Cairo.

the organization: (1) strengthening relations between member states, (2) coordinating their policies in order to further cooperation and safeguard their independence and sovereignty, and (3) a general concern for the affairs and interests of the Arab countries. In particular, the article provides for "close cooperation" between member states in matters concerning economic and financial affairs, communications, cultural affairs, problems of nationality, social affairs, and health. No mention is made of defense against external attack, coordination of military resources, or uniformity of foreign policy, unlike the Alexandria Protocol, which provided for coordination of foreign policy. The League is, however, to act as a mediator in disputes between members or between a member and a third state according to Article 5. The Pact also provides, in Article 3, for future cooperation with such international bodies as may be formed "in order to guarantee security and peace and regulate economic and social relations." In the vocabulary of functionalism, the primary purpose of the League is to foster non-political activities and only incidentally to enter the political arena.

2. *Membership and Relations between Members*

Membership is restricted by Article 1 to independent Arab states; subsequent to the establishment of the League, any such state may apply for membership. Members pledge themselves by Article 8, to respect the sovereignty of other member states and not to take any action "calculated to change established systems of government." Member states which voluntarily elect to form "stronger bonds" than provided by the Pact may do so. Resort to force to settle disputes is, however, prohibited by Article 5. Member states assume an obligation to support the League financially, on a prorated basis to be determined from time to time by the Council. Withdrawal of a member upon one year's notice is permitted, and provisions are made so that errant states may be "separated" from the organization, according to Article 18. The terminology of the Pact leaves little doubt that the League is to be regarded as no more than a device to coordinate the activities of its members and to keep them from quarreling among themselves. The prospect for political unity under the Pact of the League of Arab States is forsworn by its emphasis on preserving the sovereignty and independence of its members.

An interesting feature of the Pact is its provision for future relations with non-members, particularly in the Arab World. Article 2, which establishes the purpose of the League, includes "general concern with the affairs and interests of Arab countries" and not just for the interests of member states. Article 4 permits non-member [Arab] delegations to participate in the work of the technical committees. These provisions are reinforced by Annex 2 to the Pact, "Annex Regarding Cooperation with Countries Which Are Not Members of the Council of the League," which establishes a policy for future cooperation with non-member Arab states. Annex 2 and the other referenced articles of the Pact refer to the expressed desires of the then-dependent Arab areas of Algeria, Libya, Morocco, Palestine, and Tunisia. As a special case, Annex 1 of the Pact provides that Palestine shall be represented on the League Council, by a person to be selected by the Council, until full independence has been achieved. The membership policy is also oriented toward these potentially independent states, since the Pact was originated by all the independent Arab states of the period.

Articles 9 and 17 contain two additional provisions for regulation of relations between member states. Article 9 provides that: "Treaties and agreements already concluded or to be concluded in the future between a member state and another state shall not be binding or restrictive upon other members." Nor shall such treaties become null and void. According to Article 17, all such treaties, including both existing and future treaties between members, must be deposited with the Secretary General. This provision, which resembles that of Article 18 of the Covenant of the League of Nations, is less restrictive than the requirement for unified foreign policy contained in Article 1 of the Alexandria Protocol.

3. *Institutional Structure*

According to the Pact, the principal organs of the Arab League are the Council and the permanent Secretariat. The Pact specifies that the seat of the League is Cairo. Provision was made for future establishment of an "Arab Tribunal of Arbitration," which would work closely with other international bodies on problems of peace and security; this provision has been debated extensively but never implemented. Technical committees, one for each of the functional areas mentioned in Article 2, are provided to assist the League Council. No other organs were provided by the Pact; an Economic Council and a Joint Defense Council, however, were later provided by a special treaty, in 1950 (see Appendix C). Table 1 illustrates the organization of the League.

The organization established by the Pact appears to have combined the principal provisions of the Covenant of the League of Nations and the operating experience of the League's Council. The Arab League Council, unlike that of the League of Nations, comprises all members of the organization. The need for an Assembly such as that of the League of Nations was therefore obviated. On the other hand, the Arab League Pact specifically provides for technical committees to assist the League Council. The League of Nations Council developed the institution of the technical committee over a period of years outside the specific provisions of the Covenant.

The Council is made up of representatives from the member states of the Arab League and meets twice a year, in regular session. Each state has one vote regardless of the number of representatives it sends to the Council.[12] The principal functions of the Council are to supervise the execution of agreements concluded between members, to determine the means by which the League is to cooperate with the United Nations and other international agencies, to mediate disputes between members or between members and non-members, and to coordinate defense measures in the event of attack or threat of aggression. The Council also has internal legislative functions, including the approval of the budget, preparation and approval of administrative regulations for the Council, the technical committees, and the Secretariat, and the regulation of certain personnel matters, including appointment of the Secretary General.

The Secretariat provided by Article 12 consists of a Secretary General, an unspecified number of assistant secretaries, and "an appropriate number of officials." Aside from preparation of the League budget and support of Council meetings, neither organization nor functions of the Secretariat are prescribed by the Pact. The Council is given the responsibility for regulations concerning functions and staff of the Secretariat.

The technical committees are composed of representatives of the member states according to Article 4. Their principal function is to study conditions and to draft agreements on technical cooperation for consideration by the Arab League Council. Representatives of the non-member Arab states may sit on these committees and frequently have. In addition to the six functional committees provided by Article 4, a political committee and a

[12] See Article 4/6, League Covenant, which provided one vote per country but limited the number of representatives to one.

TABLE 1

ORGANIZATIONAL STRUCTURE OF THE ARAB LEAGUE

COUNCIL OF THE LEAGUE OF ARAB STATES[a]

Composition: Delegations of member states, one vote per member state; permanent delegations/delegates.
Functions: Principal decision-making body of League.
Voting Rule: Unanimity required except as specified by League Pact.
Meetings: Two regular meetings each year, March and October; special meetings on request.

JOINT DEFENSE COUNCIL[b]

Composition: Ministers of Defense & Foreign Affairs from states adhering to 1950 Security Treaty.
Function: Coordinate Arab security affairs. Permanent Mil. Commission provides continuity.
Voting Rule: 2/3 majority.
Meetings: Annual, special sessions on request of one member state.

PERMANENT COMMITTEES[a]

Composition: Delegates of member states of Arab League plus observers from non-member states.
Function: Coordinate programs in areas of responsibility, prepare draft programs & recommendations for League Council.
Voting: Simple majority.
Meetings: Annual; interim actions coordinated by Secretariat Dept. concerned.

ECONOMIC COUNCIL[b]

Composition: Ministers of Economic Affairs from states adhering to 1950 Collective Security Treaty.
Function: Coordinate economic development programs & mobilize resources for regional security actions.
Voting Rule: Simple majority.
Meetings: Annual.

GENERAL SECRETARIAT[a]

Composition: Secretary General, Assistant Secretaries General, Departmental staffs, Special Agencies and Offices.
Function: Administration of League affairs; execution of decisions of League Councils and other organs.

[a] Provided by League Pact [b] Added by Security Treaty of 1950

permanent committee on information have been established which directly support the League Council.

The Joint Defense and Economic Cooperation Treaty

The original seven members of the League of Arab States completed a supplemental treaty in 1950 officially known as the Joint Defense and Economic Cooperation Treaty Between the States of the Arab League (see Appendix C). The treaty, usually known as the Arab Collective Security Pact, was signed by Egypt, Lebanon, Syria, Saudi Arabia, and Yemen on June 17, 1950. Iraq signed on February 2, 1951, and Jordan signed on February 16, 1952. The treaty became effective on August 23, 1952. The treaty is somewhat unique in its juncture of functional and security problems, though the ostensible reason for the treaty was to bring the Arab League in line with the United Nations Charter in matters of collective security. The preamble states that the participating governments desire "to cooperate for the realization of mutual defense and the maintenance of security and peace according to the principles of both the Arab League Pact and the United Nations Charter." The treaty also restates the objectives of the Pact of the League which relate to consolidation of relations between members, maintenance of independence, and development of economic and social welfare. In fact, however, the treaty is based on Article 51 of the UN Charter, as was the defense pact of the Organization of American States.

Relations between members are altered in the 1950 treaty to the extent that, according to Article 10, the contracting parties "undertake to conclude no international agreements which may be contradictory to the provisions of this Treaty." This recalls the earlier attempt, under the terms of the Alexandria Protocol, to secure uniformity of foreign policy. But outside the context of Arab unity, to which this provision is often linked, the provision also resembles that of Article 20 of the Covenant of the League of Nations.[13]

From another point of view, relations between members of the Arab League have been affected to the extent that only signatories of the 1950 treaty were permitted to join the three new Arab League organs which it established. The League had thirteen members at the end of 1962, but only nine of them had adhered to the treaty. The role of the supplementary organs created by the 1950 treaty has been limited by this provision during most of the intervening period since none of the new members adhered to the treaty until 1961. Although non-adherents could attend meetings as observers, they could not participate officially in the decision-making process. This situation has been particularly embarrassing in the case of the Economic Council.

The new Arab League organs established under the terms of the 1950 treaty were the Joint Defense Council, the Economic Council, and a Permanent Military Commission.

The organization and functions of the Joint Defense Council were established by Article 6. The Council was to comprise the foreign ministers and ministers of defense of the contracting states, or their representatives. It was designed to function under the supervision of the League Council in matters of collective security, including "the use of armed force to repel the aggression and restore security and peace," coordination of available military resources, and the preparation of plans for joint defense.

The Permanent Military Commission, made up of representatives of the general staffs of the contracting states, was charged with drawing up plans for joint defense and,

[13] Article 20 of the Covenant states: "The Members of the League [of Nations] . . . solemnly undertake that they will not hereafter enter into any agreements inconsistent with the terms hereof [i.e. the Covenant]."

presumably, with effecting the necessary coordination to ensure their implementation. The Commission was supposed to work directly with the Joint Defense Council; its headquarters was established at Cairo. As a concomitant of its military functions, the Military Annex to the treaty provided that the Commission was to submit "proposals for the exploitation of natural, agricultural, industrial, and other resources of all Contracting States in favor of the inter-Arab military effort and joint defense."

The Economic Council was established to coordinate the development of the Arab economies and "generally to organize . . . their economic activities and to conclude the necessary inter-Arab agreements to realize such aims." The Council presumably works under the supervision of the Arab League Council, though this is not specified in the treaty. It is composed of the ministers of economic affairs of the contracting states, or their representatives, and cooperates with the Economic Committee established by Article 4 of the Arab League Pact. In 1960, however, steps were taken to permit representatives of non-contracting Arab states to attend sessions of the Economic Council. In September 1964, all the remaining non-signatories adhered to the Arab Collective Security Treaty as a gesture of Arab brotherhood and thus became full voting members of the Economic Council. By this time, however, the economic aspects of the treaty were rapidly being taken over by the newly organized Council of Economic Union and the projected Arab Common Market.

PART II POLICY FORMULATION AND
EXECUTION

PART II POLICY FORMULATION AND EXECUTION

SINCE its inception in 1945, the League of Arab States has dealt intimately and extensively with both regional security problems and the problems of functional integration. It has a well-developed history of activity coordinate with the United Nations and its Specialized Agencies. But during the intervening period, the League has been consistently condemned by two types of critics: (1) those within the Arab world who object that the Arab League is an inadequate substitute for genuine Arab unity, and (2) those outside the Arab world who maintain that the League has failed because it has failed to achieve Arab unity. Both sets of critics are guilty of the same error. To evaluate the organization in terms of its approach to or withdrawal from Arab unity is to misunderstand the problem or to substitute another problem and other terms of reference. The discussion above has shown that the founders of the League of Arab States made a definite, if reluctant, decision against Arab unity and in favor of regional organization.

The five chapters that follow focus attention on the characteristic functioning of the Arab League as a regional organization. Insofar as possible, the approach is analytical. In addition to the parameters developed in Chapter I, certain aspects of Kaplan's developmental theory of international systems have been adapted to the analysis.[1] Although the Arab League does not fall neatly

[1] Morton A. Kaplan, *System and Process in International Politics* (New York: John W. Wiley and Sons, Inc., 1957), particularly Chap. II and Part II, Processes.

into any one of the international systems postulated by Kaplan, functionally it most closely resembles the non-directive universal international system. In Kaplan's typology non-directive systems rely on democratic decision-making processes; directive systems are authoritarian. The principal characteristics of the non-directive system according to Kaplan, are:

1. the international system operates on other political subsystems (i.e., the member states) to determine jurisdictional limits of its members with respect to some functions while other functions are regulated by the national subsystems;

2. the international system possesses integrating mechanisms performing judicial, economic, political, and administrative functions;

3. internal formal or informal coalitions may be formed for purposes of achieving national objectives through the international system;

4. competition between members of the system will occur but will not be carried to the point where other members of the system are destroyed; preservation of the system takes precedence;

5. the international system possesses facilities and resources superior to those of any national member and is in a position to allocate these within the system membership;

6. instability is inherent in the system: success will tend to call for transformation of the system to a "hierarchical international system," while crises will tend to result in resort to traditional centers of power and devolution to a "balance of power" system.[2]

Successful functioning of the international system just characterized also requires that the value structures of the subsystems (nation members) be such that the interna-

[2] In Kaplan's typology, a hierarchical system operates directly upon individuals.

tional system can coordinate and integrate them. The common heritage of the Arab world would seem important here. Furthermore, while nation members legitimately attempt to increase their own shares of the rewards of the system, in case of conflict between national goals and system goals, the system predominates. As a final point, the individuals (delegates and functionaries) who hold decision-making roles in the international system—who are usually also members of another subsystem—must function in accordance with the objectives and rules of the international system.

The internal structure of the Arab League is essentially non-directive; its decision-making processes, discussed in the following chapter, require close coordination at the same time that they permit a wide range of effective action. Certain factors, however, alternately enhance and detract from the efficient functioning of the League; these are discussed as "integrative—disintegrative processes" in a separate chapter. The development of the League's policy of cooperation with the United Nations and an analysis of Arab neutralism are included under the heading of "External Policies." And, finally, the administrative and executive mechanisms are examined from the point of view of determining their contribution to the efficiency of the system.

LEGAL CONTROLS

ACCORDING to the Pact, policy-making and legislative functions of the Arab League are exercised by the League Council. The Council is composed of representatives from each member state and a representative from "Palestine" and meets twice a year, now usually in March and September, although the Pact stipulates meetings in March and October.[1] Chairmanship of the League Council is rotated among the member states, in alphabetical order. Special meetings may be called at the request of two or more member states. Council sessions are usually held in Cairo, the seat of the Arab League, but they may be held elsewhere at the option of the Council. Forty-two regular Council sessions were held between July 1945 and the end of 1964, not including several extraordinary sessions. Appendix G summarizes the discussions and/or decisions of these meetings.

Voting procedures for the Council are established by the Pact and are enumerated for various situations. The listing, however, is not exhaustive. The voting procedure

[1] In recent years, the October meeting has been moved back to September to permit the Council to review the agenda for the UN General Assembly. Resolution 17, December 4, 1945, provided for up to three Palestinian representatives, empowered to vote on "Palestine questions and other matters of interest." The representatives are appointed by the Council itself. In September 1963, the Council appointed Ahmed Shukairy, formerly an Assistant Secretary General and UN representative for Saudi Arabia.

for election of new members, for example, is not stipulated and became a matter for heated debate during the Kuwait crisis in the summer of 1961. In general, Article 7 provides that substantive matters must be approved unanimously in order that the decision may bind all members; majority decisions bind only those states which accept them.[2] When the Council is considering measures to repel overt aggression from within its membership, decisions are taken by unanimous vote except that the vote of the aggressor member is not counted. The same rule is applied in the case of a vote to expel a member from the League. Decisions of arbitration and mediation, on the other hand, require only a simple majority vote.

Administrative and procedural matters require only a majority vote of the Council and are generally specified by the Pact. Confirmation of the Secretary General and approval of amendments to the Pact require a two-thirds' majority. Other administrative actions require only a simple majority: adoption of the annual budget, personnel matters, establishment of the regulations for League organs, and decisions to adjourn Council sessions. Among these are such specified actions as decision on the proportion of expenses to be borne by member states, the rules of procedure for the Council itself, the approval of Assistant Secretaries and other principal officers of the Secretariat (the League Council confirming nominations presented by the Secretary General), and the determination of the conditions under which representatives of non-member Arab "states" may participate in the work of the technical committees.

[2] This is a departure from the Alexandria Protocol, which specified that all decisions would bind only those members that accepted them. The present provision was the result of a compromise sponsored by Egypt between those members who wanted a stronger union and those who upheld the importance of national sovereignty (Foda, *op.cit.*, p. 9).

Outside the League Council, voting in League organs is normally by simple majority. An exception must be made for the Joint Defense Council, which is required to use the two-thirds' majority. With this exception, however, these other agencies—i.e., the Economic Council and the technical committees—are consultative in nature and serve principally to recommend actions to the League Council for decision.

Much criticism has been directed at the Arab League because of the requirement for unanimous Council decisions in order to bind its members. Considering its historical identification with the Covenant of the League of Nations, however, the Pact's insistence on this provision is not surprising. Under Article 5/1 of the Covenant, both the Council and the Assembly used the unanimity rule. The United Nations Security Council incorporated the unanimity rule to the extent that all *permanent* members must agree on substantive matters. More recently, the EEC established unanimous voting for its Council. Unlike the situation in the UN Security Council, on the other hand, the members of the Arab League Council have no direct veto power. Technically, a dissenting member can refuse to implement the decision if it is otherwise approved but cannot block all action. In theory, at least, this procedure is an improvement over that of both the League of Nations and the United Nations. In practice, of course, unanimity is sought by the Arab League Council. Either opposition is smoothed over before the matter comes to a vote or, if the opponents are intractable, the vote may never be taken.

More significant, perhaps, is the fact that the unanimity rule of the League Council serves as a brake on the inherent tendency of the organization either to evolve into a unitary state or to collapse completely. Unanimous decisions lack the coercive character of majority decisions and require considerably more give and take by member states. Persuasion and cooperation are enhanced and authoritarian tendencies are repressed.

The unanimity rule of the Council also serves to obviate the permanent domination of the organization by a single powerful member—or a membership bloc—capable of enforcing its will on the majority. A successful move to alter the voting procedure of the League Council to provide for simple majority decisions could destroy the equilibrium of the organization and even bring about its collapse.[3] This could be brought about by either of two developments: (1) misuse of the majority rule by a dominant power or group of powers could encourage the minority members to bolt the organization, since the League Council has no enforcement powers or, (2) misuse of the majority rule by a dominant power or group of powers and concurrent development of sanctions and proscriptions against minority members, backed by the coercive force of the dominant power, could in effect permit the dominant power to substitute its national goals for those of the organization. In Kaplan's system theory, an important requirement is that member states must be prepared to subordinate national goals to common objectives. Some Arab League members feel that the drive for the majority vote in the League Council, on the plea that it will foster "Arab unity," disguises imperialistic objectives of one or another of the dominant Arab powers.

Other than formal voting procedures, the Arab League Pact also provides generalized procedures for peaceful settlement of disputes, on the basis of mutual repudiation of resort to force. According to the Pact, differences which arise between members may be referred to the Council; in these instances, the decision of the Council is "enforce-

[3] Proposals for a majority vote in the League Council have been supported by the Secretary General since about 1955 and members were circulated on the question in 1958. In March 1964, the Political Committee was reported to favor this proposed change in procedure, but no action was taken.

able." The Council is also empowered to mediate all differences that threaten to lead to war, whether between member states or between a member and a non-member state. If aggression has already occurred, the state under attack may demand immediate convocation of the League Council. Or, in event the attacked state cannot communicate with the Council, a meeting may be requested by the state's representative to the Council or by any other member state.[4] The 1950 Collective Security Pact added nothing to this procedure except that it provided for a Joint Defense Council, and appropriate military agencies, to deal with aggression from within and without the region. The 1950 treaty, however, reaffirms the resolve of its adherents to regard an attack against one member as an attack against all.

Procedures for arbitration and mediation are not detailed in the Pact, and this fact has evoked much criticism. The basis of the criticism is that arbitration is voluntary and that disputes concerning a "state's independence, sovereignty, or territorial integrity" are not subject to League Council jurisdiction according to Article 5. While the intent of the provision was apparently to distinguish between justiciable and non-justiciable disputes, the effect has been to prevent League Council action.[5]

The Arab League Pact is extremely flexible, nevertheless, and the development of operating procedures and establishment of administrative regulations have been left

[4] Article 6. Elsewhere (Article 11), the Pact requires that at least two members request a meeting of the Council.

[5] Early in the history of the Arab League, the Council convened to hear a complaint by Syria against Jordan, in connection with Abdullah's "Greater Syria Plan." On November 26, 1946, the Jordanian prime minister observed to the Council that the Arab League had no competence to consider any dispute or disagreement between two member states unless it was submitted for arbitration by *both* sides (see Khalil, *op.cit.*, Document No. 20, pp. 33-34). An amendment to the Pact to provide for compulsory arbitration was reportedly discussed by the Council in March 1964.

almost entirely to the League Council. But the relative brevity of the provisions for peaceful settlement of disputes, for example, does not in itself detract from their usefulness. There was little real need to include elaborate articles on techniques of mediation, arbitration, and the peaceful settlement of disputes. These techniques have been developed over a period of a century or more and applied often enough not to need detailed repetition in a document such as the League Pact. Whether these tested techniques have been applied effectively, or at all, is another matter. Because of the vagueness which surrounds the subject of peaceful settlement of disputes, further discussion of this subject will be deferred until Chapter X. At this point, the problem is to determine how decisions are made and not what they concern.

THE DECISION-MAKING PROCESS

According to the Pact of the Arab League, decisions are made by the League Council under fairly well defined rules. (Appendix D provides the text of the internal regulations of the Council.) Over a period of years, however, informal processes which lead to the final decision in the League Council have evolved along a pattern which is only partially defined by the Pact itself. Some of the formal organs, particularly those associated with the 1950 Collective Security Pact have only recently entered into the process. This is particularly true of the Joint Defense Council and the Permanent Military Commission, which held no formal sessions between 1954 and 1961.

The Economic Council, the other principal organ established by the 1950 treaty, remains active but it was handicapped by the fact that some of the Arab League members did not sign the treaty and until 1960 were ineligible to take part in the activities of the Council. Nevertheless, the Economic Council has gained increasing importance in the past few years. Even before 1960, non-member states were represented by observers who participated in discussions without vote. In 1958, the Economic Council authorized the Secretary General to seek a legal formula by which all members of the Arab League could participate fully in the activities of the Council. An annex to the 1950 treaty was subsequently drafted and approved on June 2, 1960, to permit all members of the Arab League—as well as non-member Arab states—to accede to membership to the Economic Council. With this step, the Economic Council should have become a major organ in the functioning of the Arab League because of the organization's emphasis on economic development. At the present time, however, the Economic Council remains in an anomalous position as a consultative organ without real power, threatened with oblivion as a result of the establishment of the Council of Economic Union.

The Arab League Secretariat, on the other hand, given only administrative and executive functions by the Pact, assumed an important role in the decision-making process from the beginning of the organization. The first Secretary General, Abd ur-Rahman 'Azzam Pasha, was bitterly opposed by some of the member states for his alleged usurpation of the League Council's authority. Even under the present Secretary General, Abdel Khalek Hassouna, the Secretariat has continued to exert great influence on the decision-making process if only because it is the only permanently functioning organ of the League.

The staff members of the several departments of the Secretariat, primarily concerned with administrative and technical support functions, are in constant contact with the member states and their problems. They have the technical capacity—or access to it—to conduct long-range studies and programs which eventually move upward toward the League Council for approval. Over a period of years, furthermore, the permanent committees established under the Pact have come to rely on the technical departments of the Secretariat for the long-range studies which the committees consider in annual meetings. Of the permanent committees, only the Political Committee, usually made up of foreign ministers, is relatively independent of the Secretariat. The Economic Committee is essentially coordinate with the more recently established Economic Council (comprising ministers of economic affairs).

Within the Secretariat, the several technical departments work closely with the permanent committees, develop long-range studies for ultimate consideration by the League Council, and prepare the agendas for League Council meetings. A group of senior staff advisors (*mushrifiin*), including the chairman of several of the permanent committees, reports directly to the Secretary General.[6] Weekly staff meetings, presided over by the Secretary General or one of the Assistant Secretaries, insure continuity of effort and permit adjustment of policies by the department heads. Control over the agenda of the League Council, of course, permits the Secretariat to determine in advance the nature and scope of the problems to be discussed. As a result of this close coordination between the Secretariat and the permanent committees and other consultative groups, recommendations that reach the League Council are normally approved without discussion.

Under actual operating conditions, the Political Committee has taken over the functions of the League Council in all but name. The Committee, normally composed of the foreign ministers of the member states but often made up of Arab diplomatic representatives in Cairo,

[6] In December 1960, the principal advisors were Taha Hussein (cultural affairs), Dr. Shusha (public health), Mohammed Hassan Assmowy (social affairs), and Mohammed Ali Nimazi (economic affairs).

is formally charged only with drawing up recommendations for the League Council. In practice, the Political Committee meets immediately before or during the sessions of the League Council, as well as at other times, and debates the recommendations of the other technical committees as well as those within its own competence. In the 1957 session, for example, the Political Committee debated a plan for an Arab common market which developed out of the Economic Council. Its decisions, adopted by simple majority, are then drafted as resolutions and passed to the League Council where they are normally approved without serious debate. For all practical purposes, the Political Committee often acts as the principal decision-making body of the Arab League.

An *ad hoc* "conference of foreign ministers" has also developed outside the Arab League Pact. This group, whose membership may be identical with that of the Political Committee and the League Council at any given session, frequently informally fulfills the role of the Political Committee. Decisions reached by this group are unofficial and hortatory, since they have not passed through the constitutional Arab League decision-making process; but they carry considerable weight. In recent years, the conference of foreign ministers has simply transformed itself into the Political Committee and, subsequently, into the League Council; and the unofficial recommendations have passed into the official records of the League.

Thus the League Council, while still the legal decision-making body, has often been little more than a "rubber stamp," ratifying without discussion approved recommendations for programs and specific actions which reach it through the Political Committee. Some of the administrative actions reserved for League Council approval by the Pact appear to be approved by the Political Committee instead. For example, the Political Committee reportedly *approved* the appointment of two Assistant Secretaries in a meeting on April 28, 1958, a decision which is specifically designated by the League Pact as the responsibility of the League Council. However, since this decision may be made by *majority* vote, there seems to be no reason to insist on referring it to the League Council in formal session. This situation appears to be less a derogation than a delegation of authority.

The Arab League Pact does not specify the composition of either the League Council or the Political Committee. However, both organs have often made use of the same members. Available information indicates that about half the meetings of the Political Committee have been at the ambassadorial level—i.e., Arab diplomatic representatives in Cairo—while the remainder have been at the foreign-minister level. In recent years, increasing use has been made of permanent delegates to the Arab League, who may not be identical with the diplomatic representatives in Cairo accredited to member states. In any case, the assumption of authority by the Political Committee, usually over matters of internal procedure, is more a technical matter than not.

The decision-making processes of the Arab League are illustrated in Figures I and II. Figure I depicts the intricate coordination involved in processing a resolution through the League Council, while Figure II completes the decision-making cycle by including the execution step. The diagrams should be regarded only as a guide, of course, since the decision-making process may be initiated at any level.

The decision-making process, moreover, is subject to external controls which cannot be diagrammed adequately. It is perhaps sufficient to recall that the technical committees, the Economic Council, and the Political Committee include representatives of all the member states and may include from time to time observers from

FIGURE I

ARAB LEAGUE DECISION-MAKING PROCESS

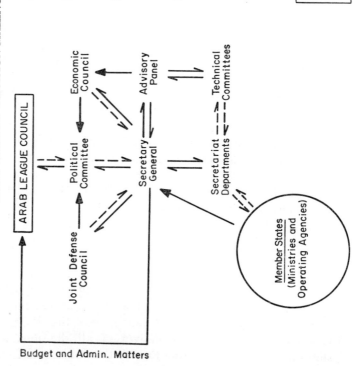

4. Final decision; resolutions approved after review by Political Committee.

3. a. Recommendations debated; final resolutions drafted.
   b. Decisions in areas of responsibility.

2. Recommendations, plans, etc., reviewed and forwarded. Administrative decisions in areas of responsibility.

1. a. Plans and recommendations drafted.
   b. League Council agenda formulated (Secretariat).
   c. Weekly coordinating and policy meetings.

DECISION PROCESS (Read Up)

LEGEND

——— Flow of primary information
----- Flow of secondary information

non-member or dependent Arab territories, such as Bahrain, Oman, or Qatar. Proposals by national representatives may therefore be introduced directly into these agencies for discussion and/or study. Or projects may be referred initially to the League Council by national member representatives, though this body will usually refer them to one of the technical committees or to the Secretary General for appropriate action. Because proposals may flow upward, downward, and laterally within the process, the decision-making processes of the League are non-directive in nature. The resulting "ventilation" of the system, while it may encumber the actual process of making decisions, insures a healthful airing of views at all levels.

EVALUATION OF THE DECISION-MAKING PROCESS

Two factors inherent in the operations of the Arab League appear to condition the effectiveness of the decision-making process. First, member states attempt to realize their national goals through the mechanisms of the League. Second, member states sacrifice some of their jealously guarded sovereignty to promote the collective goals of the organization: i.e., they attempt to realize the rewards of the system. These factors are by no means mutually exclusive, but the interplay between member states emphasizing one or the other factor to a different degree at the same time encourages a continuum of conflict.

The League Council, unfortunately, is inherently unqualified to act as an agency of conflict resolution. Council membership is unspecified in the Arab League Pact, and over the years member representation has ranged from diplomatic representatives in Cairo to heads of state and prime ministers. Although the Council is legally in continuous session, meetings are held for only about three weeks out of the year, and official member

FIGURE II
DECISION-MAKING AND EXECUTION CYCLE

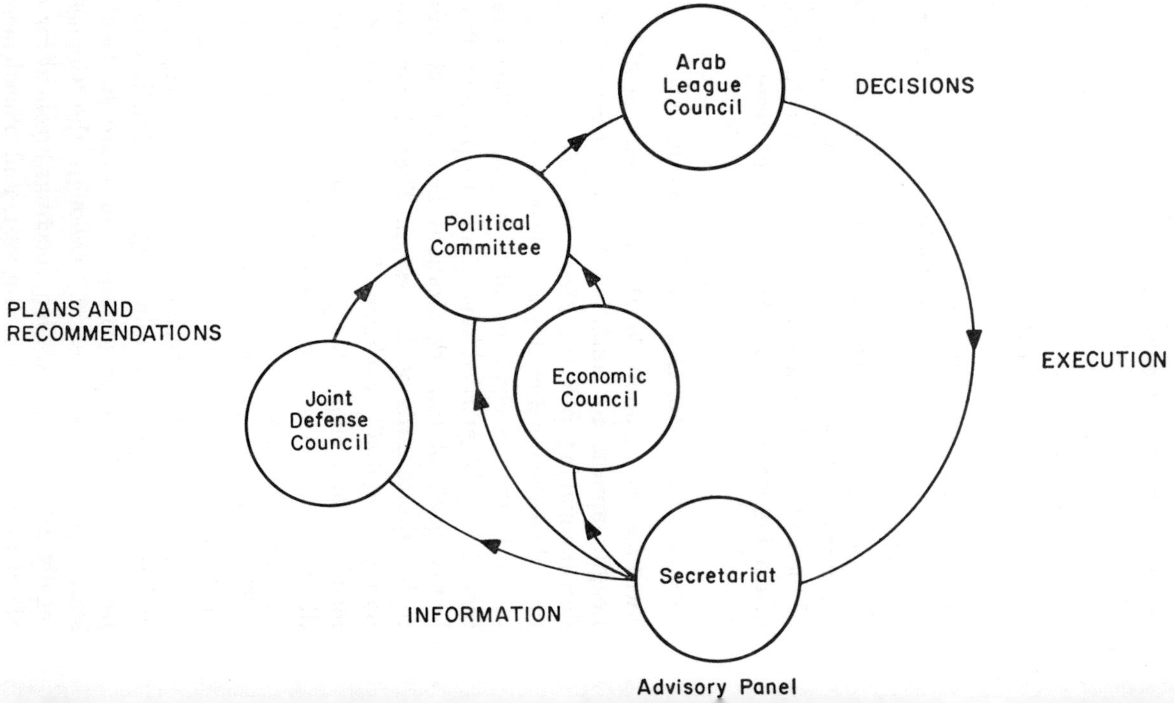

contact between sessions is often minimal. The permanent diplomatic representatives of the Arab League member states in Cairo, do, however, meet from time to time at the call of the Secretary General, either informally or as the Political Committee. The Secretary General is also in contact with these representatives as individuals. Recently several states have appointed permanent representatives to the Arab League, comparable to those at the United Nations.

It could be postulated that a League Council composed of such permanent delegates to the League would improve the operations of the Council. Long and continued association between permanent representatives should tend to modify national viewpoints in favor of collective action for joint goals. Arab opinion, however, has apparently come to expect the Council to be made up of heads of state and prime ministers, or—at the least—foreign ministers; a fact formalized in January 1964, when Arab leaders agreed to meet annually. Council sessions at lower levels (e.g., ambassadorial level) are usually pro forma in nature and unexceptional in results. The net result has been that participants in the League Council sessions tend to be either active political leaders with partisan interests in critical problems or functionaries with no power of decision. This situation is hardly conducive to calm, dispassionate discussion and settlement of outstanding differences between member political units, especially when the rules require unanimous decisions. The measure of the effectiveness of the decision-making process, therefore, cannot be sought only in the operations of the League Council.

The somewhat complicated decision-making process illustrated by Figure I seems to provide a key to evaluation of the efficiency of the process. Recommendations are subject to discussion and review at various levels in the decision-making process by competent representatives

of all members of the League. As a result, final drafts
of recommendations which reach the Political Committee have run the gauntlet and are fairly certain of approval by the League Council. Under the circumstances,
however, the screening process which occurs below the
League Council level automatically culls out most controversial issues which fail to receive general support.
Thus, while the decision-making process works well with
routine problems, it fails when really critical political
issues arise. In a crisis, the League Council may not arrive
at the point of voting on the political issue either because
of roadblocks encountered on the way or because in-
sufficient time is available to permit the full operation of
the screening process.

Not unexpectedly, therefore, it is under conditions of
internal crisis that the decision-making processes of the
League fail most conspicuously. For it is here that self-
consciously asserted national political goals come into
play, personified in the political leaders who sit on the
League Council. Examples of such conditions are the
failure of the Arab League to coordinate planning for
the Arab-Israeli War of 1948, the unilateral accession of
the remnants of Palestine (the so-called "West Bank"
of the Jordan) to Jordan in 1950, the protracted internal
conflict in the mid-1950's caused by Iraq's adherence
to the Baghdad Pact, and the recent crisis over Yemen
(in 1962) when League members split ranks to support
the royalists and the republicans.

Under the best of conditions, the decisions of the Arab
League Council are in the form of resolutions which
"recommend," "request," and "urge" member states to
take joint action. This is a logical outcome of the fact
that the League is by design an agency of coordination
which lacks the coercive powers of government. In the
final analysis, therefore, the League Council is a policy-
making body and not a legislative organ. Directive de-

cisions are applied only to the internal organs of the League: the Secretariat and the operating agencies of the organization.

The controversial unanimity rule is useful because it requires all members to confront issues before the Council and at the same time makes certain that only those policies will be adopted which have been agreed upon in advance. The unanimity rule would therefore appear to operate to modify particularistic national policies in favor of joint cooperation in the long run. In opposition to those who argue that the unanimity rule is the cause of the dissensions and weakness sometimes demonstrated by the Arab League, it could be held that the requirement for unanimity is one of the most effective institutions of the League. The unanimity rule does not cause dissension; rather, lack of unanimity is a symptom of the failure of the member states to subordinate particularistic national objectives to those of the organization.

It is doubtful that either the scope of action or the effectiveness of the League would be enhanced by elimination of the unanimity rule, unless it were replaced by a qualified majority vote. Since the organization has no coercive authority, employment of the simple majority rule in the League Council—which would alter the entire intermediate screening process—could lead to heightened tension and increased fragmentation, if not utter collapse of the League. If a majority-minority relationship were to solidify, the minority group might well withdraw from the Arab League; and, so far, despite the internal conflicts which have rocked the League, no member state has seriously proposed resigning.

The decision-making process as it has been described above serves to limit the scope of agreement on concrete issues within the range of the League's purposes and objectives. Nevertheless, the decisions reached by the

League Council during its first eighteen years covered a remarkable range of subjects. Adaptation of decision-making processes to the requirements of the situation has been more important than formalistic legal restraints. The adaptation of voting procedure—i.e., the legal requirement for unanimous decision at the League Council level—has followed the empirical adaptation of the decision-making processes. At the same time, and conversely, the formalistic restraint of the unanimity rule in the League Council has encouraged a high degree of internal coordination in subsidiary bodies; this decision-making process, however, works best when applied to relatively routine problems. As one authority has suggested, the League Council is too often little more than a permanent inter-governmental conference with accommodation at the level of the least common denominator.[7] This is not very damning, however, when one recognizes the intense nationalisms within the region which generate regional tensions and frustrate consensus on questions that threaten hard-won Arab sovereignties. But this problem is a central one in the remainder of this study.

[7] See Ernest B. Haas, "International Integration: The European and the Universal Process," *International Organization*, xv (Summer 1961), 379.

CHAPTER 4 INTERNAL DYNAMICS AND POLICY FORMULATION

In the preceding chapter, it was suggested that crisis situations limit the decision-making processes of the Arab League because they short-circuit established procedures for developing consensus and tend to paralyze the League Council. A corollary to this proposition is that routine problems pass through the decision-making process precisely because they are amenable to unanimous decisions at the League Council level. The purpose of this chapter is to analyze the circumstances that condition the decision-making process of the Arab League and to evaluate their impact on the policies of the organization.

In general terms, the discussion will be concerned with three factors which condition policy formulation: (1) the polarization of power and the formation of blocs within the membership of the Arab League, (2) regional dynamics, and (3) external stimuli. The last two factors will be examined under the general heading of integrative and disintegrative processes, terms that will be explained below. The effects of all three factors will be discussed by reference to actual situations. And, finally, the major operating policies of the Arab League will be discussed in terms of the influence of these factors on League policies.

The Polarization of Power

The rivalry between Iraq and Egypt for leadership of the Arab League has been one of the distinctive factors of the organization since its earliest days. This rivalry has been institutionalized in and through the Arab League in the intervening period and has been a persistent component of the continuum of conflict evident at the League Council level, the level examined in this chapter. The natural outcome of this rivalry has been the development of a balance of power system within the Arab League. In order to understand the internal functioning of the decision-making process, therefore, it is necessary to understand the causes of this relationship and the influence it exerts on policy formulation.[1]

The reasons for the polarization of power within the Arab League are partly objective and partly subjective in nature. Historically, both Iraq and Egypt have been centers of important pre-Islamic civilizations and, later, of great Arab empires. Both countries later passed through periods of British tutelage, developed political consciousness in the years following the First World War, and briefly participated in the activities of the League of Nations in the period just prior to World War II. While the experience of the two countries have been comparable in quantitative terms, the quality of their experiences has been somewhat different.

Before the arrival of the British in the last quarter of the 19th century, Egypt had enjoyed almost 75 years of virtual independence within the loose framework of Ottoman suzerainty. This period had been one of rapid development of commerce and industry, considerable borrowing of Western cultural and political institutions, and the development of a politically conscious elite.

By the First World War, Egypt had experienced the growth of a cultural nationalism which found its origins in the pre-Islamic Egypt of the ancient Pharaohs and developed under the concurrent influence of the Islamic

[1] For a provocative discussion of recent inter-Arab relations, see George A. Kirk, *Contemporary Arab Politics* (New York: Praeger, 1961).

reform movement and of the coordinate Pan-Islamic movement. Inevitably, Egyptian nationalism developed an indigenous character that ran counter to that of the developing Arab nationalism (Pan-Arabism) rooted among Syrian intellectuals of the same period. Even after the First World War, when the British had relaxed their hold on the Egyptian protectorate, Egyptian nationalists had little time for Arab nationalism. Their real concern was with the Nile Valley and the Sudan. Subject to continuous pressure from the British until the end of the Second World War, the major concern of the Egyptians always seemed to be to get rid of the British and get on with their own affairs. Thus, domestic Egyptian politics are characterized by pragmatism; doctrinaire movements affect only the fringes of society.

Iraq, on the other hand, was a backward province of the old Ottoman Empire, meagerly participating in the Arab nationalist movement developing in Syria and Lebanon, and became a political entity only after the defeat of the Turks in 1918, largely as a result of historical accident. Before the First World War, Iraqi adherents to the Arab nationalist movement—many of whom were officers in the Ottoman army—concerned themselves primarily with achieving some form of autonomous Arab state, subordinated to the Ottoman Empire and enjoying a federal status. The projected Arab state was essentially coextensive with the contemporary states of Iraq, Syria, Lebanon, Jordan, and Israel—the area of the so-called Fertile Crescent. The movement was also one of cultural nationalism but, unlike the Egyptian movement, it was oriented to the more illustrious eras of the Arab-Islamic epoch and had no well-defined territorial objectives.[2]

[2] Baghdad, the seat of the illustrious Islamic Abbassid dynasty (AD 750-1258), was the center of an Arab empire that rivaled Byzantium and maintained diplomatic relations with Europe. Its wonders are related in the *Tales of a Thousand and One Nights.*

Instead of unity after the defeat of the Turks, the Arabs of the old Ottoman Empire saw the traditional Ottoman administrative units converted to political entities by the French and British and administered as mandates under the League of Nations. Paradoxically, as a semi-independent state, Iraq became a center of Fertile Crescent Arab nationalism after 1920 at the same time that Arab nationalists were licking their wounds over the failure of postwar political unity. And, revived Arab nationalist movements in the Fertile Crescent area have generally been doctrinaire in nature.

Iraq was given virtually complete authority over her internal affairs in 1932 after a few years of political tutelage. And thus one of the most backward provinces of the Ottoman Empire became the first independent modern Arab state. Subjectively, however, the major concern of the Iraqis seemed less to get on with their internal affairs then to maintain their leadership in the Arab nationalist movement. In the balance, Iraq's relatively happy experience with British control was a source of irritation to the Egyptians, especially since the latter had to follow in the Iraqi footsteps on the road to independence.

Thus if the two responses to Anthony Eden's 1941 suggestion of an Arab union were those of Nuri Sa'id (Iraq) and Nahhas Pasha (Egypt), the reasons were quite different. The Egyptians moved largely, if not completely, to head off the proposed union of the Fertile Crescent that would greatly strengthen Iraq vis-à-vis Egypt. That a few Egyptian leaders felt it was time to join the mainstream of the Arab national movement was a secondary consideration.[3] Of more importance was the

[3] Egyptian leaders who favored the Arab nationalist movement were few but important. Nahhas Pasha reportedly had plans for Egyptian participation in the Arab nationalist movement as early as 1936 but lacked general support. 'Azzam Pasha, the first Secretary General of the Arab League, was a life-long exponent of

Egyptian plan to rally Arab opinion behind a pending move to force the British out of Egypt as soon as World War II was over.

During the period since the founding of the Arab League, the rivalry between Egypt and Iraq has been demonstrated in a number of concrete situations which form part of the history of the Arab League. The League's policy, assiduously promoted by Egypt, of non-cooperation with the West until Arab national objectives had been realized has frequently found Iraq and Egypt in opposite camps. The controversy over Iraq's participation in the Baghdad Pact is, of course, an outstanding illustration of the differences between the two countries and one which almost wrecked the Arab League. Paradoxically, Egypt, now the leader of the Arab nationalist movement, has persistently opposed the plans for unification of Iraq and Syria (a limited form of Fertile Crescent union) which are periodically proposed to the Arab League Council by both Syrians and Iraqis. Iraq, on the other hand, has generally opposed alleged Egyptian domination of the Arab League and was particularly vehement in the denunciation of the first Secretary General of the League for allegedly exceeding his authority and modeling League policies on those of Egypt, without consulting member states.

It is interesting to note that the disputes between the two countries did not cease with the overthrow of the Iraqi monarchy in 1958, though the Egyptians hastened to sign a mutual defense treaty with the Kassem government a few days after the revolution. Significantly, the Kingdom of Iraq participated in League Council meetings to the end, though annual dues were withheld after 1957. The Republic of Iraq, however, boycotted the

the idea of Arab unity and one of the best informed Egyptians of his era on the Arab nationalist movement. See T. R. Little, "The Arab League: A Reassessment," *Middle East Journal*, x (1956), 144.

League Council between 1959 and 1960 until, in the winter of 1960, Iraq was threatened with expulsion. After Kassem's unsuccessful bid to annex Kuwait, in 1961, Iraq again carried out a partial boycott of League activities and withheld dues amounting to more than $2.5 million.

A balance of power system usually encourages the formation of blocs within the system, and the Arab League is no exception. Table 2 illustrates the shifting nature of the Arab League power blocs, keyed to the two polar powers. These blocs are largely informal and have seldom depended upon military treaty or convention; the spate of bilateral military agreements between Egypt and other members of the League in 1955-57 was an exception. The North African members of the League have had their own grudges against Egypt at times, but they have not always moved toward Iraq, largely because the radical Kassem government in Iraq coincided with their adherence to the League Pact.

The traditional dynastic rivalry between the Saudi royal house and the Hashemite kings of Jordan and Iraq operated on the League Council at least until the 1956 ouster of Glubb Pasha from Jordan. Subsequent to this time, the Saudis undertook to furnish a major portion of the annual subsidy the British had paid to maintain the Arab Legion. The Saudis also moved closer to friendly relations with Iraq, and away from Egypt, both before and after the 1958 Iraqi revolution; but from 1959 to 1961 the tendency was for improved relations between the Saudis and the Egyptians. Nasser's support of anti-regime Saudi princes and the Yemeni Republic in 1962 however, reversed the trend and led to a new low in Egyptian-Saudi relations.

Lebanon has tended to remain aloof from both polar powers during most of the period, at times taking the role of mediator between Iraq and Egypt, partly because of the Christian orientation in the early days of the

78

TABLE 2

BLOC PATTERNS IN THE ARAB LEAGUE

Year	Alignment		
	Egypt	*Neutral*	*Iraq*
1946	Saudi Arabia Syria Yemen Lebanon		Jordan
1950	Saudi Arabia Yemen	Lebanon	Jordan Syria[a]
1955	Saudi Arabia Jordan Yemen Syria	Lebanon Libya	None[b]
1958	Yemen Syria[c]	Lebanon Libya Sudan Jordan Tunisia Morocco	(Morocco and Saudi Arabia)[d]
1960	Yemen Syria Sudan Morocco[f]	Tunisia Lebanon Libya Saudi Arabia Jordan	None[e]
1963	Algeria Kuwait Yemen	Tunisia Morocco Libya Saudi Arabia Sudan Jordan	Syria Lebanon

[a] As of the time Jordan annexed Western Palestine.

[b] Influence of the Baghdad Pact controversy.

[c] Egypt and Syria formed the UAR; Yemen joined the first two as a member of the United Arab States, in a loose federation.

[d] Prior to the Iraqi revolution of 1958, Jordan and Sudan could be listed under the Iraqi bloc. Following the revolution, Morocco and Saudi Arabia were friendly to the Kassem regime because of their opposition to Nasser.

[e] Iraq was threatened with expulsion from the League for its boycott of the League Council and its flirtation with the Soviets.

[f] Morocco drawing closer to Egypt.

League and, later, because of her opposition to Nasser's bid for leadership of the Arab nationalist movement.

Largely as a result of internal politics during a series of military-supported governments between 1948 and 1955, Syria's course during the period 1945-1958 was an extreme one. In 1945, Syria was the only Arab state willing to sacrifice her sovereignty to the cause of Arab unity, presumably because of the influence of Iraq. By 1955 Syria had moved to the opposite pole by means of a military alliance with Egypt in protest to Iraq's membership in the Baghdad Pact. And, finally, in 1958 Egypt and Syria merged to form the United Arab Republic. Following the breakup of the UAR, in September 1961, Syria tended to resume her traditional oscillation between the two polar powers by improving relations with Iraq.

Jordan, like Syria, has shifted back and forth between the polar powers, attracted first by the pull of the Hashemite ties with Iraq and then (1955-57) by the support of Nasser's Egypt against continued British control of the country. Jordan's military alliance with Egypt, Syria, and Saudi Arabia in 1957 was transitional, however; in 1958 she moved back into the Iraqi orbit in a loose federal union of the two states. After the Iraqi revolution of 1958, Jordan tended to remain aloof and tried to improve relations with its dynastic enemy, Saudi Arabia. In 1964 Jordan renewed relations with Egypt.

Of the original members of the Arab League, only Yemen has been a consistent supporter of the Egyptians and, even so, she abstained on the 1950 Egyptian-inspired vote to expel Jordan from the League as a result of that country's annexation of the West Bank (eastern Palestine). The newer members of the Arab League (Libya, Sudan, Morocco, and Tunisia) have tended to form a neutralist bloc between Iraq and Egypt, though Tunisia refused to participate in League activities between 1958 and 1961 because of overt differences with Egypt. Kuwait owes its existence to Egypt, in return for its support against Iraq in 1961, but tends toward a neutralist role. Algeria was at least nominally aligned with Egypt in 1963-64.

The polarization of power and the operation of power blocs within the Arab League has tended to narrow its range of action. On the other hand, it would be wrong to conclude that the polarization of power is the only factor which conditions the decision-making processes of the Arab League. Even in the midst of the most bitter disputes between Iraq and Egypt, there has been substantial agreement on some fundamental Arab League issues between the two states.

Thus, in 1955-56, when the dispute over Iraq's membership in the Baghdad Pact was threatening to destroy the Arab League, the Iraqis took the initiative in proposing a Joint Arab army, to be maintained by the Arab League, with the mission of defending the borders of Palestine.[4] In April 1956, the Iraqi delegate requested the League Council to direct the almost defunct Military Commission to examine the cases of alleged Israeli aggression against Syria, Jordan, and Egypt with a view to implementing the 1950 Collective Security Pact. Later the same year, after the Egyptian nationalization of the Suez Canal, Iraq reaffirmed her support of Egyptian policy and, when Egypt was attacked by Israel, offered to implement her obligations under the 1950 treaty in the event of further conflict. In August 1959, while Iraq was boycotting the Arab League in protest against alleged Egyptian control of the organization, Iraqi experts met with others from Arab countries to discuss a common Arab League policy on Palestine. And even while he was boycotting the League, Iraq's General Kassem affirmed his country's support of

[4] Reported by *al-Akhbar* [Cairo], November 17, 1955. Critics argue that Iraq was merely attempting to outmaneuver Egypt, but the effect is that of at least limited consensus.

the League's principles, declaring that Iraq "works strenuously for bolstering cultural, economic, and political ties with all Arab states." After the admission of Kuwait to the League in 1961, Iraq continued to implement Council resolutions but boycotted League activities in which Kuwait was represented.

Aside from the fact that polarization is not complete and is far from inflexible, the increasing disengagement of member states from the influence of the two polar powers and the resultant formation of neutral blocs tends to promote mediation. On substantive matters, competition between the two dominant members of the League must take into consideration the positions of member states uncommitted to either member at any given time. It is necessary, therefore, to look beyond the polarization of power in order to understand the operations of the Arab League.

INTEGRATIVE AND DISINTEGRATIVE PROCESSES

Most of the policies, programs, and activities of the Arab League can be classed as "internal" and "external" according to the focus of the issue. About ten general categories suffice to gather together the diverse policies of the Arab League; these are shown in Table 3, based on the Pact and the 1950 Collective Security Treaty or on operating experience.

Even though an effort has been made to pair related issues, the arrangement of activities as "internal" and "external" provides little information about the operation of the Arab League. If anything, indeed, it provides an erroneous view of the League because the opposed items fit rather neatly together as enumerated. The maintenance of state sovereignties relates well to the policy of political independence for all Arab peoples. Economic and social development and cooperation with the UN seem to complement each other. And the issues of Palestine and Arab

TABLE 3

ANALYSIS OF ARAB LEAGUE ISSUES

Internal Issues/Policies	*External Issues/Policies*
1. Maintenance of state sovereignties	1. Political independence for all Arab peoples
2. Political unification (Arab unity)	2. Afro-Asian solidarity
3. Military cooperation	3. Neutralism
4. Economic and social development	4. Cooperation with the UN
5. Palestine problem	5. Relations with Israel

relations with Israel are obviously two sides of the same coin. The pairing of military cooperation with neutralism, however, does not provide insight into the failure of the League to achieve military cooperation; nor does the achievement of Afro-Asian solidarity in the face of outright Arab disunity add to understanding the situation.

In Table 4, these same issues have been rearranged as *Integrative Processes* and *Disintegrative Processes* on the basis of the historical experience of the Arab League. Using these processes as parameters, a more realistic analysis of the complex workings of the organization can be attempted in an effort to evaluate its successes and failures.

TABLE 4

INTEGRATIVE AND DISINTEGRATIVE PROCESSES

Integrative Processes	*Disintegrative Processes*
Economic and social development	Maintenance of state sovereignties
Collective security	Political unification
Cooperation with the UN	Neutralism
Political independence for all Arab peoples	Palestine problem
Afro-Asian solidarity	
Relations with Israel	

The suggestion has already been made that members of the Arab League, or of any other inter-governmental organization, attempt to realize particularistic goals through the organization and, if necessary, despite the organization. In this context, integrative processes are those which favor consensus on joint policies and collective action toward common objectives: i.e., toward the goals of the organization. Disintegrative processes tend to impede or negate consensus and collective action, largely because particularistic goals conflict with group objectives.

The key question, therefore, becomes that of the relative ability of member states of the Arab League to subordinate particularistic national goals to the common good. The integrative processes listed in Table 4 are generalizations of types of issues on which a large measure of effective consensus between Arab League members exists *a priori*. Disintegrative processes interact with the integrative processes in the course of decision-making and may prevent the realization of objectives which otherwise appear to be of mutual benefit to the entire membership. Furthermore, even the integrative processes are not always mutually reinforcing. On these grounds the policies and procedures of the Arab League cannot be categorized in any such simple manner as that favored by some commentators when they assert that the Arab League is unable to agree on internal issues because of permanent polarization and is, therefore, ineffectual.

It is, of course, true that polarization of power within the membership of the Arab League operates more or less directly to prevent or impede effective action on some issues. The relative positions of Iraq and Egypt on most disintegrative processes have been in complete opposition during most of the life of the League, as illustrated below (plus indicates history of general support and minus general opposition).

	Egypt	Iraq
Maintenance of state sovereignties	+	—
Political unification	—	+
Neutralism	+	—
Palestine problem	+	+

But this type of analysis cannot adequately explain the failure to adopt policies, or to implement policies already adopted, from within the field of integrative processes. Only by an analysis of the interaction of the disintegrative processes with the integrative processes, in terms of their influence on the total membership, may a more accurate insight into the internal dynamics of the League be obtained. The following sections show that the polarization of power is not the only villain.

1. *The Palestine Problem and Israel*

The question of Arab relations with Israel is, of course, the fundamental issue for the Arab League. It is the issue best known by non-Arab observers and the one on which the organization is most often judged. Far-reaching in its effects, the Arab-Israeli issue interacts with and influences the operation of most of the other integrative and disintegrative processes listed above. The Arab-Israeli problem and its corollary, the "Palestine problem," have already been described as two sides of the same coin, though the first has been termed *integrative* and the other *disintegrative*. A brief review of the Arab positions on these two critical issues, therefore, seems in order.

The establishment of Israel in 1948 was the result of a half century of vigorous Zionist activity dedicated to the establishment of a Jewish state in Palestine. The movement acquired great impetus and marshalled powerful non-Zionist supporters just before and during the Second World War as a result of the infamous German atrocities against Europe's Jewish communities, but its success was not due entirely to these developments. Rather, in the Arab view, Israel was established by force of arms in a prolonged and dramatic struggle that led to the displacement of about two-thirds of the population of Palestine—about 85 per cent of the Arab population, or some 650,000 persons—to provide a new refuge for the remnants of Europe's ravished Jewish communities. The Arabs fear further armed encroachments upon Arab territory as a result of Israel's avowed policy to gather in all the remaining Jews of the diaspora.

Arab opposition to the Zionist movement to take over Palestine dates at least from the end of the First World War, but the Arabs proved to be powerless and ineffectual in the face of the overwhelming pressures exerted by the victorious Allies to implement the historic Balfour Declaration through the League of Nations mandate over Palestine. In 1917 the British had bound themselves by the Balfour Declaration to support a movement for a "Jewish national home" in Palestine, a seemingly innocuous objective since the Declaration provided that "nothing shall be done which may prejudice the civil and religious rights of existing non-Jewish communities in Palestine." But, as one astute observer has written, the British administration of the Palestine mandate (1922-48) "created a situation of irreconcilable discord which was bound to make the exercise of force inevitable."[5]

The Arab League owes its existence to a large extent to joint Arab efforts after the First World War to frustrate the Zionist program for a Jewish national home in an area where only 10 per cent of the inhabitants were Jewish. Joint Arab conferences in 1937 and 1938 protested accelerated Jewish immigration and reflected general Arab concern for the future of Palestine. In 1939 the

[5] H. B. Sharabi, *Government and Politics of the Middle East in the Twentieth Century* (New York: Van Nostrand, 1962), p. 169.

British invitation to the governments of Egypt, Iraq, Trans-Jordan, Saudi Arabia, and Yemen to attend the London Round Table talks on the deteriorating situation in Palestine confirmed the view that any solution to the "Palestine Question" required the approval of all Arab states. After 1942, Nuri Sa'id's "Blue Book" and the other Arab plans and schemes that eventually led to the formation of the Arab League were at least partly motivated by the necessity for a joint Arab solution to the Palestine problem.

After the formation of the Arab League, Arab determination to keep Palestine in the Arab camp was underscored by the special treatment given Palestine in the League Pact, the reservation of a seat on the Arab League Council for a Palestine representative, and the League's strenuous efforts to coordinate joint Arab military action during the Arab-Israeli War of 1948-49. Despite its failure to prevent the establishment of Israel, the League Council has continued to act as the legal surrogate for all Palestine Arabs, maintaining a seat on the League Council for the Palestine representative, sponsoring the "Palestine delegation" to the United Nations, and at least nominally supervising the remaining pieces of Palestine in the Gaza Strip and the "West Bank" region of Jordan.

Arabs consider that the establishment and continued existence of Israel, with the official sanction of the British and Americans, is a fundamental moral issue and a serious affront to Arab sovereignty and the principle of self-determination. They condemn the British for their perfidy and the Americans for political expediency in carrying out policies that led to the Zionist occupation of an "indivisible part of the Arab homeland" and created a "bridgehead of Western imperialism." They refuse to recognize publicly even the *de facto* existence of Israel as a state, and their radios support their claim that the "liberation of Palestine" has become a "sacred Arab cause." They regard the provisional boundaries of Israel as temporary armistice lines, as, indeed, they are under the terms of the 1949 United Nations armistice agreements.

In their efforts to seek redress against the "Zionist occupation of Palestine," the Arab states have generally worked together within the Arab League. In an attempt to rectify the situation, short of a resumption of hostilities, the Arab League has inaugurated a far-reaching economic boycott against Israel, supported Egypt's policy to deny Israel the use of the Suez Canal, refused to cooperate with Israel on any regional undertaking (including boycotts of international meetings attended by Israel), and persistently demanded the implementation of United Nations resolutions affecting Israel and its relations with its Arab neighbors. As a minimum, the Arab position now looks to the United Nations for the rectification of Israel's present boundaries in accordance with the 1947 partition plan, the establishment of an international regime for Jerusalem, and the implementation of a UN resolution that supports the right of the Palestine refugees to elect to return to their former homes or to receive compensation for their lost property and other assets in Israel.

The establishment of Israel has provided the main impetus for the collective security arrangements established by the Arab League. All the original members of the League, including Iraq and Egypt, adhered to the 1950 Arab Collective Security Pact. And, in spite of its subsequent adherence to the ill-fated Baghdad Pact, Iraq repeatedly offered to implement the 1950 agreements in the event that any Arab state was attacked by Israel.[6] In 1964, the formation of a Joint Arab Com-

[6] In February 1955, Iraq insisted that her commitment to the Baghdad Pact did not affect her membership in the 1950 Arab

mand under the general terms of the 1950 security pact provided another instance of this consensus on a vital League issue. But most Arabs concede the impracticability of any military move to destroy Israel in the face of current Western policy, and most observers agree that the Joint Arab Command was designed to be a deterrent force rather than an offensive force aimed at Israel.

The Arab League has not hesitated to take its arguments against recognition of Israel to Afro-Asian bloc conferences, where it also urges the extension of the Arab League boycott. The Arabs have achieved some success with this tactic, particularly since the 1955 Bandung Conference. The Arab League has also exploited its neutralist position to secure military and other assistance from the Communist bloc when the West refused to furnish arms for fear they would be used against Israel. Conversely, of course, Western support of Israel has nudged the Arab League toward a neutralist position and sympathetic relations with the "anti-imperialists" of the Communist bloc and the Afro-Asian bloc. In Arab eyes, the establishment of Israel "represented the final and most dramatic encroachment by the West on Arab society and served to spark the radical postwar revolution in the area which is still going on."[7]

In this situation, several of the integrative processes listed in Table 4 interact and reinforce each other: the Arab League's *relations with Israel* influence the organization's orientation toward *collective security* and its attitude toward *Afro-Asian solidarity*. The League's policy of *cooperation with the UN* is also affected by the Arab-Israeli problem, while the League's policy of *neutralism* —normally a disintegrative process—reinforces other

Collective Security Pact but, rather, enhanced the Arab position vis-à-vis Israel. See H. Hall, "The Arab League States," *Current History*, xxix (August 1955), 97.

[7] Sharabi, *op.cit.*, p. 169.

League policies on the question of relations with Israel.

If the Arab League has managed to present a united front in its policy toward Israel, it has usually been less than successful in its attempts to coordinate policy with respect to the vestiges of the Palestine problem. In this context, the "Palestine problem" as it is discussed here refers principally to (1) Arab policies toward the Palestine refugees, (2) attempts to administer a Palestine government in exile, and (3) pressures to dislodge the Israeli bridgehead and restore Palestine to its former Arab inhabitants. The problem is, of course, complicated by the far-reaching effects of the ignominious failure of Arab League policy on Palestine in 1948.

The Arab states most concerned (Jordan, Egypt, Lebanon, and Syria) have refused to resettle the hundreds of thousands of Palestine refugees still living in UNWRA refugee camps in their territories. Criticism of this policy is met by the legal argument that assimilation of the refugees would play into the hands of Israel since the United Nations has supported the Arab demands that the refugees be allowed to return to "Palestine" if they wish to or to be compensated for lost property. (There is also the moral argument that the problem was created by the United Nations—at the urging of the United States and other Western powers—and that the Arab states should not be required to absorb these victims of high policy at the expense of the welfare of their own citizens.) However, there is also reason to believe that resettlement is resisted because the refugees are considered, at the least, a potential cause of political instability. They form a restless force for rapid political change within the Arab community, often becoming the prey of demagogues and professional Palestinians who press for radical programs to recover their lost homeland.

The problem of who shall govern the remnants of

Palestine (Gaza and the "West Bank" of the Jordan River) has never been satisfactorily solved under the circumstances. An All-Palestine Government was formed by the Arab League Council in September 1948 and recognized the following month by all the Arab League members except Jordan. Composed of the supporters of the Higher Arab Committee, headed by the controversial former mufti of Jerusalem, Hajj Amin al-Husseini, the All-Palestine Government has had a tenuous existence. The nominal government was headed by the venerable Ahmad Hilmi until his death in Beirut in 1963, but it had little to do in recent years. The "West Bank" was incorporated into the Kingdom of Jordan in 1950, ostensibly in trust for the Palestinians. Hajj Amin had a falling out with the Egyptians and moved his apparatus from Cairo to Beirut, while the Egyptians set up an independent government in Gaza in 1959, also in trust for the Palestinians. The North African Arab leaders were too busy with their own problems to be much concerned.

The problems of reconciling political rivalries and the inability of the All-Palestine Government to capture the imagination of the Palestinians led the UAR to propose the formation of an ill-defined "Palestine entity" at the September 1959 session of the League Council at Casablanca. Under study by a committee of five Palestine "experts" (League Secretary General Hassouna, chairman) between 1960 and 1963, the plan was finally implemented in the spring of 1964 in the era of good feeling that followed the January 1964 Arab summit conference in Cairo. The death of Ahmad Hilmi in June 1963 had already broached the problem of a successor to represent the Palestinians in the League Council. This was solved in September when the League Council approved the nomination of Ahmad Shukairy, a one-time Assistant Secretary General and former Saudi Arabian representative to the United Nations.

Shukairy and his staff worked through the fall and winter of 1963-64 to draft a "Palestine National Charter" and a constitution for the so-called "Palestine Liberation Organization," meanwhile traveling extensively for consultations with Arab leaders. This activity was climaxed on May 28, 1964, with the proclamation of the Palestine Liberation Organization at the first significant convocation of Palestine representatives since 1948. The meeting, symbolically convened at Jerusalem, was opened by Jordan's King Hussein and addressed by League Secretary General Hassouna. Inasmuch as Hussein's grandfather had refused to recognize the All-Palestine Government of Hajj Amin, this step represented a giant stride forward in inter-Arab relations. Moreover, delegates of all the Arab states except Saudi Arabia attended. Hajj Amin's Higher Arab Committee, along with several other splinter groups, withheld its cooperation after first denouncing Skukairy and his whole scheme as illegal. Shukairy nevertheless promptly cabled the Secretary General of the United Nations that, henceforth, the Palestine Liberation Organization was the official spokesman of the Palestine people.

Much publicity was given in the Arab press to the fact that the emblem of the Palestine Liberation Organization conference bore a huge map of Palestine on which was superimposed the slogan: "We Shall Return!" The oath by some 350 delegates to the congress declared among other things that "Palestine is our homeland . . . repatriation is our goal . . . struggle is our road . . . unity is our guide . . . Palestine is ours . . . and [we] shall accept no substitute homeland. God and history are our witness that we shall sacrifice our blood for your liberation."[8] Nevertheless, the decisions of the conference were largely dedicated to procedural matters: levying token taxes on Palestinians everywhere, setting up ex-

[8] *The Arab World* [Beirut] (May 29, 1964).

ecutive offices and a nominal governmental structure, providing for a worldwide information campaign, and discussing arrangements for the future election of Palestinian representatives. One potentially explosive issue, the question of constituting a Palestinian armed force, was resolved in favor of training refugees by the new Joint Arab Command and a plan to establish the "Palestine" units within existing national armies, two devices calculated to keep the Palestinians out of trouble. In the final analysis, moreover, the resolutions of the congress required ratification by the Arab League Council, thus keeping the activities of the new organization within an established institutional framework.

Thus the Arabs publicly demonstrated for the second time in 1964 that they did not intend to attack Israel, at least in the foreseeable future. While no Arab will publicly disavow the Arab pledge to recover Palestine, and few will do so privately, the question was obviously being accorded only a relatively low priority. For the Arabs were acutely aware of the military, technological, and economic superiority of Israel and had no desire to experience another humiliating defeat like those of 1948 and 1956, even supposing that the major powers did not intervene.

Beyond the immediate issue of "liberation," a disintegrative factor (maintenance of state sovereignty) comes into play along with an integrative factor (economic development). No Arab leader can afford to agitate the Palestine issue to its ultimate conclusion if he has the slightest fear that he will thereby forfeit his own position of power and possibly even lose a portion of his country in the bargain. Furthermore, it was recognized years before the 1948 disaster that the only possible way for the Arabs to defeat the Zionist encroachment on Palestine was by drastic economic reform. It is, therefore, interesting to note that it was subsequent to 1948 that Arab writers on the subject of economic reform seemed almost by agreement to turn to the socialist experience as a model for rapid modernization. It is also pertinent to note that the 1950 Arab Collective Security Treaty provided the first mechanism for economic reform, as a concomitant of military reorganization, in a sweeping effort to make efficient use of the economic resources of the area in the future.

2. *The Arab Independence Movement*

Despite the League's failure in Palestine in 1948, one of the most successful programs carried out by the Arab League has been that of promoting independence for all Arab peoples. The central League policy of encouraging independent status for dependent Arab areas operates in a field of integrative processes dominated by *Afro-Asian solidarity* and *cooperation with the UN*. The League's subsidiary orientation toward strengthening these two policies permits it to exploit them in favor of regional independence. Meanwhile, the growth of the League's policy of *neutralism* has helped it to interact with the integrative processes in a positive sense. The League states have not shrunk from accepting Soviet bloc assistance with the regional "national liberation movement," but none of the new Arab states has fallen prey to Communist machinations.

While the details of the movement toward independence of Arab states are properly the subject of a separate study, a few principles of action may be deduced here. In the first place, representatives of the North African dependencies were present at Alexandria during the preliminary discussions that led to the Arab League and they participated in the ceremonies by which the League was formally established in March 1945. Annex 2 to the Pact of the League of Arab States, furthermore, provides for cooperation with and assistance to "Arab countries which are not members of the Council" and promises the "safeguarding of their future with all the political means" at the disposal of the League. As early as 1945, League Secretary General 'Azzam told a press conference that formal contacts were to be made between the Arab League and political leaders in North Africa and the Persian Gulf area.[9]

The actual techniques employed by the League, drawn from an analysis of League Council decisions, illustrate a fairly consistent pattern of action:

1. representatives of dependent territories are encouraged to look to the Arab League for encouragement and support of their "national" aspirations, including financial support and participation in League activities and programs;

2. the Arab League makes direct representations to the "imperialist power" (Britain and France), offering in some instances to serve as trustee for the dependent territory until independence has been achieved (e.g., Libya, Tunisia, Persian Gulf sheikhdoms);

3. member states of the Arab League act through established diplomatic channels to bring pressure to bear on the "imperialist power" and/or to gain sympathy for the Arab cause among other Western powers (e.g., NATO powers were requested in 1959 not to support France in her military campaign in Algeria);

4. member states act through diplomatic channels to win support of the non-Arab members of the Afro-Asian bloc powers to recognize the newly established provisional Algerian government in Cairo;

5. Arab League states' representatives at the United Nations attempt to gain the support of the Afro-Asian bloc, and other powers, in behalf of motions for com-

[9] For an account of the Arab League's role in the independence of Libya, see Majid Khadduri, *Modern Libya* (Baltimore: Johns Hopkins, 1963), pp. 118-20, 224-26, *et passim.*

missions or investigations by the Security Council and/or the General Assembly into conditions in the dependent Arab territories (the Arab seat on the Trusteeship Council was useful in this respect).

Cooperation among the members of the Arab League has been and continues to be outstanding on the issue of independence for the Arab dependencies. Since 1945, the number of independent Arab states has risen from seven to thirteen. Polarization within the League has not had a noticeably adverse influence on the programs undertaken by the League and, indeed, seems to have acted in quite the opposite way in most cases—with the possible exception of Iraq's obstruction of Kuwait's independence in 1961. Both Iraq and Egypt contributed heavily to the Algerian struggle during a period when the two powers were at each other's throats (1955-60). Even when Iraq was actively boycotting the League (1959-62), General Kassem was pointedly receiving delegations of Algerian rebels and signing over to them sums of money which had been voted by the Arab League Council on a pro-rata basis. The focus has now shifted to the Persian Gulf sheikhdoms, however, where UAR and Iraqi national goals may come into open conflict in the future.

3. *Afro-Asian Solidarity*

Similar success has been achieved with the programs of Afro-Asian solidarity, which have been supported by all Arab League members and which pre-date the 1955 Bandung Conference. The key integrative processes interacting with *Afro-Asian solidarity* are those of League *cooperation with the UN* and *relations with Israel.* Once again, *neutralism* plays a positive role in determining the League's attitude toward Afro-Asian solidarity.

In this situation, a major impact is on the formation of voting blocs in the UN, which will be discussed in

Chapter XI. The interacting process, *relations with Israel,* is a factor here because of the endeavor of the League to secure the support of the Afro-Asian bloc against Israel, including the extension of the Arab League boycott and nonrecognition. The nominal neutralism of a large part of the Afro-Asian bloc operates as a positive factor for the most part and reinforces the Arab League in its dealings with both the East and the West. Conversely, the Arab League has supported the non-Arab states of the Afro-Asian bloc in various undertakings, starting with active support for the Indonesian independence movement in 1946. At various times, for example, the Arab League has attempted to mediate the Kashmir dispute between India and Pakistan, supported Vietnam's independence movement (but not partition), promoted the idea of a mission to the Far East in an effort to keep the Communist Chinese military forces in Korea from crossing the 38th parallel in 1951, and supported independence for Cyprus after 1955. Most of these activities have been in the context of *cooperation with the UN.*

Prior to the Bandung Conference, the League's Secretary General had participated in the New Delhi conference of Afro-Asian nations, in January 1949, and had assisted with the development of a common Afro-Asian policy at several UN sessions.[10] In December 1952, a special Afro-Asian bloc meeting on the situation in North Africa was held in Cairo under Arab League auspices. The non-League participants included India, Indonesia, Afghanistan, Ethiopia, Pakistan, and Iran.[11]

[10] Mohammed Abdel Khalek Hassouna, *The First Asian-African Conference, Held at Bandung, Indonesia* (April 18-24, 1955), (Cairo: Imprimerie Misr, SAE, 1955), Chap. 1.

[11] *Middle East Journal,* vii (1953), 203. The conference resolved that the participants should work for a solution to the North African problems through the United Nations.

In December 1954, when the League Council approved Arab participation in the Bandung Conference, special emphasis was given to "efforts to put on the conference agenda Arab questions, foremost the Palestine question, along with world problems such as the fight against colonialism and racial discrimination and the regulation of armaments and the use of atomic energy and other problems." The resolution also recommended special efforts "to enlist the support of the sponsors of the Conference . . . for Arab policy."[12] The League Council had earlier recommended that Arab member states "strengthen their diplomatic representation" in the countries of the Afro-Asian bloc. In his report to the League Council on the Bandung Conference, the Secretary General recommended that the Arab League Secretariat in Cairo be made the principal liaison center for Afro-Asian cooperation in the Near East and that the League's permanent office in New York serve the same function at the United Nations.[13]

The polarization of power within the Arab League, however, has affected the development of the League's policies toward Afro-Asian solidarity from time to time. While the Arab League supported the Greek Cypriots at the United Nations after 1955, Iraq's ties to Turkey, within the Baghdad Pact, led her to soft-pedal the issue. When the Arab League member states' delegates at the United Nations voted against Turkey in a General Assembly resolution on the Cyprus issue in 1958, Iraq recalled her UN delegate and formally apologized to the Turkish Government. The incident is inconclusive, but it suggests the incipient development of an Arab League policy independent of the policies of the League's members.

[12] Hassouna, *op.cit.*, p. 20.
[13] *Ibid.*, p. 174.

4. *Other Dynamic Processes*

Although generally effective programs have emerged from the three situations discussed above, the League's experience with the important questions of economic development, regional collective security, and cooperation with the UN has been somewhat more ambivalent. In particular the interactive processes which influence any program of economic development envisaged by the Arab League minimize hopes for the success of such programs unless some basic approaches are changed. This situation will be discussed more fully in Chapter IX.

The integrative processes working toward regional economic integration do not always interact positively. *Cooperation with the UN*, for example, is adversely affected by another integrative process: *relations with Israel.* Moreover, the normally integrative processes are more or less in equilibrium with disintegrative processes.

Formal relations with Israel are prohibited to member states, and the possibility for intra-Arab League development in the areas of trade and industry—not to mention such U.S. supported proposals as a regional Jordan River Authority—are greatly reduced. At the same time, the attitude toward Israel has precluded full realization of the potential assistance which could be provided by the United Nations. For example, no Middle East Economic Commission has ever been formed. Other things being equal, however, there is considerable scope for concrete action in the area of economic development, including fruitful cooperation with the United Nations and the Specialized Agencies. The realization of concrete projects is blocked to a large degree by the combination of strong disintegrative processes:

a. The question of *maintenance of state sovereignties* is geared to divergent internal economic policies and conditions (commerce and banking in Lebanon versus an autarchic industrial development program in Egypt, for example) which cannot easily be altered, though their external effects could be harmonized.

b. *Political unification* counteracts economic development programs in two ways: (1) anything less than total political unification poses a threat to the continued leadership of Egypt (or other leader) in the economic sense and, (2) premature political unification poses a threat to particularistic economic interests in the unified states. By deviating from its established policy against partial unity in order to "save" Syria in 1958, Egypt inadvertently threatened the economic viability of an otherwise fairly healthy economy. The United Arab Republic broke down when the Egyptians showed a real intent to integrate the economies of the two countries, in July 1961.

c. The process of *neutralism* is economically and politically disruptive since it threatens established extraregional commercial ties (e.g., Kuwait and Lebanon to Europe; Algeria, Morocco, and Tunisia to the franc bloc) and eventually extends even to the internal political structures of the affected states. As an illustration of the dependence on ties to the West, both Morocco and Lebanon refused to support a proposed Arab League economic boycott of France during the final phases of the Algerian war.[14]

The three more or less successful programs carried out by the Arab League are heavily weighted on the side of the integrative processes, while the integrative process of *economic development* has normally formed an equilibrium with other integrative and disintegrative processes. The processes influencing the *collective security* programs of the League are also essentially in equilibrium, and this helps to explain the fact that the collective

[14] *Middle East Journal*, xiv (1960), 294.

security mechanism has remained weak and ineffectual. The final integrative process, *cooperation with the UN*, has functioned more freely than either of these two noted above, but the Arab League has never been able to establish the kind of relationships it would like with either the United Nations or its specialized agencies. These three problems which, ironically, are considered fundamental to regional organization, will be examined in considerable detail in Part III of this study.

CHAPTER 5 EXTERNAL POLICIES OF THE LEAGUE

THE relatively clear-cut objectives set forth by the League Pact determine the input of Arab League regional programs, and the several interactive processes already discussed help determine the output of the same programs. At this point it is essential that a closer look be taken at three clearly identifiable policies affecting the League's operational approach—and often its response—to specific problem situations external to the region.

The first policy is that of cooperation with the United Nations, in the context of adherence to the principles and purposes of the UN Charter for the benefit of the region. This policy was foreshadowed, at least, by the Pact of the League of Arab States in March 1945. The second is that of neutralism or non-alignment, a policy articulated from an early posture of non-cooperation with the Western powers until the stated national aims of Arab League member states had been realized. Interacting with these two policies is a third externally applied policy, the Arab League boycott of Israel.

COOPERATION WITH THE UNITED NATIONS

Cooperation with the United Nations was initially a manifestation of the Arab League's emphasis on the functional approach to peace and regional security. The founders of the Arab League understood the significance of fruitful mutual cooperation with the United Nations, particularly in the economic, social, and cultural realms.

The point has already been made that Arab League spokesmen at UNCIO in 1945 emphasized the necessity for regional economic and social development in cooperation with the United Nations. Subsequent Arab League spokesmen have never hesitated to reaffirm the League's commitment to United Nations objectives and principles.

Although League spokesmen at San Francisco had emphasized functional problems, the political role of the United Nations has never been overlooked. One of the first actions of the Arab League Council was to refer the open conflict between France and the former League of Nations mandates of Syria and Lebanon to the Security Council, where a settlement favorable to the Arabs was devised in April 1946. In May 1946, when five Arab League leaders met at Inchass, Egypt, to discuss Arab problems of the postwar era, they resolved that the best road to peace lay in Arab League cooperation with the United Nations. Following discussions of the future status of Palestine, Libya, and other dependent Arab territories, the conference resolved that the Arab League should "undertake the realization of the wishes of their people [to be independent] and [ensure] their participation in the League of Arab States."[1] The Secretary General of the League was requested to transmit the Inchass resolutions to the Arab League Council. Finally, still early in the history of the Arab League, the important Political Department of the Secretariat was made responsible for UN matters.

The Arabs soon discovered, however, that the Charter did not always mean the same thing to all men. Their bitterness over UN handling of the Palestine mandate in 1947-48 and the failure of the UN to act on Egypt's case

[1] The meeting at Inchass (May 28-29, 1946) was attended by King Farouk (Egypt), Prime Minister Shukri Quwatli (Syria), Crown Prince Faisal (Saudi Arabia), the Emir Abdullah (Trans-Jordan), and Prince Abdullah (Yemen). See Khalil, *op.cit.*, Document No. 139, pp. 224-26.

against continued British occupation redirected the attention of Arab League member states in the United Nations toward attempts to expand the power of the General Assembly. But these failures only confirmed the League in its effort to secure formal recognition as a regional organization under the UN Charter and to employ the resources of the United Nations to solve such major regional issues as the question of the independence of the North African states. The Arab League Council resolution of February 2, 1951, formalized the attitude of the Arab League toward the United Nations:

"The Arab League declares that it makes the principles underlying the United Nations its own and pledges itself under those principles to help eliminate war.

"But it points out that its member states cannot undertake fully their obligations under the United Nations Charter while some of them have not attained their complete national sovereignty and rights and the right of self-defense."[2]

Since 1951, the Secretary General of the Arab League has been a regular and official observer at UN General Assembly sessions, and the permanent Arab League offices in New York and Geneva coordinate programs and policies affecting both organizations. It is, however, difficult to determine with any precision the degree to which the Arab League has influenced the larger organization. Certainly the persistent efforts of the Arab League states—one of the oldest and most cohesive voting blocs in the United Nations—have helped increase the powers of the General Assembly vis-à-vis those of the Security Council. The vigorous efforts of Arab League states to secure independence for all Arab territories through the

[2] Resolution No. 332, February 2, 1951, summarized in Egyptian Society of International Law, *Egypt and the United Nations* (New York: Manhattan Publishing Co., 1957), p. 128 (hereafter cited as *Egypt and the UN*).

agency of the United Nations have paid off handsomely. And the Arab League actively supported and encouraged the development of the Afro-Asian bloc that now dominates the General Assembly.

Within the context of functionalism, the Arab League states at the United Nations have sought to enlarge the operational scope of the Economic and Social Council (ECOSOC) and have been prominent in the moves for special UN agencies for accelerating economic development and regulating world commodity trade. Informal relations with several UN Specialized Agencies began early in the history of the Arab League, and formal instruments of cooperation have been concluded between the League and the World Health Organization, the Food and Agriculture Organization, the International Labor Organization, and UNESCO.

A detailed analysis of the relations between the Arab League and the United Nations and its Specialized Agencies is included in Chapter XI, and further discussion of this subject will, therefore, be deferred for the present. The major points to be made are that the Arab League has usually exploited the United Nations in the realization of its regional goals, that it has more or less consistently implemented a policy of cooperation with the United Nations and its Specialized Agencies, and that these policies have affected both organizations, not to mention their influence on international society and power factors in the aftermath of World War II.

Neutralism and Non-Alignment

The Arab League's policy of cooperation with and support for the United Nations is to a large extent a corollary of the other major operational policy of the organization. Cold War non-alignment policy, too, has been influenced at least as much by functional considerations as by political considerations. The preoccupation of the less-developed areas of Asia and Africa with economic and social development was already well-articulated before the end of World War II, although the importance of this factor on the subsequent development of Afro-Asian non-alignment is frequently overlooked.[3] In the Arab world, however, non-alignment policy also incorporated a conscious policy of non-cooperation with major Western European powers until certain Arab national political goals had been realized. It was nurtured and strengthened in the Cold War environment of the 1950's, particularly after the Bandung Conference of 1955, but its roots were firmly planted in the 1930's.

Immediately prior to World War II, frustrated nationalistic Arab leaders were strongly attracted by the apparent success of European fascism. The attraction was only to a slight degree ideological, though some Arab intellectuals found in fascism a virile politico-economic system superior to other Western models then available. More important to Arab leaders was that the suddenly powerful fascist states represented a real challenge to traditional French and British hegemony over the Mediterranean basin. And, although they had no desire to substitute one imperial master for another, some Arab politicians were fully prepared to accept Axis help to secure their political independence from Great Britain and France. The advent of the Second World War spoiled these plans.[4]

Egypt was a hotbed of Axis intrigue in the early years of the war, and the Egyptian Government neglected to join the Allied (or United Nations) war effort until 1945.

[3] For cogent discussions of the postwar regional objectives of some Asian leaders, see K. M. Panikkar *et al.*, *Regionalism and Security* (London, 1948).

[4] An interesting inquiry into this situation is available in Majid Khadduri, "General Nuri's Flirtation with the Axis Powers," *Middle East Journal*, xvi (Summer 1962), 328-36. See also Elsa Marston, "Fascist Tendencies in Pre-War Arab Politics," *Middle East Forum* [Beirut] (May 1959), 19-22.

Iraq severed diplomatic relations with Germany (but not with Italy) in September 1939, but an Axis-supported coup d'etat almost put Iraq in the Axis camp in the spring of 1941. Axis sympathies remained strong in Syria and Lebanon under the Vichy French regime at least until de Gaulle's Free French forces "liberated" these French mandates in June 1941. To de Gaulle's embarrassment he was unable to recruit any significant Arab force from among the French-trained troops in Syria and Lebanon that would give the liberation a "native" flavor.

The Arabs failed to see the advantage in supporting British and French war aims when these forces had already frustrated Arab dreams of independence. The possibility of an Axis victory also seemed to mean the end of the British and French hegemony in the area. On the other hand, if few Arabs fought for the Allies or "United Nations," fewer fought for the Axis. In the jargon of the Cold War, the Arabs were in effect maintaining a posture of "positive neutrality," but no one had yet invented the term.

British military victories in Africa in 1941 and political gestures to secure Arab participation in the war effort—by supporting independence for Syria and Lebanon, for example—eventually encouraged Arab leaders to hope for a better future. And in the first optimistic months after the end of the war, the Arab leaders felt that they would soon achieve the final independence for which they had worked and waited so long. The initial success achieved in the United Nations Security Council in 1945-46, whereby France acknowledged the unqualified independence of Syria and Lebanon, served to bolster this optimism.

When, in 1947, Egypt sought in its turn to bring about the end of the British military presence in that country, however, a different reaction occurred. The British held to their rights under the 1936 treaty with Egypt and refused to budge. Egypt subsequently developed, with the cooperation and sympathy of the other members of the Arab League, the general policy of non-cooperation with Great Britain until Arab aims had been satisfied. A British observer foresaw the possibility of this event as early as 1946. Noting that "the League has the blessing of the British government" and that "support for its long term aims is a declared principle of British policy," he wrote that Egyptian domination of the Arab League would pose a dilemma to other members because of the Anglo-Egyptian controversy. If Egypt gained the support of the other members of the League, he observed, "hostility to Britain will become its driving force."[5]

The other members of the League not only supported Egypt, but they extended the policy of non-cooperation to other Western powers with interests in the Middle East and North Africa—particularly to France. In this context, it is of some significance that no such policy was or has since been applied to Spain, which at the time had extensive areas of Morocco under its control, or to Italy, which retained residual interests in Libya and the former Italian colonies of Eritrea and Somaliland.

In the case of Spain, General Franco, conscious that he was ostracized by the international community, had made friendly gestures to the Arab League as early as December 1946. In April 1953, the Spanish foreign minister made a goodwill tour through the Arab League states, after which Franco offered to negotiate treaties of friendship and non-aggression with the Arab states. In January 1954, the League reportedly invited Franco to visit the Arab states. In turn, the League Secretary General visited Spain as the official guest of the Spanish government in April of the same year. Most of this display of mutual admiration, incidentally, took place while the League was rejecting Western approaches for a "regional security

[5] H. S. Deighton, "The Arab Middle East and the Modern World," *International Affairs,* xxii (1946), 518-19.

pact" in the Middle East that represented an extension of the North Atlantic Treaty Organization.

The failure of the Middle East Defense Treaty proposed by Secretary of State Dulles undoubtedly represented a landmark in the development of Arab non-alignment policy. But Egypt had already taken the lead in advocating a policy of neutralism once the dimensions of the Cold War schism between the Soviet bloc and the West became clear. The real turning point may have been reached as early as June 27, 1950 when the Egyptian representative to the UN Security Council refused to participate in the vote on a resolution calling for all member states to contribute to the UN effort in Korea. On June 30, the Egyptian delegate explained that he had lacked instructions on the vote but that, in any event, he would have abstained because the Korean situation was simply a manifestation of the dispute between the East and the West that already threatened world peace and security (and, presumably, the United Nations should not participate in this partisan struggle). Moreover, he said, the United Nations had not taken such strong action in the case of similar serious breaches of the peace in other areas.[6]

During the rest of the Korean crisis, most of the Arab League members at the United Nations underwrote Egypt's position. Only Iraq supported the UN action in Korea; the other Arab delegations abstained from voting on the issue when the General Assembly became involved in the Korean problem. However, other Arab League members reportedly joined Iraq to oppose an Egyptian bid during the League Political Committee meetings of

[6] The episode is summarized in the *United Nations Yearbook*, 1950 (New York: United Nations, 1951), pp. 222-24. Egypt voted for the earlier resolution of June 25, 1950, condemning the North Korean government for its invasion of South Korea. The reference to other breaches of the peace was obviously intended to include Palestine.

January 1951 to secure general Arab League endorsement of a thoroughgoing neutralist policy. In 1954, in a review of the debate of the period on the League's Cold War policy, Nuri Sa'id asserted that the Arab League Council had refused to sanction neutralism as a political principle in 1950, although it insisted upon the satisfaction of Arab political demands as a precondition for cooperation with the West.[7]

Neutralism has remained a controversial (i.e., disintegrative) issue within the Arab League, although the policy of non-cooperation with the West (Britain, France, and the U.S.) until legitimate national aims have been satisfied has received general approval and support. In January 1954, for example, the League Council supported Egypt's stand against Great Britain but refused to commit itself to neutralism despite some equivocal language:

"The Council firmly supports Egypt in her just and firm attitude and urges Arab countries to reconsider their policies on the basis of insisting that there should be no cooperation or friendship with others, whoever they may be, except on the basis of justice and right, dignity and partnership. The Arab countries will extend their hands to whoever proves by deeds and not words his sincere friendship, good will, loyalty to peace, and real regard for human dignity."[8]

Considering the Arab League's display of friendship for Spain in 1953 and 1954, however, it would be as logical to conclude that the "neutralist" overtones of this resolution imply a favorable attitude toward Spain's Franco as to conclude that the Arab League was leaning toward the Soviet bloc—which at the time was playing no large

[7] *Middle Eastern Affairs*, v (1954), 352.
[8] League Council Resolution No. 597, January 11, 1954, quoted in *Middle Eastern Affairs*, v (1954), 67.

role in the Arab world. In support of this conclusion, it is perhaps worth noting that at about the same time the League Council issued a declaration supporting General Franco in his disputes with the French over Morocco and with the British over Gibraltar.

By 1955, however, outside pressures—largely from India—had pushed the Arab League into the "third force" arena. Nehru's visit to Cairo in August 1953, during which he talked to Arab League Secretary General Hassouna as well as to Egyptian political leaders, undoubtedly exerted considerable influence in the direction of neutralism. Moreover, India's astute anti-Western ambassador in Cairo, K. M. Panikkar, is said to have indoctrinated key Egyptian and Arab League officials with the tenets of neutralism before he left Egypt in 1954.[9]

It would be facile to ascribe to Panikkar the entire credit for turning Egypt onto an irreversible neutralist course, a course along which President Nasser has urged the other Arab League states. Nasser has been a major proponent of non-alignment since Bandung, but Egypt was already veering toward neutralism before Nasser arrived on the scene. It is interesting, incidentally, that the Egyptian delegate's failure to vote on the Korean resolution in the Security Council in June 1950 was shared by the Indian delegate—who may or may not have influenced his colleague. What is certain is that the Arab League had already established ties with the small bloc of new Asian nations by the late 1940's, although the initial motive may have been associated with the vague idea of an "Islamic Commonwealth" advocated by the Secretary General. Moreover, the League Secretary General had attended the 1949 Afro-Asian conference in New Delhi. In more specific regional terms, Egypt and some other Arab states of the Arab League had always en-

[9] See James W. Spain, "Middle East Defense: A New Approach," in *Middle East Journal*, VII (1954), 258.

visaged the eventual withdrawal of the non-regional powers from the League's self-proclaimed jurisdiction. And
this meant the withdrawal of the Western powers which
had established imperial claims in the area in the
19th century and had strengthened them as a result of
the First World War.

On the other hand, it is likely that Panikkar's influence
struck a responsive chord among the new generation of
Arab leaders who came to power after, indeed largely as
a result of, the Palestine disaster. His assignment to Cairo
following a tour of duty in Communist China more or less
coincided with Nasser's rise within the Revolutionary
Command Council. His writings and personal discussions with the young revolutionary Egyptian leaders sure-
ly helped provide a rational basis for Egyptian foreign
policy decisions after 1952.[10] The frankly functional approach to regionalism already adopted by Egypt and the
Arab League, largely as an outgrowth of the thinking
being applied to other regional movements in the less
developed areas, helps justify a policy of accepting help
with regional economic and social development and of
establishing cultural ties with all friendly nations. Since
there are no necessary political consequences to this type
of international relations (according to functionalist theory), non-alignment or neutralism should therefore logi-
cally be the normal extension of regionalism. Most Arab
advocates of non-alignment point to the lack of tangible
political advantages enjoyed by the Communist bloc nations in the region after a decade of close association
with the Arab League states. Indeed, the tone of Khru-
shchev's statements in Cairo during his 1964 visit to the
United Arab Republic suggested that the Soviets were
more than a little chagrined at the lack of political impact

[10] Scholar, geopolitician, statesman, and diplomat, Panikkar was
influential in the development of the concept of the Afro-Asian
"third force" in the polarized postwar world. See his *Regionalism
and Security*, cited above.

resulting from their economic and military assistance programs in the Arab world.

It is of more than passing interest to note that, historically, regionalism has generally been exclusive and that this exclusiveness has usually been justified on a doctrinal basis. Americans, who dominate the Organization of American States, have long relied on the Monroe Doctrine to keep European influence out of the Western hemisphere, for example. The abortive World War II Japanese scheme for an "Asian Co-Prosperity Sphere" generated considerable regional interest by promising "Asia for the Asians," while the Japanese systematically replaced European interests in Southeast Asia. Arab nationalism and the urge for Arab unity are the calls to arms in the Arab world. These regional motivations are essentially negative. Non-alignment or neutralism at least offers the advantage of continued contact with the extra-regional Great Powers (if only to exploit their superior economic power and their technology) at the same time that it bars the way—at least in theory—to the maintenance or establishment of political beachheads within the region by either the West or the East. Moreover, it facilitates inter-regional contacts and cooperation. And, finally, of course, the logic of non-alignment with its essentially functionalist basis is to increase the importance of the United Nations as the coordinator of functional programs and the guarantor of world security.

Arab participation in the Bandung Conference of Afro-Asian nations in April 1955 marked the point of no return for the Arab League on the question of non-alignment. In his report on the conference prepared for the Arab League Council, League Secretary General Hassouna noted that the meetings discussed the following subjects of particular interest to the League: (1) the Palestine problem, (2) the liberation of Arab dependencies in North Africa, Aden, and the Persian Gulf protectorates,

(3) cooperation with the United Nations, and (4) the matter of strengthening regional representation on the UN Security Council.

At the conclusion of his report, the Secretary General recommended that, since the goals of the Bandung Conference are essentially those of the Arab League, the League Secretariat should act as a coordinating center in the Near East for Afro-Asian activities and that the League's office in New York should perform the same function at the United Nations. In the Far East, the Columbo Plan Secretariat was to carry out Afro-Asian programs in its area of interest. The report also recommended prior consultation on all Bandung resolutions that might be brought to the attention of the UN for action. Furthermore, the Secretary General suggested that Arab League economic and trade agreements might usefully serve as models for other Afro-Asian regional groupings and proposed that the Secretariat serve as a clearinghouse for the exchange of information on petroleum affairs and trade within the Afro-Asian community.[11]

Western observers viewed events in the Arab Middle East after the Bandung Conference through a pink haze, in which "positive neutrality" seemed to mean positive rejection of anything Western and positive acceptance of anything connected with the Soviet bloc. The 1955 Soviet bloc arms deal with Nasser was followed by the Suez Crisis, the Eisenhower Doctrine, and the near-subversion

[11] Hassouna, *op.cit.*, pp. 173-78. The Secretary General appears to have been attracted primarily to the non-aligned segment of the Afro-Asian bloc, dominated by India, and failed, like most Arab leaders, to see the movement as a potential instrument of Communist policy. However, the virtual withdrawal of Arab support from the Communist-infiltrated Afro-Asian Peoples' Solidarity Organization in Cairo in 1964 and Nasser's drive for the leadership of the non-aligned nations after the death of Nehru seems to confirm the original intent to support the Afro-Asian movement as an independent force.

of Syria. In 1957, even such staunchly pro-West Arab leaders as Iraq's King Faisal and Saudi Arabia's King Saud climbed on the bandwagon. During the brief Saudi-Iraqi "honeymoon"—designed to counteract Egyptian pressures on their conservative regimes—the two kings issued a statement condemning both Communism and Western "imperialism."

In the face of Western pessimism, the Arabs insisted that they meant what they said about "positive neutrality." And in 1959 another turning point arrived when Republican Iraq became so involved with the Soviet Union that even the Arabs concluded that it was little more than a satellite. An unprecedented meeting of the Arab League Political Committee, in Beirut in April 1959, condemned Iraq for its ties with the Soviet bloc. Noting that the Arab League states adhered to a policy of non-alignment "which is the policy which safeguards the independence and sovereignty of the Arab states," the Political Committee resolution of April 7 went on to condemn "any external influence . . . which aims at the division of the Arabs" and called on Iraq to adhere to the decisions of the meeting.[12]

In June 1961, an official Arab League information bulletin published a definition of neutralism developed at a Cairo conference of 22 non-aligned nations, including most of the Arab League states. According to the statement, participants in the proposed Belgrade conference of non-aligned states must:

1. follow an independent policy, based on non-alignment and peaceful coexistence with nations of differing social and political structure;

2. consistently support popular liberation and independence movements;

[12] Text in Khalil, *op.cit.*, pp. 204-5. Besides Iraq, three pro-Western League members were absent: Jordan, Libya, and Tunisia. Sudan was present but abstained from voting, *Middle Eastern Affairs*, x (1959), 205.

3. refuse to participate in collective military pacts or become involved in East-West Cold War disputes;

4. refuse to enter into any agreement to establish military bases on its territory for either side in the Cold War.[13]

By 1963 non-alignment was hardly a controversial subject among Arab League members, although many reservations continued to be expressed and some sound lessons have been learned the hard way. The Ba'th Party coup d'etat in Iraq in February 1963 brought forth a torrent of abuse from Soviet bloc propaganda weapons and demonstrated to most Arabs what happened when non-alignment policies were allowed to veer off course. But, also in 1963, Kuwait and Jordan established diplomatic relations with Soviet bloc countries for the first time, Lebanese leaders repeatedly emphasized their neutrality, and even Crown Prince Faisal of Saudi Arabia was rumored to be under pressure to establish relations with the Soviet Union.

As they achieved their independence, the North African members of the League, interestingly enough, seemed to succumb rather readily to the appeals of non-alignment, with the temporary exception of Tunisia and Libya. In an address to the National Press Club in Washington on May 5, 1961, two months before the Bizerte incident, Tunisia's President Bourguiba said that member states of the Arab League felt "very uneasy" about Nasser's claim to the leadership of the Arab unity movement and Arab nationalism. He added that the North African countries were not in favor of positive neutrality because they "did not want to stand against the Western world."[14] At the time, however, Morocco was already engaged in negotiations with the Soviet bloc for military and economic assistance and the rebel Algerians were reportedly solicit-

[13] *Arab News and Views* [New York], July 1, 1961.
[14] Reported by *Middle East Journal*, xv (1961), 317.

ing the bloc nations for aid in fighting the French. Only Libya and Tunisia seemed staunchly allied with the West.

The Bizerte incident changed things for the doggedly pro-West Bourguiba, and in January 1964 he even announced that Tunisia was about to take the rather extreme step of establishing diplomatic relations with Communist China. The Libyan government was forced into at least partial acknowledgement of non-alignment later in 1964 when President Nasser called for the end of foreign military bases in the Arab world. The only important foreign bases in the independent states of the Arab world were the British Army base at Tripoli and the American Air Force base at Wheelus Field. After some hesitation, the Libyans demanded that the British and the Americans remove these bases. Libya did not move immediately toward diplomatic relations with the Communist bloc, however.

For the Arab League, non-alignment has been a reasonably successful policy. And, in the final analysis, it probably is the only sound policy that a regional organization could follow. Non-alignment permits the Arab League both greater freedom of action and greater influence in the United Nations, a circumstance which Arab League officials fully appreciate. Arab League cultivation of and cooperation with the Afro-Asian nations inside and outside the United Nations has added to the effectiveness of its policies with respect to the United Nations and has increased Arab League leverage with respect to the unsettled problems of the Palestine refugees, for example. On the question of "popular liberation movements" in the remaining Arab dependencies, the Afro-Asian bloc has given substantial support to Arab League policies. And, in the context of regional economic and social development, Arab League non-alignment has at least contributed to the circumstances that the Soviet bloc and the West are competing for opportunities to build dams, power stations, factories, and schools in the Arab world.

Western observers have long been disturbed, however, by the fact that the impetus to the Arab League non-alignment policy has often seemed to have a negative character. In the first instance, although the device of bargaining with the West for independence and sovereignty is a legitimate political tool, the reactions have too often been spiteful on both sides. The best example of this is, of course, the Suez Crisis of 1956, apparently encouraged by the somewhat spiteful withdrawal of a U.S. offer to help finance the Aswan Dam. In the second place, the Arab League's preoccupation with the problem of Israel, which it considers an example of Western perfidy, has led the Arab League and its member states into dangerous terrain in search for armaments denied by the West. There are, hopefully, indications that non-alignment will be used less as a tool against the West in the future. But from the Arab point of view, at least, Western encouragement of and support for the Arab League's regional development programs through the agency of the United Nations might be a useful way to restore Arab confidence in the West and, at the same time, take the sting out of non-alignment.

THE BOYCOTT OF ISRAEL

The economic boycott of Israel has long reflected a basic Arab League policy to obstruct the development of Israel, which the Arab states regard as "Zionist-occupied Palestine." Under the terms of Resolution 16 of the Arab League Council, December 1945, all members of the Arab League agreed to boycott goods produced by Zionist firms in Palestine. The boycott was originally envisaged as a simple operation to prevent smuggling, and the Arab League Boycott Office was headed by an Egyptian Coast Guard officer until 1951. But since 1948, when Israel established itself as a state, the boycott has been elaborated into an instrument of economic warfare by which all financial and commercial transactions between Arab states and Israel are banned; foreign industrialists and entrepreneurs who establish factories or branches in Israel are denied the opportunity to sell to or operate in Arab states; and attempts are made to restrict land, sea, and air communications serving Israel.

The Arab League boycott policy is known in the United States chiefly for its humorous or irritating aspects. The United States government takes no official cognizance of the boycott, and information on the effect of the boycott on U.S. firms is not widely disseminated. Everyone knows Elizabeth Taylor and all her films are banned in Arab countries because she contributes generously to Zionist causes, for example. Tourists soon learn that they cannot enter an Arab country from Israel, and that Arab customs officials refuses to stamp a passport containing an Israeli visa. But there are more serious aspects of the boycott that make it a formidable weapon against Israel. In October 1962, about eighty American business concerns and seventy U.S. owned ships were said to be blacklisted by the Arab League because of business relations with Israel.[15] Several hundred other companies in other countries (mostly in Western Europe) are also blacklisted.

Although it is generally agreed that the Israeli economy has been hurt by the boycott, there is no way of telling how much harm has been done. Moreover, Israeli spokesmen maintain that the Arab League states are hurting themselves more than Israel because the boycott policy is hindering economic development in the Arab world. Perhaps one of the principal benefits of the boycott program, in Arab League eyes, is that it keeps the issue of Israel constantly before the Arab people. No Arab country

[15] According to a report of the American Jewish Committee cited by the *Middle East Journal*, xvi (1962), 75.

has seriously proposed discontinuing the boycott, and—even when internal relations are at their worst—Arab states' representatives to annual Arab League boycott conferences almost always show up. For example, a boycott conference at Tripoli held during June and July 1960 was attended by representatives of all Arab League states at a time when Iraq and Tunisia were boycotting Arab League activities as a result of their differences with Egypt's Nasser. On the other hand, the political effectiveness of the boycott program was attested to by the late Dag Hammarskjold in 1957 when he condemned the Arab League action as a major obstacle to UN efforts for peaceful settlement in the Middle East.

In a few instances, the Arab League has used the boycott as an international political weapon, though the usual method is to "blacklist" individual foreign concerns on a case basis. One of the more notable instances of a politically important boycott was the action taken against Air France in 1957, when the Arab League announced that its members would henceforth deny overflight and landing rights to the airline. The case involved Air France investments in Israeli development projects and the alleged production of "propaganda films" for Israel. The Arab League ban halted Air France operations at Cairo and Damascus. After holding out for 18 months, the company finally capitulated to Arab demands.

In 1959, a similar case against Renault, the French automobile company, led to the collapse of Renault's plan to establish an assembly plant in Israel. The Arab League Boycott Office threatened to deny Renault the entire Arab market for its products. In this case, French-Israeli diplomatic relations were reportedly strained and Israel reportedly cancelled a contract for a 650-passenger ocean liner that was to have been built in France.[16] Since both Renault and Air France are owned by the French govern-

[16] *Washington Post*, October 19, 1959.

ment, the two boycott cases were undoubtedly intended as retaliation to French support for Israel during and after the Suez Crisis of 1956.

The boycott at the political level was also used in 1957 to dissuade Czechoslovakia, Hungary, and Bulgaria from trading with Israel. Relations between the Arab states and Turkey have been cool for years because of Turkish-Israeli commercial ties. Cyprus has also been of special interest to the Arab League Boycott Office because of its alleged use as an entrepôt, from which Israeli-made goods are transhipped to Arab states (and *vice versa*) on Cypriot manifests. In July 1960, the United Arab Republic (Egypt) broke off diplomatic relations with Iran after the Arab League Council condemned the Shah's confirmation of an earlier *de facto* recognition of Israel. An attempt to extend the boycott to Iran was threatened.

Of more concern to the Arab League, however, has been the question of West German recognition of Israel, which caused considerable anxiety in Arab capitals in 1963-64. League pressure was brought to bear on German diplomatic representatives in the Arab states, and Arab diplomats exhorted German officials in Bonn not to take any precipitous action. A thinly veiled threat that the Arabs would retaliate by according diplomatic recognition to the East German regime backed a very real threat to boycott German industry and trade in the Arab area. The threat of boycott was also used in 1962-63 against members of the European Economic Community who, the Arabs feared, were about to conclude an agreement to make Israel an associate member of the European Common Market.

Arab League officials and political leaders of member Arab states have made every effort to extend the boycott of Israel. The League's ties to the Afro-Asian bloc have been exploited for this purpose, and many Asian states refuse even to recognize Israel out of respect for Arab policy. In some instances, the identity of Muslim religious interests between Arab states and such countries as Iran, Pakistan, and Indonesia has served to bolster Arab League arguments against economic relations with Israel. Since 1961, the Arab League has been particularly concerned about Israeli economic and technical assistance activities in Africa. Despite a number of countermeasures, however, the Arab League has not been very successful in persuading newly established African states to turn down Israeli offers of training, technical assistance, and commercial ties. The Arab League has taken credit for the collapse of joint ventures in the shipping field between Israel's Zim line and the governments of Sierra Leone and Ghana. And the program has been partially effective in a few other instances, including Somalia and Nigeria. Israeli ties with West African countries continue to develop, however.

The Arab League policy is based on the Arab position that the 1948 Arab-Israeli War never ended and that a state of belligerency continues. For its legal precedent, the League also leans on the example of the League of Nations' boycott of Italy during the mid-1930's.[17] This state of affairs not only accounts for the penalties and sanctions levied against blacklisted companies, but also for Egypt's claim of the right to search and seize ships transiting the Suez Canal with cargoes for Israel or with Israeli products aboard. An official statement issued by the Arab League Secretariat, December 7, 1963, in connection with the threatened boycott of the British Norwich Union Insurance Company, aptly illustrates the rationale behind the boycott: "There are a number of facts that rebut the allegations of world Zionism which is trying to depict the incident as interference in British domestic affairs. World Zionism thus ignores the fact that by boycotting Israel,

[17] More recently, the Arabs have derived considerable comfort from U.S. attempts to maintain an economic embargo against Cuba.

the Arabs are only defending themselves against the aggressive forces which occupy a part of their land and with whom they are in a state of war."

According to the release, the facts were:

1. The Arab boycott is not an act of revenge or aggression, but a defensive, protective one.

2. The Arab boycott is not based on any racial or religious discrimination. The Arab states have dealings with companies owned by Jews who do not support Israel.

3. The Arab boycott is a legitimate weapon which does not conflict with international law.

4. The Arab states are careful not to harm the interests of foreign companies, and for this reason the Arab states contact the companies which have relations with Israel to discover the nature of these relations. If these relations prove to be strictly commercial, no action is taken against the company; but if these relations prove to strengthen Israel's economy, its war effort, and expansionist aggressive intentions, then the company is asked to choose between the Arabs and Israel.

The boycott of Israel is decentralized to the member states of the Arab League (and to some non-member territories like Qatar and Bahrain), but the League Secretariat exercises close control over the program by means of a permanent League Boycott Office in Damascus. Semi-annual meetings of member-country "boycott liaison officers" help coordinate boycott policies and programs throughout the world, under the general guidance of the Arab League Council and the Economic Council.

CHAPTER 6. ADMINISTRATIVE ORGAN-IZATION AND FUNCTIONS

THE center of gravity of the contemporary international organization is the permanent Secretariat, where the day-to-day administration is carried on, where technical support is provided for the organization's programs, and where established policies are put into execution or supervised. A discussion of the organization and functions of the Arab League Secretariat is therefore an essential part of the development of the over-all analysis of policy formulation and execution. The present chapter is devoted to the administrative functions of the Secretariat, while the following chapter is concerned with the role of the Secretary General as executive, mediator, and principal spokesman for the Arab League.

INTERNAL ORGANIZATION OF THE SECRETARIAT

The permanent General Secretariat provided for by Article 12 of the Pact of the League of Arab States was to be located in Cairo and was to consist of a Secretary General, an unspecified number of Assistant Secretaries, and "an appropriate number of officials." The details of the Secretariat's functions and organization and the procedures to be used by the Secretary General were largely left to the discretion of the League Council, which subsequently approved the necessary administrative regulations in 1953 (see Appendix F). The Pact restricted itself to naming the first Secretary General and to providing him with the authority to prepare the draft of the annual budget and to convene the League Council. The Secretariat was also designated the depository for copies of treaties and agreements concluded between member states or between member states and a third state (see Appendix B).

The appointment of the Secretary General carries with it the rank of ambassador, since this officer is not only the chief administrator of the Arab League but also its principal representative, whether operating within the League membership, as a visitor to foreign (i.e., non-Arab) states, or as the organization's representative at international conferences or the United Nations. The Arab League has had only two Secretary Generals in its history: Abd ur-Rahman 'Azzam (1945-1952), and Abdel Khalek Hassouna, who began his third five-year term in September 1962. The Secretary General is appointed by the League Council, in accordance with Article 12 of the Pact of the Arab League, with the approval of two-thirds of the member states. The first appointment was for a period of two years, but the Council later established the term of office as five years, subject to renewal, and extended 'Azzam Pasha's term accordingly.[1]

The administrative regulations of the Secretariat provide for an unspecified number of Assistant Secretaries General, though there have never been more than four at any one time and usually no more than two or three.[2] The Assistant Secretaries are nominated by the member governments, appointed by the Secretary General, and approved by the League Council, in accordance with Article 12 of the League Pact. They work directly under the

[1] Mohammed Abdel Aziz Badr, "La Ligue des Etats Arabes," *Oriente Moderno*, xxxii (1952), 114. The term of five years is provided by the Internal Regulations of the Secretariat General, May 10, 1953 (see Appendix F).

[2] Some Arab commentators refer to a provision for four Assistant Secretaries in the Internal Regulations; a fifth Assistant Secretary for Economic Affairs has also been mentioned. The text of the Internal Regulations of the Secretariat (see Appendix F) does not specify the number of Assistant Secretaries, however.

Secretary General and normally exercise supervisory control over one or more departments of the Secretariat.[3] As senior officials of the League, each Assistant Secretary holds the rank of minister plenipotentiary.

The office of the Secretary General also includes the four so-called supervisors (*mushrifiin*), experts in the fields of cultural affairs, economics, public health, and social affairs. Directly subordinate to the Secretary General is the Conference Secretariat, to which are attached the archives and the library.

The Secretariat has grown from a nucleus of six men in the Egyptian foreign office in 1945 to a complex organization with a staff of about 175 professional personnel. (See Table 5.) In addition to its nine departments, the Secretariat also administers various bureaus, including the Boycott Office in Damascus; the Arab Narcotics Bureau, the Institute of Advanced Arab Studies, and the Institute of Arab Manuscripts, all in Cairo; and the League's Social Service Centers in several member states. Two autonomous agencies, affiliated with the Arab League are also domiciled in Cairo, near the Secretariat: the Arab Postal Union and the Arab Telecommunications Union. Other "specialized agencies" of this general type, including the authorized but inactive Arab Development Bank, will presumably operate in close coordination with the Secretariat as they are established. The Secretariat also maintains permanent offices in New York and Geneva for liaison with the United Nations and its Specialized Agencies and operates a growing number of "Arab Information

[3] The first Assistant Secretary General was Ahmed Shukairy, a Palestinian, who served as Assistant Secretary General for Political Affairs, 1951-57. In 1964, the Assistant Secretaries General were Ahmed ed-Dardiri Isma'il (Egypt), Dr. Said Nawfal (Egypt), Aref Taher (Iraq); and Lt. Gen. Mohammed Fawzi (Egypt), for Military Affairs. Other Assistant Secretaries General have included Dr. Ra'if Abu'l-Lam' (Lebanon), 1953-57; General Mohammad Ibrahim (Egypt), 1954-58; Mohammed Abdel Moneim Mustafa (Egypt), 1958-60; Lt. Gen. 'Ali 'Ali Amer (Egypt), 1961-64.

TABLE 5
ORGANIZATION OF THE ARAB LEAGUE SECRETARIAT

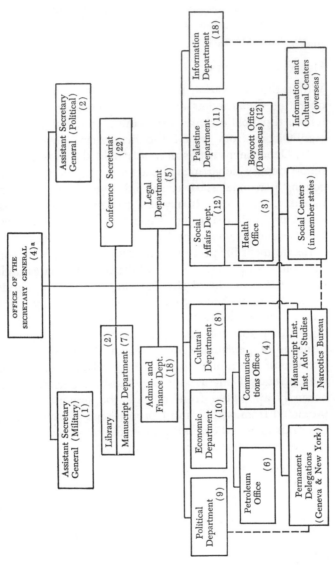

[a] Numbers in brackets refer to staff, December 1960; dotted lines show supervision/coordination.

Centers" in New York (with branches at Washington, Chicago, San Francisco, Dallas, and Ottawa), Geneva, Paris, London, Bonn, Rome, Buenos Aires, Rio de Janeiro, New Delhi, and other world capitals.

PERSONNEL POLICIES

Within the Secretariat, professional staff members in the operating departments are graded according to the system of diplomatic ranks prevailing in the Egyptian Foreign Office—from which the Secretariat developed in 1945. Department heads normally hold the rank of counsellor; deputy department heads are first secretaries. Incoming personnel start as second attachés and are promoted, usually after two years, to first attachés. Subsequent promotions through the ranks are to third secretary, second secretary, and eventually counsellor.

Recruitment for professional personnel is by open competition, held periodically in all the member states under the direction of one of the Assistant Secretaries. Service with the League Secretariat is financially attractive, since pay in the graded service is established as two-grades higher than that for the Egyptian Foreign Service.[4] The turnover of personnel, however, has been considerable because of the limited potential for advancement. Since the Secretary General and the Assistant Secretaries are normally appointed from outside the organization, not promoted from within, most professional personnel leave the Arab League Secretariat after they have attained the rank of counsellor and return to their own country's for-

[4] The graded service of the League does not include the Secretary General, who receives a salary equal to that of an ambassador in the Egyptian foreign service; in 1960, the basic monthly salary of the Secretary General was 500 Egyptian pounds (or about $1,450 at official rates of exchange). The Secretary General also receives additional allowances. The basic monthly salary for an Assistant Secretary General was 150 Egyptian pounds, plus allowances that brought the total to 265 pounds a month in 1960 (approximately $765 at official rates of exchange).

eign services.[5] Furthermore, many of the staff members in the past have been "seconded" to the League from the foreign services of the member countries; in these instances, too long a stay at the Secretariat is considered to be detrimental to individual careers.

There is no pension system, but a provident fund is in effect; 7.5 per cent of each month's pay is deducted and matched by an equal amount contributed from Arab League funds. The total amount is available to the staff member when he leaves the service of the Secretariat. Generous separation pay has also been provided, paid at the rate of one month's pay for each year of service, based on the pay of the highest grade attained.

One of the problems that has plagued the League Secretariat, like the secretariats of other international organizations, is that of equitable national composition of the staff, approximating proportional representation of member states. Data on 150 Secretariat officers, including those assigned to the Boycott Commissariat in Damascus, reveal a predominance of Egyptian personnel. This is not a surprising discovery considering that the Secretariat is located in Cairo. There is a rough analogy with the situation in New York, where about one-fourth of the professional staff of the UN Secretariat is American.

Table 6 shows the national composition of Secretariat staff as of December 1964, with the representation of each member state compared to its population as a per cent of all the Arab League states. At the time, there were no staff members from Kuwait or the North African states. Strict proportional representation in the future Secretariat staff, however, is improbable because of the scarcity of

---

[5] Exceptions to this general rule are made. Ahmed Shukairy was director of the League's Political Department, with the rank of counsellor, immediately prior to his appointment as Assistant Secretary General in 1951. In 1963, Aref Taher, Director of the Economic Department, was made an Assistant Secretary General and given responsibility for Economic Affairs.

TABLE 6

NATIONAL COMPOSITION OF THE ARAB LEAGUE
SECRETARIAT, 1964

Country of Origin[a]	Number of Staff Members[a]	Per Cent of Total Staff	Member State Population as Per Cent of Total (Approximate)
United Arab Republic (Egypt)	92	61.3	28.6
Lebanon	12	8.0	1.8
Syria	11	7.4	5.3
Palestine	10	6.7	—
Iraq	9	6.0	7.0
Jordan	6	4.0	1.8
Sudan	6	4.0	13.1
Saudi Arabia	2	1.3	7.1
Yemen	2	1.3	4.7
TOTALS	150	100.00	69.4[b]

[a] Data furnished by Arab League Secretariat, December 1964.
[b] Discrepancy due to absence of staff members from Algeria, Libya, Kuwait, Tunisia, and Morocco.

properly qualified personnel in some of the member countries of the League, or, even when they are available, of the difficulty of attracting them to serve on the Secretariat staff under somewhat temporary conditions. Thus, while Egypt, Syria, Jordan, and Lebanon were over-represented in the Secretariat in 1960, Saudi Arabia, Sudan, and Yemen were under-represented.

At least as important as national composition of the entire Secretariat staff is the national representation among the key graded officials. Table 7 shows the country representation at the end of 1960.[6] The Egyptians

[6] Data from Administrative and Financial Department, Secretariat, December 1964.

TABLE 7

NATIONAL ORIGINS OF KEY GRADED OFFICIALS, 1960

Country of Origin	Number	Departments or Offices Controlled
Egypt	5	Conference Secretariat; Political, Social, and Cultural Depts.; and Communications Office
Iraq	3	Finance Dept., Economics Dept., Petroleum Office
Sudan	1	Press and Information Dept.
Syria	2	Legal Dept., Boycott Commission (Damascus)
Palestine	2	Palestine Office, Health Office

obviously enjoy a relative superiority within the League Secretariat, though important posts are held by representatives of several other member states.

No precise evaluation of the loyalty of the Secretariat staff to the organization—as opposed to the occasionally contradictory interests of their own home states—can be made, but it would appear from personal observation that relations between the various national representatives are good and that the primary objective of the staff is to advance the interests of the League as a collectivity.

Intra-staff harmony in the Secretariat may be of fairly recent vintage, however, as suggested by the observation of an Egyptian journalist in 1954 that "only the Zionists can enjoy the goings-on in the Arab League Secretariat!"[7] Since 1958, however, a new spirit of cooperation and purpose has been in evidence which is at least partly due to the influence of the Secretary General.

SECRETARIAT FUNCTIONS

The functions of the Secretariat staff tend to combine administrative and executive tasks. The Secretary Gen-

[7] H. Gamati in *al-Musawwar* [Cairo], quoted in *Middle Eastern Affairs*, v (1954), 356. It should be noted that this was the time of crisis over Iraq's decision to join Turkey and Pakistan in the Baghdad Pact.

eral holds weekly staff meetings with department heads throughout the year to assure continuity of policy. The Secretariat is responsible for preparing the agenda for the semiannual meetings of the League Council. The Conference Secretariat, attached to the Secretary General's office, prepares the physical environment for conferences and provides administrative support during the proceedings. The new Secretariat building in Cairo, dedicated on March 22, 1960 (the fifteenth anniversary of the Arab League) includes a hall for the League Council and smaller halls for meetings of other committees and League organs, as well as offices and other facilities.

In addition to its routine tasks in support of the activities of the League—including keeping records, gathering statistics, maintaining contact with member states and the permanent committees, and preparing technical studies and drafts of policies to support the permanent committees, the League Council, and other League organs—each department has special functions.

The Political Department, the second largest department after the Financial and Administrative Department, has the over-all responsibility for coordinating UN affairs. But the Department of Social Affairs is also actively engaged in programs which require cooperation with the United Nations or with such Specialized Agencies as the World Health Organization and the International Labor Organization. And the Cultural Department coordinates the League's relations with UNESCO. In the future, the Political Department would seem to be the likely agency to coordinate activities carried out jointly with other regional or international organizations. A cooperation agreement between the Arab League and the Organization of American States is reportedly under negotiation; the proposal provides for the exchange of documents, publications, and technical assistance.[8] A cooperation agreement

[8] *Akhbar al-Yom* [Cairo], May 4, 1963.

132

with the European Economic Community has been discussed as another future possibility.

The Palestine Department was established by Resolution 469, September 23, 1952, to handle all matters connected with Palestine; it was placed under the supervision of one of the Assistant Secretaries.[9] Upon its establishment, the Palestine Department assumed the responsibility for the education of the children of Arab refugees, previously a function of the Social Affairs Department. The boycott program, directed against Israel and originally established under the now defunct Palestine Committee, was also transferred to the Palestine Department.[10]

Although the economic boycott against "Zionist" goods and services very early became a fundamental policy of the Arab League, the full effect of the boycott program was not registered until it was placed under the supervision of the Secretary General in 1952. After some indecision, the League Council on May 19, 1951, approved the recommendation of the Political Committee that a coordinated policy be drawn up and administered by an officer appointed by the Secretary General.[11]

The League Council resolution provided for the establishment of a central Boycott Office in Damascus to maintain "security of communications between the [affiliated] boycott offices in each country," to coordinate the activities of the local offices, and to maintain "continuous activity." Each participating Arab government—not limited to members of the Arab League—was requested to appoint a "liaison officer" to the central Boycott Commission in Damascus. In addition, each participating state

[9] Butros-Ghali, "The Arab League," *International Conciliation*, 498 (May 1954), 414, n22.

[10] Although according to Butros-Ghali, *loc.cit.*, the boycott program was later placed under the control of the Military Secretariat, it is doubtful that this step was taken.

[11] Council Resolution No. 357, May 19, 1951, cited in *Egypt and the UN*, p. 172.

was to organize a national boycott office, under the supervision of the Damascus headquarters. The Boycott Commissioner was empowered to convene annual meetings of the liaison officers. He was also directed to make quarterly reports to the Secretary General on the progress of the boycott, copies of which were to be provided for member states. Nineteen meetings of boycott officials had been held between 1952 and the end of 1963—averaging two meetings a year instead of one. Despite a minor scuffle between the Secretariat and the Syrian Government in early 1963, when the Secretary General replaced the Boycott Commissioner (a Syrian) with an Egyptian, the program has operated with remarkable consistency and efficiency.

The Press and Information Department has gained in stature since the Suez crisis as the League's information programs have expanded on a worldwide scale. The department is the focal point of two distinct programs, one directed to the Arab world and the other directed to the world at large. In the aftermath of the January 1964 Arab summit meeting an expanded information program was developed and placed under the supervision of the Arab Information Council—a newly formed Arab League agency composed of the ministers of information of the member states. The program was budgeted at $4.6 million, according to regional press reports, and it was expected that the expansion of the staff of the Information Department of the Secretariat from 18 to an eventual 80 members would be required to carry it out.[12]

Within the Arab world, the League's information organs publicize the activities of the organization by means of the usual bulletins, reports, and documentary films. The sixth session of the Permanent Committee on Information, meeting at Algiers in June 1963, considered a number of proposals for expanding Arab League informa-

[12] *Arab World* [Beirut] (February 25, 1964).

tion activities and the ways and means of financing an expanded program—including benefit artistic performances during an annual "Arab League Week," a series of special Arab League stamps, and special excise taxes. Arab governments were urged to supply the Secretariat with information and publications about economic, educational, and social developments. The recommendation was made that each news agency in the Arab states maintain a bureau at the Secretariat to facilitate the dissemination of news about League activities. In June 1964, the establishment of the first Arab League Information Center in the Arab world, at Jerusalem, inaugurated a long-planned program to establish a series of such centers in each member country.

The Press and Information Department coordinates and services the activities of the expanding number of Arab League information offices abroad, under the general supervision of one of the Assistant Secretaries General. Information bulletins, reports, background data, photographs, and documentary films flow from Cairo to Arab League information centers in key world capitals, where bulletins and other publications are prepared in the appropriate languages for local distribution. For the United States and Canada, the New York office produces the slick paper English-language monthly, *Arab World*; a news bulletin, *Arab News and Views* (distributed monthly in 1964, but previously produced biweekly); and a series of research reports. The Geneva office produces the French-language monthly *Le Monde Arabe*, and the London center distributes *Arab Outlook*. A monthly is produced in Spanish for distribution in Latin America, and other publications are distributed in German and Italian by League offices in Bonn and Rome.

The League's overseas information centers also carry on other informational and cultural activities. They prepare and distribute news releases on Arab affairs for the local press, they distribute documentary films, and they provide lecturers and panelists for appropriate functions. In 1962, the Secretariat was reported to have arranged with an Italian company for the production of 50 documentary films on Arab League countries on a cooperative basis; the League would pay only 35 per cent of the cost.[13] In October 1963, the Geneva information center inaugurated an ambitious seminar on Arab world history and geography, with a staff of three lecturers, as a pilot project in a plan to increase cultural activities abroad. In 1964, $230,000 was earmarked for the establishment of Arab League information libraries in foreign countries.[14] Several proposals have been made for League-sponsored traveling exhibits on Arab world affairs. In 1964, increased emphasis was placed on the role of the offices in promoting tourism. And, of course, one of the fundamental functions of the League's information offices abroad is to coordinate the activities of the member states in the information fields. Joint press releases are frequently originated by the Arab League information centers, in the names of the Arab diplomatic representatives in the host country.[15]

The United States has been given special attention by the Arab League information program, partly, at least, because of the Arab contention that Israel is kept alive by means of dollars collected from American Jews. The program in the United States was initiated early in the League's history, but its full scope was not attained until after 1954, when the Arab Information Center in New York was opened under the direction of Kamal Abdul Rahim, former Egyptian minister to the United States

[13] Ibid., November 23, 1962.

[14] *al-Ba'th* [Damascus], March 24, 1964.

[15] According to the April 1964 issue of the *Bulletin of the Republic of Iraq* (Washington), the activities of the press attachés assigned to Arab embassies in Great Britain are coordinated by the League's information office in London.

and present head of the Arab League office in New York.[16] Since then, branch information offices have been established in Washington, Chicago, San Francisco, and Dallas under the control of the New York office. An Arab Information Center in Ottawa, Canada, is also administered by the New York center.

Fragmentary information on expenditures by the Arab Information Office (and its several branches) in the United States does not indicate a very large program, however. A reported $106,265 was expended in 1957 and nearly doubled that amount, $208,294, in 1958.[17] Although these sums represent significant shares of the Arab League's operating budget (about 5 per cent in 1957 and 10 per cent in 1958), it is a small amount if it includes the cost of publications, salaries, rent, and other overhead expenses for the five offices in the United States and Canada then in operation.

Other Arab Information Centers are located in Bonn, Rome, London, Paris, Buenos Aires, Rio de Janeiro, and New Delhi, while the Arab League's Permanent Delegation in Geneva includes an information section. According to a Cairo press report on the activities of the League's information offices abroad, the total budget for 1963 for all offices was just under $1.5 million.[18]

In 1964, new Arab League information centers were planned or under discussion for Japan, Pakistan, Indonesia, Ethiopia, Nigeria, and Senegal. The pattern reflects increased emphasis on the Afro-Asian area, motivated to

[16] An Arab Office was established in Washington in 1947 by Musa al-Alami, the well-known Palestinian; it was closed in May 1948 at the beginning of the Arab-Israeli War. See *Middle East Journal*, ii (1948), 321.

[17] *Oriente Moderno*, xxxix (1959), 591. The Arab Information Center in New York reported expenditures of $186,000 in 1963, according to the U.S. Attorney General's annual report on the Foreign Agents' Registration Act of 1936.

[18] *Ben'a al-Watan* [Cairo], February 29, 1964.

some extent by recent Israeli activities in the fields of trade and economic development, particularly in Africa. The first Arab League information office in the Afro-Asian area, established at New Delhi in 1960, planned to emphasize the Arab position on the boycott of Israel, the question of the Palestine refugees, and Arab cooperation in oil and commerce.[19] Branch offices were planned for Burma, Ceylon, and Indonesia at the time the New Delhi office was established.

The Economic Department actively promotes economic development planning for the Arab League and its member states and supports the annual meetings of the Economic Council. Its functions are becoming increasingly important as the League moves toward some form of regional common market, complete with an active development bank and other activities and agencies. Within the Economic Department, the Petroleum Office has been responsible since 1959 for organizing the annual Arab petroleum conferences—attended by observers from the non-Arab oil producing countries as well as from the producing companies—and for efforts to promote a coordinated Arab petroleum policy. The Department's Communications Office is primarily concerned with improving rail, highway, and air links between the Arab states but also generally supervises the programs of the Arab Telecommunications Union and the Arab Postal Union, two autonomous bureaus located in Cairo.

The functions of the Legal Department and of the Administrative and Financial Department are more or less self-evident. It is worth noting in passing, however, that the Legal Department has conducted original studies in international law in support of a proposal to establish an Arab Court (to handle regional disputes along the lines of the existing World Court), in support of such Arab League programs as the boycott of Israel, and in

[19] *New York Times,* October 29, 1960, p. 3.

connection with the problems involved in international rights to the waters of the Jordan River and its tributaries.

The relative success of the administrative programs of the Arab League, carried out under the direction of an active Secretary General, is noteworthy. As one observer of the situation has pointed out, the technical bureaus of the Arab League are making progress toward the goal of improving the life of the peoples of the Arab world in political, economic, social, cultural, and health matters, "working quietly and with determination."[20] It is perhaps a truism that government by administration is highly developed in the Arab world, but the traditional administrative service is by nature conservative and a stabilizing factor. The executive and administrative personnel of the League Secretariat, on the other hand, are apt to be young liberals fired with missionary zeal and impatient with inept political leadership. In any event, whether the operations of the Secretariat represent a continuation of an established area pattern of government by administration or are symptomatic of a new order of international cooperation, the fact is that much of the superficial rivalry between Arab leaders at the League Council level is moderated at working levels in the Secretariat. The ability of Arab national representatives of diverse backgrounds and interests to work together toward common goals is nowhere better demonstrated.

BUDGET AND FISCAL PROBLEMS

One of the most important administrative functions of the Secretariat is the preparation of the annual operat-

[20] Wendell Cleland, "The League of Arab States after Fifteen Years," *World Affairs* [Washington], CXXII (Summer 1960), 52. On occasion, however, the harmony has broken down. On April 23, 1962, *al-Akhbar* [Cairo] reported that two Iraqi staff members had been withdrawn from the Secretariat and that others would return to Iraq as a result of the dispute about back dues owed by Iraq.

ing budget. Apparently because of the sensitive nature of some of the League's programs, for example, the Israeli boycott, exact data on budget allocations are not available and even information on the annual operating budget for the Secretariat is difficult to obtain. Figure III, based on data from a number of official and unofficial published sources, provides a picture of the almost steady growth of the Arab League Secretariat's ordinary annual budget from $500 thousand in 1952 to $3.0 million in 1964-65. Special assessments, such as the annual payments voted to the provisional Algerian government from 1958 to 1961 and the special annual defense fund authorized in January 1964 by the Arab League Council, are not included in the ordinary budget.

Each member state of the Arab League is obligated to pay a pro rata share of the annual operating budget. The shares are determined by the League Council on the basis of national incomes and are revised from time to time to take into account new members. Table 8 illustrates the influence of expanding membership on the percentages allocated member countries since 1945. The allocation to the United Arab Republic of about 24 per cent of the annual budget compares somewhat to the heavy budgetary contributions made to the United Nations by the United States.

Not surprisingly, allocating national contributions to the Arab League budget is easier than collecting the money. The Secretary General has frequently issued urgent appeals for payment of arrears. In October 1953, the Secretary General complained that not a single member had paid its assessment for 1953; some members were in default of two years' dues. A 25 per cent increase in the 1957 budget strained the League's meager resources. By March 1958, the Secretary General reported, there was only enough money to pay salaries and essential ex-

FIGURE III

DEVELOPMENT OF THE SECRETARIAT BUDGET, 1952-1964

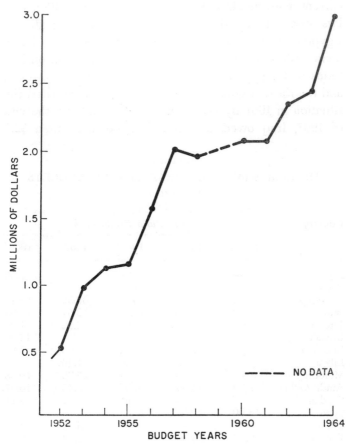

penses.[21] Telegrams were sent to all delinquent member governments to pay their dues immediately or risk expulsion from the League.

The League's treasury benefited briefly from the era of Arab good feeling following the 1958 coup d'etat in

[21] *Oriente Moderno,* XXXVIII (1958), 385, 498, 669.

Iraq and the successful resolution of the Lebanese crisis. The new Republic of Iraq promptly paid past dues and current assessments amounting to almost a million dollars—withheld by the old monarchy to protest alleged Egyptian domination of the League and attacks on Iraq's membership in the Baghdad Pact. Iraq was soon on bad terms with Egypt and other League members, however, and the Kassem government in Baghdad exacerbated the situation in 1961 by laying claim to Kuwait. By the end of 1962, Iraq owed the Arab League more than $2.5

TABLE 8

MEMBER SHARES OF ARAB LEAGUE BUDGETS
(per cent)

Country	Date Ratio Established				
	1945[a]	1953[a]	1958[b]	1960[c]	1964[d]
Algeria	—	—	—	—	5.00
UAR (Egypt)	42.00	40.00	50.29	39.56	23.73
Iraq	20.00	17.00	15.98	12.57	10.94
Jordan	3.00	3.00	2.82	2.22	1.93
Kuwait	—	—	—	—	14.00
Lebanon	6.00	6.00	5.64	4.43	3.85
Libya	—	2.00	1.88	1.48	1.50
Morocco	—	—	—	15.73	10.68
Saudi Arabia	7.00	15.50	14.57	11.46	10.97
Saudan	—	—	6.00	4.72	4.11
Syria	16.00	13.50	[e]	[e]	7.69
Tunisia	—	—	—	5.61	4.67
Yemen	6.00	3.00	2.82	2.22	0.93
	100.00	100.00	100.00	100.00	100.00

Source of data: [a] Butros-Ghali, *International Conciliation* (May 1954); [b] *The Arab World* [New York] (April 1959); [c] *Middle East, 1960* (Europa Publications); [d] *ad-Difa'* [Jerusalem], May 22, 1964. [e] After union with Egypt, Syria's share was included under UAR.

million in dues and other assessments. Egypt, Jordan, and Syria also withheld dues for varying reasons in 1961-62. The financial situation was so critical at the beginning of 1963 that the Secretary General was again obliged to curtail all but the most essential activities.

Happily enough, the Arab unity moves that excited the Arab world in the spring of 1963, following the violent overthrow of Kassem's regime in Iraq, focused attention on the critical condition of the Arab League. The new government in Iraq began to pay its arrears, having declared its support of the Arab League. By mid-year, Jordan, Saudi Arabia, and Egypt were once again paying into the League's coffers at the urging of the first important League Council session in almost two years. Another fiscal crisis passed, and the League revived under the dual influences of new injections of hard currency and renewed optimism about the future.

There seems to be no simple solution to the budgetary situation. In the future, political expediency and policy conflicts will probably continue to threaten the solvency of the organization as member states withhold dues in an effort to exert pressure. In the long run, however, the fiscal problems of the Arab League are probably little worse than those of the United Nations, which relies on the same form of voluntary payment of annual dues and special assessments.

If annual budget data are difficult to obtain, information on individual budget items is almost totally lacking, probably because of the inclusion of items for what the League considers "classified" programs. Partial data for 1954, however, are shown in Table 9.

Although it is quite possible that the 36.6 per cent for "other" expenses was entirely allocated to administrative expenses and salaries, data for one annual budget do not provide an adequate base upon which to erect any generalizations about the relative cost of various programs, or the type of program for which the League provides. In 1954, however, about 16 per cent of the budget was allocated to what may be termed

TABLE 9

ARAB LEAGUE BUDGET ALLOCATIONS, 1954[a]

Budget Item	Allocation	Per cent of Total
Joint Defense Council	$ 63,580	6.2
North Africa Fund	43,350	4.2
Israel Boycott Office	57,800	5.7
Conferences	10,115[b]	1.0
Press and information	71,650	7.0
Arab Information Office (USA)	260,100	25.4
Social affairs activities	52,020	5.1
Anti-Narcotics Bureau	12,370	1.2
Institute of Higher Arab Studies	72,250	7.0
Statistical Institute (with UN support)	5,780	0.6
Other (not allocated)	375,490	36.6
TOTALS	$1,024,505	100.0

[a] Source: *Oriente Moderno* xxxiv (1954), 2.
[b] Included $5,780 for Economic Council meeting.

"security" matters (Joint Defense Council, the boycott of Israel, and the North Africa fund) compared to about 14 per cent for "functional" programs (social affairs, Narcotics Bureau, etc.). No conclusions are possible concerning the relationship between these two budget areas in previous or later years. Furthermore, the relatively large proportion of the budget allocated for an information office in the United States (25.4 per cent) may have been non-recurring.

In addition to the regular budget of the League, the Council has approved assessments from time to time. In 1958 the Council voted to provide the provisional government of Algeria an annual subsidy of 12 million

Egyptian pounds ($34,400,000) to be contributed by League members, presumably in the same ratio as that shown in Table 9. The Arab summit conference meeting which took place in Cairo in January 1964—actually, the Arab League Council in a special session—approved the establishment of an annual "defense fund" of $42 million, plus a special $17.5 million assessment to cover the cost of preliminary work related to the proposed diversion of the tributaries of the Jordan River. The formula reported for payment of the defense fund by member states departed from the usual formula for budget payments. Of the total $42 million, Kuwait was to pay $14 million, the UAR and Saudi Arabia were to pay $8.4 million each, Iraq was to pay $4.2 million; the balance of $7 million was to be apportioned among the remaining members of the Arab League.

CHAPTER 7 EXECUTION: THE ROLE OF THE SECRETARY GENERAL

UNLIKE the United Nations Charter, which characterized the Secretary General as "the chief administrative officer of the Organization" (Article 97), the Pact of the Arab League failed to specify the duties and functions of the Arab League Secretary General beyond those already noted. As a consequence, therefore, the role of the Secretary General has tended to develop along with the scope and activities of the Arab League. Through usage, the functions of the Secretary General tend to fall into two broad categories: (1) *internal functions* (execution of League Council decisions, recommendations of policy, and mediation between member states), and (2) *external functions* (principal spokesman of the Arab League, principal diplomatic representative to non-Arab League powers, and principal liaison officer with the United Nations). The development of these functions over the course of years has been somewhat erratic and, at times, arbitrary—influenced to some extent by the personalities of the two Secretary Generals.

DEVELOPMENT OF THE ROLE OF THE SECRETARY GENERAL

The first Secretary General, Abd al-Rahman 'Azzam Pasha, was an old-time Arab nationalist who championed Pan-Arabism in Egypt in the 1920's without conspicuous success.[1] As one of the few Egyptians who sincerely ad-

[1] Reportedly 'Azzam once attempted to convince Egyptian nationalist leader, Sa'ad Zaghlul, of the merits of Arab nationalism,

vocated his country's participation in the Arab nationalist movement, 'Azzam Pasha became well-known throughout the Arab world in the 1930's, partly, at least, because of his article in a 1932 issue of the Palestinian journal, *al Arab*: "The Arabs are the Nation of the Future." Immediately prior to his appointment as the first Secretary General of the Arab League, he was serving as minister of Arab affairs in the Egyptian foreign office. On the face of things, his choice as Secretary General seemed quite appropriate.

It soon became apparent, however, that in the absence of a clearly defined role for the new office, 'Azzam Pasha felt that he *was* the Arab League. As one early observer pointed out in 1949, under 'Azzam Pasha the Secretariat had come to play "an influential and frequently autonomous role in the formation of League policy."[2] His own dynamic personality and his belief in the rightness of those causes which he personally championed inevitably brought him into conflict with the political leaders who were ostensibly his superiors. Three of his personal preoccupations played large roles in the policy of the League in its early years: (1) he was a vigorous opponent of "imperialism," (2) he had long advocated independence for Libya, and (3) he had a vaguely defined inclination toward a future Pan-Islamic commonwealth in which the Arab states would assume their rightful leadership of the world's Muslims. 'Azzam's inclinations toward a Pan-Islamic movement, in which he involved the League, will not be rehearsed here because they failed to be a signifi-

---

whereupon the latter replied, "If you add one zero to another zero, then you add another zero (in which the zeroes were the Arab states), what will be the sum?" (Anwar G. Chejne, "Egyptian Attitudes toward Pan-Arabism," *Middle East Journal*, xxi (1957), 253).

[2] Paul Seabury, "The League of Arab States: Debacle of a Regional Organization," *International Organization*, iii (1949), 637.

cant part of the League's program. Although 'Azzam Pasha's interest in an "Islamic Commonwealth" helps explain the League's support of remote Indonesia in 1947, it earned him little support from the secularist Arab nationalists of the Fertile Crescent countries.

Under the circumstances, 'Azzam Pasha reacted with vigor and imagination in the early days of the League when he denounced French "imperialist designs" in Syria and Lebanon and called for the first working meeting of the Arab League Council in May 1945. Characteristically, 'Azzam Pasha denounced France on May 21, 1945, and called for a meeting of the League Council only on May 22. When the Council met in June, it supported 'Azzam.[3] He was instrumental in lining up League members in support of independence for Libya and other Arab territories in North Africa; and he apparently originated the League policy of non-cooperation with the West until Arab national goals had been realized—the latter with initial reference to the Anglo-Egyptian controversy between 1946 and 1954.

'Azzam Pasha was also instrumental in initiating the contacts between the Arab States and newly independent Asian nations, operating through the Indian ambassador in the United States to contact Nehru in support of Indonesian independence in 1947.[4] Thus, the first Secretary General was often more active as a policy maker in the *political field* than as an administrator and executive, much to the chagrin of several member states of the League, who castigated 'Azzam Pasha as the chief protagonist of Egyptian foreign policy.

Following the failure of the Arab League's policies in Palestine during 1947-48, 'Azzam Pasha came under in-

[3] George Kirk, *The Middle East in the War* (London: Oxford University Press, 1954), p. 342. See also *Egypt and the UN*, pp. 180-81, for Resolutions 1 and 2 of the League Council.

[4] *Egypt and the UN*, pp. 73-74.

creasing attack because of his tendency to take things into his own hands. Speaking in the Iraqi Chamber of Deputies on May 3, 1949, Fadhil al-Jamali, then the Iraqi Foreign Minister, attacked 'Azzam Pasha for having exceeded his authority, and he demanded revision of the League's administrative regulations to curtail the powers of the Secretary General.[5] Jamali charged that the Secretary General had manipulated his office to interfere with League policy, to embarrass member states without having to answer to people or parliament, and to carry on negotiations with foreign powers through a head of state without regard to the policies of member states of the Arab League.

The Secretary General's lengthy written response was a classic statement of the role of the Secretary General of any international organization.[6] In answer to al-Jamali's characterization of the office of Secretary General as little more than that of a glorified file clerk, 'Azzam Pasha wrote: "The function of the Secretary General of any international organization is not restricted to the supervision of records and the communication of decisions, but he has to exercise the powers granted to him by the organization, by its pact, its regulations, and its decisions." He challenged al-Jamali to document a single instance in which he acted on his own.

Furthermore, 'Azzam wrote, the Secretary is responsible to a League Council composed of representatives of member states. Admitting that he had no authority over any Arab government, 'Azzam pointed out that the powers he had exercised during the Palestine War resulted from the exigencies of the situation: the League Council had entrusted him with the supervision of certain critical programs and projects in order to im-

[5] See Khalil, *op.cit.*, Vol. ıı, pp. 61-64 for text of al-Jamali's remarks.

[6] See *ibid.*, pp. 65-72 for text of 'Azzam's response of May 14, 1949.

149

plement Council resolutions—which, he observed, were approved unanimously. In some cases he had been empowered to act in behalf of the League Council, on a temporary basis. As for negotiations with heads of foreign states, 'Azzam Pasha insisted, the League Council and the Political Committee had empowered the Secretary General to act on certain matters concerning Libya, North Africa, Indonesia, and other problem areas.

Although some proposed changes in the administrative regulations of the Secretariat were approved in October 1949 at the subsequent League Council meeting, 'Azzam Pasha's position was essentially irrefutable. As the principal officer of the Arab League, he had been responsible for formulating and executing a joint policy at a level above that of the member states—the beginnings of a distinct Arab League policy. Iraq's protest was said to be based on the lofty principle of "cooperation on the basis of equal sovereignty," a position to which she had retreated only after Egypt had frustrated the Iraqi move for union with Syria and Jordan and one which would have denied any power to the Secretary General.

The public attacks on 'Azzam Pasha continued and he was held personally responsible by many Arabs for the Palestine disaster, the subsequent handling of the "Palestine Problem," and opposition to the plan to unite the Fertile Crescent. With the revolution in Egypt, 'Azzam lost what remaining support he had. He yielded to pressure on September 4, 1952, resigning at the same time from his post as Secretary General and from the Egyptian foreign service.

Mohammed 'Abd al-Khaliq al-Hassouna, 'Azzam's successor as Secretary General and the present incumbent, also came to the Arab League from the Egyptian foreign office, where he had served briefly as foreign minister. But Hassouna's career in the foreign service apparently had a different effect on him, and his other government service prepared him for some of the *functional* programs basic to the establishment of the Arab League. Hassouna served as under secretary of state for social affairs in the Ali Maher government in 1939, as governor of Alexandria, 1942-48, and as minister of social affairs (1949) and minister of public instruction (1952). His diplomatic service, 1926-1932, included assignments to Egyptian legations in Prague, Brussels, Berlin, and Rome. He served as director general for political affairs in the foreign ministry (1938), and under secretary of state for foreign affairs (1948).

While 'Azzam Pasha was "Mr. Arab League," the functions of the Secretariat remained relatively undeveloped. Opposition to his personal assumption of authority, indeed, made it appear advisable to Council members that the Secretariat not be built into a powerful organ under the personal control of 'Azzam. Thus, the functions of the present Palestine Department were maintained in the hands of the Palestine Committee until 1952, when, following 'Azzam's resignation, they were transferred to the supervision of a newly created Palestine Department in the League Secretariat, under the control of an Assistant Secretary General.[7] The Boycott Office has a similar history. Its functions had been carried out somewhat haphazardly by a politically constituted Boycott Committee until 1951, when its activities were absorbed by a newly created Boycott Office within the Secretariat.[8]

In fairness to 'Azzam Pasha, it must be noted that proposals for both these moves had been drawn up during his term of office. But there is ample evidence that the League Council was reluctant to give added authority to the Secretary General and, therefore, maintained control

[7] Resolution 471, September 23, 1952, *Egypt and the UN*, pp. 176-77.
[8] Resolution 357, May 19, 1951, *ibid.*, pp. 171-72.

of the programs by means of committees responsible to the Council and not to the Secretary General.

The Secretariat has prospered under Dr. Hassouna, perhaps because of his administrative background, while its activities have tended more and more to emphasize constructive functional programs. Although some observers claim that Hassouna is even more influenced by the exigencies of Egyptian foreign policy than was 'Azzam, most agree that he has generally managed to maintain his position as an impartial executive and administrator of the affairs of all the members of the Arab League. In any event, Hassouna has expanded the role of Secretary General, with the obvious support of the League Council, and has augmented the physical assets and staff of the Secretariat. It was under Secretary General Hassouna, for example, that the permanent Secretariat building in Cairo was planned and constructed. The permanent staff has quadrupled under Hassouna's administration as the emphasis on functional programs of a highly technical nature has grown. Despite the financial and political limitations under which it operates, the League Secretariat is more and more performing the normal functions of an international secretariat. At any rate, conditions have changed since 'Azzam Pasha declared bitterly: "The Secretariat General is nothing but a mirror of the Arab States. The conditions seen in the Secretariat are nothing but reflections of those existing in the Arab countries."[9]

INTERNAL FUNCTIONS OF THE SECRETARY GENERAL

The Secretary General's policy-making role is no longer so controversial as it was in 1948 and 1949, and more emphasis is placed on his role as the principal executive officer of the Arab League. As the League's executive, the Secretary General is assigned tasks by the decisions

[9] Chejne, *op.cit.*, p. 260.

and/or resolutions of the League Council. These decisions may include specific instructions to dispatch a letter agreed upon by the League Council or general instructions to prepare a study on a technical subject for consideration by a later Council meeting. Or, they may authorize the Secretary General to carry out complicated negotiations, with minimum guidance.

The various departments of the Secretariat are, of course, at the disposal of the Secretary General and assist him to carry out his functions. Thus the Legal Department prepared a brief on the legality of Jordan's annexation of Western Palestine in 1951. The Secretariat staff was called on to prepare background data for use by Arab delegations to the United Nations in 1953 in connection with the League Council's decision to raise the Algerian issue before the General Assembly. A technical working group studied the 1954 Johnston Plan for Jordan Valley development and made various recommendations; another drew up plans for an Arab Development Bank. Other groups have studied such problems as the effect of the European Common Market on the Arab economies, or the means by which relations between the Arab League and the Afro-Asian bloc could be consolidated.

The Secretary General is also charged with executing broad programs with only general supervision by the League Council. The boycott of Israel, already mentioned, is in this category. For a long time a major responsibility of the Secretary General was the coordination of all Arab League activities related to North Africa.[10] The establishment of the Palestine Department within the Secretariat is another example whereby executive responsibility for a continuing operating program is delegated to the Secretary General.

[10] According to Resolution 523, April 9, 1953, "The Secretariat is requested to arrange for the unification of the efforts of all organizations and parties interested in North African problems." *Egypt and the UN*, p. 152.

From time to time the Secretary General is charged with determining the attitude of member governments toward possible future actions by the League Council. In 1947, for example, the Secretary General was requested to determine the attitude of member governments toward a proposed referendum in Libya, to be supervised by the Arab League, and to propose other steps by which the independence of Libya could be assured.[11] In 1954, the Secretary General was requested to make a survey of member states to determine their positions on a proposed joint Arab League-UNRWA program for the education of Arab refugees.[12] The Secretary General and his staff are, in short, in constant contact with member governments, either to determine their attitudes toward specific proposals or to determine the extent to which they have implemented earlier Council decisions.

While the policy-making powers of the Secretary General were somewhat curtailed after 1949 as a result of the reaction to 'Azzam Pasha's unilateral view of the role of the Secretary General, there is still scope for influencing, if not actually initiating, policy. The recommendations which inevitably accompany detailed technical studies, of course, represent one method by which policies are developed or influenced.

Occasionally the Secretary General is given a broad mission to perform, such as that in 1954 when the Secretary General was directed to maintain contact with the Yemeni government on the issue of British "aggression" in southern Yemen with the objective of deciding upon appropriate assistance to render Yemen in order to maintain the country's security.[13] A report prepared by the Secretariat on the treatment of Arabs in Israel, for another example, recommend that the issue be raised at the

[11] Resolution 157, March 24, 1947, *ibid.*, p. 144.
[12] Resolution 759, April 5, 1954, *ibid.*, p. 179.
[13] Resolution 753, April 3, 1954, *ibid.*, pp. 183-84.

United Nations; the report and the recommendation were later approved by the Political Committee.[14] In March 1959, the Secretary General was empowered to make the necessary contacts to set up a meeting to discuss a common Arab League policy on Palestine, after the Council had approved the proposal for such a meeting. More recently, in February 1960, the Secretary General was made president of a continuing commission of five experts and charged with preparing a plan for common Arab action on the "Palestine problem."

The recent tendency of the Secretary General to promote amendments to the Pact of the League that would radically change the nature of the organization is another aspect of policy formulation. The first indication of this appears to have come in January 1955, during a press conference at which Secretary General Hassouna told a group of Syrian journalists that the League Pact must be amended to make a majority vote by the Council binding.[15] In July 1955, following this feeler, the Secretary General sent all member governments proposals for amendments to the Pact, which included: (1) a consultative assembly composed of parliamentary representatives from the several member states, and (2) a binding majority vote in the League Council.[16] The consultative assembly, which would resemble the Council of Europe, was to advise the League Council. Similar proposals were made to the Political Committee, in March 1958, following the union between Iraq and Jordan and the formation of the United Arab Republic by Syria and Egypt. At this time, moreover, the Secretary General also recommended strengthening the Collective Security Pact of 1950, the establishment of obligatory arbitration procedures, and the immediate formation of an Arab

[14] *Middle East Journal*, ix (Summer 1955), 313.
[15] *Oriente Moderno*, xxxv (1955), 2.
[16] *al-Ahram* [Cairo], July 29, 1955.

Court of Justice.[17] Although these latter proposals were not acted upon at the time, they were revived with better effect at the 1964 Arab summit meetings.

The Secretary General's proposals would greatly increase the central authority of the Arab League and give it some of the attributes of the EEC, presumably as a step toward eventual Arab unity—a departure from previous League policy. In September 1958, to illustrate the trend, the Secretary General opened the League Council session "in the name of God, Arab nationalism, and Arab unity," reportedly the first time the latter two terms had been used in an inaugural.[18] The new emphasis was confirmed for observers, in March 1960, at the inauguration of the new Secretariat building in Cairo, when Hassouna called for complete Arab union. Lebanon immediately repudiated the idea; and one member of the Lebanese Chamber of Deputies forthwith urged that the Lebanese government demand the resignation of Hassouna and withdraw from the Arab League.[19]

In addition to his role in formulating and executing policy, the Secretary General has had a large role as a mediator, either between quarreling member states or between member states and an outside power. The limitations on procedures for handling disputes between member states incorporated in the League Pact have forced the Secretary General to assume the burdens of peacemaking and conciliation. Article 5 of the League Pact, it will be recalled, specifically excepts from League Council jurisdiction all disputes concerning a member state's "independence, sovereignty, or territorial integrity."

Probably the first notable example of the Secretary General's functions as a mediator was the Arab League intervention in the civil strife in Yemen, in February

[17] *Oriente Moderno*, xxxviii (1958), 385.
[18] *Washington Post*, September 7, 1958, p. A7.
[19] *Middle East Journal*, xiv (1960), 294.

and March 1948, after the murder of Imam Yahya. A delegation led by the Secretary General and comprising a delegate from each of the Arab League states was dispatched to Yemen on February 17, 1948 in an attempt to halt the hostilities between the warring factions. 'Azzam Pasha never reached San'a; he turned back to Cairo while still at Jidda, Saudi Arabia, where he received news of the victory of Imam Ahmed in Yemen. Eventually, however, both of the League's Secretary Generals played large roles in mediating the dispute between Yemen and the British concerning the border with Aden. As a result of a series of Arab League actions, a settlement was reached in 1954, ending 20 years of tribal warfare. Unfortunately, the issue became inflamed again following the formation of the Yemeni Arab Republic in 1962.

Secretary General Hassouna has frequently mediated disputes between member states and has generally shown himself to be a more skillful negotiator than his predecessor. In the fall of 1955, he was reported to be working with Lebanese leaders to settle the disagreement between Iraq and Egypt over Iraq's membership in the Baghdad Pact. Hassouna also attempted to mediate a dispute between the Sudanese and the Egyptians in February 1958, brought about by alleged Egyptian aggression. He was more successful, however, in mediating a dispute between Jordan and the UAR in 1959. Encouraged by this success, he then engaged in mediating the dispute between the UAR and Tunisia which had caused Tunisia to walk out of the League Council meetings in 1958. Despite conciliatory gestures by the UAR and the scheduling of the 1959 League Council meeting in Casablanca to tempt the Tunisians, however, the effort failed.

More recent mediation efforts by the Secretary General (and by the Assistant Secretaries) resulted in Iraq's rejoining the League Council in September 1960, after a two-year boycott. Subsequently, the Secretary attempted to mediate the vicious propaganda war between the UAR and Jordan that erupted into violence in August 1960 with the assassination of Prime Minister Majali. In 1961 Hassouna was influential in solving the crisis that developed after Iraq claimed Kuwait. At about the same time, he busied himself with conferences in Tunis concerning possible Arab League action to assist President Bourguiba following the Bizerte incident. Late in 1961, the Secretary General successfully negotiated an agreement between Syria and the UAR for an exchange of national military forces interned after Syria's break with the United Arab Republic in September. The crisis year of 1963 found the Secretary General involved in the Yemen situation, mediating between the UAR, on the one hand, and Jordan and Saudi Arabia, on the other. He toured Arab capitals in the spring and summer of 1963 in an attempt to capitalize on the Arab unity moves and bring disputing Arabs back together. In the fall, he rushed off to North Africa for talks with squabbling Algerian and Moroccan leaders.

Under Dr. Hassouna, the office of the Secretary General has taken on an institutionalized character it never could claim under the more volatile 'Azzam Pasha. Hassouna commands the general respect of the member states because of his concern for the success of the organization. Although the present Secretary General has been denounced as a tool of the Egyptian foreign ministry, he has brought to his office a conciliatory approach to the often explosive problems that have set Arabs apart in recent years. It is interesting, in this respect, that most of the mediation attempts by Hassouna have involved disputes between Egypt and another member of the Arab League—a circumstance that reportedly has failed to endear Hassouna to President Nasser. His constant travels betweeen Arab capitals undoubtedly keep him better informed about inter-Arab problems than most Arab politicians, and at the same time his presence is a token of the idealized solidarity symbolized by the League itself. To Hassouna goes much of the credit for bringing together all the League Council members in the Arab summit meeting of January 1964 that reestablished the prestige of the organization.

EXTERNAL FUNCTIONS OF THE SECRETARY GENERAL

The principal externally oriented functions of the Secretary General include his role as spokesman for the organization, as principal diplomatic representative, and as official observer at the United Nations. To assist him in the first function, he has a press and information staff at the Secretariat and the services of a growing network of information offices around the world. And, to lend weight to his office in the foreign offices of the world, the Secretary General has been provided the rank of ambassador.

The role of spokesman for any large organization is a sensitive one which requires discretion and tact. If the Secretary General is really to be the executive officer of the Arab League, he must also be content to be the mouthpiece of the League Council. On this subject, however, the two Secretary Generals the League has had thus far have taken widely differing views. 'Azzam Pasha was all too prone to consider his own opinions as the policies of the League. Dr. Hassouna, on the other hand, has generally contented himself with expressing the actual policies of the League Council. While the differences between the two men may make Dr. Hassouna seem somewhat colorless compared to the more flamboyant 'Azzam Pasha, his effect on the League has been salutary.

The official policy of the League in 1946, for example, was not to excite French fears of Arab intervention in

North Africa but rather to work the League into the position of mediator between the French and the nationalist leaders in Tunisia, Algeria, and Morocco. Thus, in October 1946, Secretary General 'Azzam declared in a French language Egyptian embassy bulletin issued in Paris: "There is no contradiction between membership in the Arab League and adherence to the French Union, so long as this association is wanted and freely entered into by these three countries. The Arab League Pact leaves intact the sovereignty of its member states."[20] The calming effect on the French was noticeably diluted, soon after the bulletin was issued, by the Secretary General's blistering attack on French policy in North Africa during a fete in honor of the Sultan of Morocco.

'Azzam's highly individualistic handling of the Palestine negotiations and other League programs provide other illustrations of policy by public statement which did little to enhance his popularity, though the details are too involved to justify discussion here. Toward the end of his term of office, however, 'Azzam Pasha's visit to Turkey provided some interesting illustrations of his personal aspirations for an "Islamic bloc" to constitute a third force between the West and the Communist bloc. At a press conference in Ankara, June 17, 1951, the Secretary General stated that the Arab League maintained an autonomous position in the face of the ideologies of the East and the West and proposed to realize its own ideals of human solidarity, respect for individual liberty, and non-recourse to war.[21] His visit, he said, was a prelude to future broad cooperation between Turkey and the other Islamic nations of the Middle East. The eventual aim was a neutral Islamic bloc serving as a barrier between the Soviet Union and the United States.[22]

[20] Quoted by Butros-Ghali, *op.cit.*, p. 427.
[21] *Oriente Moderno*, xxxi (1951), 78.
[22] *Middle East Journal*, v (1951), 496. The Turkish government

The more normal role of the Secretary General as the spokesman for the Arab League is characterized by innumerable press dispatches which start, "The Secretary General of the Arab League announced here today that . . ." Thus the Secretary General or one of the Assistant Secretaries has normally issued a statement at the end of each major conference and following League Council sessions summarizing the accomplishments and decisions of the meeting.

Statements to the press offer some insight into League Council policies with respect to actions which have occurred or programs in progress. For example, 'Azzam Pasha in July 1951 announced to a press conference that Egypt's surveillance of shipping in the Suez Canal implemented "secret" Arab League Council decisions to prevent Israel from using Arab lands or waters to strengthen itself militarily. In this instance, the announcement correlates with the provision of League Council Resolution 357, May 1951, which—it was later revealed—stated that: "the Council recommended that all Arab governments endeavor to check activity of that kind [smuggling of goods to Israel by foreign countries] . . . and/or undertake other arrangements which would assure their not trading with Israel."[23] On another occasion, Assistant Secretary General Shukairy, commenting on a speech by John Foster Dulles following his 1953 tour of the Arab States, emphasized that while Mr. Dulles viewed Arab issues in terms of the dispute between the East and the West, the Arabs had to look at the same issues from their own viewpoint. Barely a month before, the League Council had affirmed its concern for preservation of interna-

---

was upset by 'Azzam's visit, in view of the deliberate secularization of Turkey since Ataturk. 'Azzam Pasha has recorded his ideas on the Islamic Commonwealth in his recent book, *The Eternal Message of Muhammad* (New York: Devin Adair, 1964).

[23] Resolution 357, May 19, 1951, *Egypt and the UN*, p. 172.

tional peace but concluded that the major Arab problems were the Egyptian and Palestinian cases, the settlement of which would bring about Arab solidarity.[24]

After 1952, therefore, the announcements of the Secretary General and his staff were more apt to be reflections of League Council decisions on general policy than they had been in the earlier period under 'Azzam Pasha. Normally, informal verification of the "official" nature of the policy statements by the Secretary General can be made by cross reference to the national press of Arab League member states. If the press of member states generally supports the announcement, it is probably derived from a League Council decision. During 'Azzam Pasha's regime as Secretary General, the national presses of member states were as prone to denounce his statements of "policy" as to support them. In general, this change is a healthy one since it shows a greater recognition of group objectives on the part of the Secretary General; he is acting in his statutory role as executive officer and not as policy maker.

Both Secretary Generals have been active outside the immediate bloc of member states in fulfilling the function of chief diplomatic representative of the Arab League. Because the Arab League itself is outside normal diplomatic channels, the exercise of this function has some interesting aspects. Routine matters between the Arab League, as a regional organization, and individual non-Arab states are normally carried out through the embassies and legations in Cairo. On the other hand, the Secretary General has not hesitated to address directly the foreign offices of the world.

In at least one instance, a direct channel between the Secretariat and a non-member country has been established. In 1946, the British Foreign Office adopted a policy of dealing directly with the Arab League Secretary

[24] Resolution 571, May 9, 1953, *ibid.*, p. 129.

General in matters of general concern to the Arab states, and information copies of diplomatic correspondence with individual member states of the League were also to be sent to the Secretary General.[25] The British policy is the only known case of a formal relationship of this nature, which is comparable to the diplomatic recognition afforded the United Nations. The United States, for example, normally communicates with the Secretary General through its ambassador in Cairo.

The Secretary General is in frequent contact with foreign (i.e., non-Arab) diplomats in Cairo in an effort to promote Arab League policies. Two examples suffice to illustrate this technique. In early 1952, 'Azzam Pasha intervened with the Indian chargé in Cairo to warn against rumored Indian plans to recognize Israel; such action, he said, was against Arab policy and would seriously affect Arab relations with India.[26] Secretary General Hassouna has also frequently conferred with West German ambassadors in Cairo about the League's opposition to the German "reparations" agreement and other West German relations with Israel.

Cloaked with the rank of ambassador, the Arab League Secretary General has been a frequent visitor to non-Arab states, both as the official diplomatic representative of the Arab League and as a guest of the state. 'Azzam Pasha attended the Palestine Conference in London, in September 1946, and advanced a compromise League plan for settling the Palestine question. In 1947, he conferred in England with Foreign Secretary Bevin and in the United States with Secretary of State Marshall about the situation in Palestine. In 1955, Dr. Hassouna attended the Bandung Conference as the official Arab League delegate. In 1963, the Secretary General represented the

[25] *Oriente Moderno,* xxvii (1947), 36.
[26] *Oriente Moderno,* xxxii (1952), 72.

Arab League in Rome at the Vatican ceremonies for the installation of Pope Paul. Both Secretaries have been, in their turns, interested observers at United Nations General Assembly sessions, and have been officially concerned with formalizing relations between the Arab League and the United Nations. These few illustrations suggest a developing pattern of significant diplomatic activity over a period of years, initiated by 'Azzam Pasha and continued by Dr. Hassouna. The capacity for diplomatic negotiation developed by the Secretary Generals is perhaps less appreciated in the United States than in other countries, particularly in European and Asian states, where the Secretary General is given official recognition as the spokesman and official representative of Arab regional activity.

Both Secretary Generals have been inveterate travelers. Among other places outside the Arab world, 'Azzam Pasha made official trips to London (1946 and 1947), Washington (1947), Pakistan (1949), and Turkey (1951). Secretary General Hassouna has been the official guest of President Eisenhower (1953) and General Franco (1954), as well as of the governments of Italy (1954), the Soviet Union (1960), and India (1964), among others. In 1963, for example, Dr. Hassouna represented the Arab League at the Vatican (June), inspected Arab League offices in Europe (Rome, Bonn, Geneva, and London), spent a week in East Germany as an official guest (August), and attended the United Nations General Assembly session in New York (October-November) —not to mention a swing through the Arab League states in September and a trip to Yemen in early October.

The role of the Secretary General as the Arab League representative to the United Nations has been increasingly important since the League was invited to send an official "observer" to the General Assembly in 1950. In 1951, the first such observer, Assistant Secretary General

Shukairy, was attached to the Syrian delegation. The League now maintains permanent Arab states delegations in New York and Geneva.

Although semiofficial relations with the United Nations and its agencies had existed since the early days of the Arab League, it was not until 1951 that the League Secretary General received an official communication from the Secretary General of the United Nations. In September 1951, the League Secretary General forwarded a Political Committee resolution supporting Egypt's policy on Suez Canal shipping to the Secretary General of the United Nations; the acknowledgment of receipt of the resolution was reported to be the first official communication to the Arab League from the United Nations.[27] Since that time, relations between the two organizations have developed steadily. This development and its results, however, are more properly dealt with in the discussion of the relations between the Arab League and the United Nations in Chapter XI.

[27] *Oriente Moderno*, xxxi (1951), 126.

PART III THE OPERATIONAL CONTEXT

PART III THE OPERATIONAL CONTEXT

ONE conclusion drawn from the examination of the operational factors of regionalism (Part I) was that regional organizations are strongly oriented toward "functional" objectives, i.e., regional social, cultural, and economic development. In order to attain these objectives, regional organizations more or less automatically assume a status subordinate but not inferior to that of the universal agency. In biological terminology, the relationship might be called symbiotic. The regional agency needs the technological and financial assets of the universal agency in order to effect its own programs, and the universal agency can be more effective by working in close harmony with regional agencies with common goals. A corollary to this conclusion was that security matters were less significant operational factors in regional organization than would otherwise appear. Or, at the least, regional organizations do not necessarily assume the characteristics of the so-called regional security organizations developed in the aftermath of World War II.

The examination of the several aspects of the decision-making and execution processes of the League of Arab States (Part II) provided some insight into the functional objectives of that organization, as well as of its collective security problems and its relations with the United Nations. In particular, it will be recalled, a significant characteristic of the Pact of the League of Arab States is that it emphasizes functional objectives. The second major document of the League, the so-called Arab Collective Security Pact of 1950, gave about as much weight to economic cooperation as to military cooperation. Both basic documents contain provisions for close cooperation and coordination with the United Nations.

The objective of Part III is to analyze the various programs of the Arab League as they have operated over a period of twenty years. The four chapters in Part III are concerned with functional activities, the problem of collective security, and interaction with other international agencies—principally the United Nations. These discussions are not intended to be detailed historical narratives of activities and events. Rather, the primary purpose is to describe and analyze broad programs in several fields by means of a critical treatment.

CHAPTER 8 FUNCTIONAL ACTIVITIES AND PROGRAMS I: CULTURAL, SOCIAL, AND TECHNOLOGICAL PROGRAMS

THE second article of the Pact of the League of Arab States declares that one of the major purposes of the League is to foster cooperation between the Arab member countries in matters of economic and social affairs, communications, cultural affairs, personal status, social affairs, and health. These were the very types of "functional" problems that regionalists had recommended for regional solution. These were also the types of problems which had concerned the Union of American Republics, the only other proximate "regional organization" of the period before the Second World War.

The emphasis on functional programs, with their deceptively easy technique of "cooperation," was also the logical alternative to the proposed political unification that had been rejected by the founders of the Arab League. Cooperation in the functional fields, many Arabs felt, would pave the way for eventual Arab unity. According to this view, the Arab League was and is merely a step on the road to political unification.

The path of cooperation, however, has proved to be narrow, treacherous, and infinitely longer than the most optimistic Arab nationalists would have imagined. As the critics of functionalism have consistently argued, functional problems ultimately require political solutions. On the international level, cooperation represents the lowest common denominator of a matrix made up of national sovereignty, political independence, and particularistic national objectives. Under the circumstances, it could be stated as an operational rule that functional integration proceeds in inverse proportion to its impact on national sovereignty and political autonomy. Simply put, functional integration fails when its objectives come into direct conflict with national political goals.

National goals are, nevertheless, subject to revision. They are flexible and dynamic, changing according to external and internal circumstances and conditions. It is thus pertinent to ask what internal and external factors operating on the Arab League states influence the relationship between national political goals and functional objectives. The present chapter is designed to provide tentative answers to this question, by reference to two of the principal functional categories: (1) social and cultural integration and (2) scientific and technological cooperation. The following chapter discusses the problems of regional economic development.

CULTURAL AND SOCIAL INTEGRATION

The rediscovery of the common Arab cultural heritage by Arab intellectuals in the latter half of the 19th century, with the involuntary assistance of American missionaries, and attempts to modernize indigenous social institutions in accordance with contemporary regional requirements are fundamental factors in the development of Arab nationalism. Although these two processes have been in operation for about a century, their impacts are still considerable, roughly proportional to the dissemination of education and rising standards of living. The Arab League has been a major factor in channeling and coordinating previous random activity by means of institutionalized programs in the fields of cultural affairs, education, and social reconstruction. Largely because of common consensus on these matters, which only marginally affect national sovereignty or which may even assist in the realization of national goals, the Arab League's programs in the cultural and social fields have been relatively successful.

Institutionally, the activities of the Arab League in the social and cultural fields are guided by the Arab League Cultural Treaty of 1946, the League's permanent Cultural Committee, and the Cultural and Social Affairs Departments in the League Secretariat. The Cultural Treaty was the first regional treaty developed by the Arab League. It was approved by the League Council during its second session, on November 27, 1945, and initiated by League members in 1947.[1] National organizations have also been established in member states for the purpose of promoting and developing cultural cooperation between the Arab states.

In broad outline, the League's programs in the cultural field include the improvement of educational facilities; exchange of teachers and students; the promotion of youth activities and sports; the preservation and dissemination of the Arab cultural heritage; the encouragement of achievement in literature, sciences, and the arts; translations of great works of world literature; the establishment of libraries and museums; the development of professional associations; and the promotion of mass media. Programs in the social fields involve the development of common social programs, studies of current social problems, seminars for training sociologists and social workers, and work in allied fields of labor, medicine, public health, and criminology. In both the cultural and social fields, the League collaborates with the Specialized Agencies of the United Nations, including UNESCO, the Food and Agriculture Organization (FAO), the World Health Organization (WHO), and the International Labor Organization (ILO).

[1] Text in League of Arab States, *Treaty Series* (publication data not given).

The operational techniques used by the Arab League to carry out its cultural and social programs are varied. A much-used device has been the convening of an *ad hoc* conference of professional men of one sort or another, followed by the establishment of a continuing program of activities, sometimes under the aegis of a newly organized regional professional association. In the early stages of this process, the staff of the League Secretariat and the appropriate permanent committees perform the preliminary staff work, support the conferences, and publish the usual reports and proceedings.

In the cultural field, for example, the League had sponsored six Arab Cultural Conferences by 1964 (dealing mainly with educational problems); four Archeological Conferences (1947, 1957, 1959, and 1963); several Arab Writers' Conferences; four conferences for Arab teachers; a Linguistics Conference (1956, dealing with the adjustment of Arabic to contemporary developments); and several conferences for Arab journalists. In the field of social affairs, the League has encouraged, supported, or sponsored at least six Arab Social Affairs Conferences, a series of Medical and Dental Conferences, and several Arab Lawyers' Conferences (sponsored by the Legal Committee and the Legal Department). Conference sites are normally rotated among Arab League member countries; but with the completion of the new League Secretariat building, more and more activity has centered in Cairo.

The list of Arab League conferences is not intended to be exhaustive, but it does serve to illustrate the range of problems with which the organization has dealt. The principal effect of the conferences has been to stimulate regional interest in common problems, to afford a forum for the exchange of experiences and discussion of possible solutions to particular problems, and—significantly —to establish an atmosphere conducive to future collaboration. The papers and discussions of the conferences, usually published by the League Secretariat, have assumed their places in the sparse Arabic literature of the various fields. In a number of instances the conference technique has led to the establishment of autonomous professional societies with regional scope. Several such societies established as a result of Arab League sponsorship or encouragement are the Federation of Arab Lawyers, the Arab Journalists Union, the Federation of Arab Physicians, and the Arab Teachers' Federation.

In addition to the conferences sponsored by the Arab League itself, Secretariat staff members and other Arab experts attend a variety of meetings and conferences sponsored by the United Nations and its Specialized Agencies. Most of these conferences have been held outside the region, though several have emphasized problems of special interest to the region. The 1954 Palermo Conference on cultural and economic cooperation in the Mediterranean region is an example of this type, as are the various UNESCO general conferences on international cultural relations and education. In 1960, the United Nations sponsored a seminar for the Arab States on social welfare administration and training in Denmark, which was attended by Arab League officials among others. The significance of this type of activity is that it provides in-service training for the League's executive and administrative officials and helps broaden their approaches to regional problems.

On a more sophisticated level than the regional conference is the seminar approach. For example, a series of Arab Social Welfare Seminars has been held in various Arab states since 1949. The first two Social Welfare Seminars were organized and administered by the United Nations, at the request of the Arab League. In 1952, the League assumed some of the technical and administrative functions connected with the conduct of the third seminar. Beginning with the fifth (1956), the Arab League Social Affairs Department assumed the burden of conducting the seminars, with the cooperation of the Arab host government. Experts of the United Nations and the interested Specialized Agencies have continued to attend as observers.

This series of seminars illustrates the developing competence of the Arab League staff to plan for and conduct meetings concerned with regional problems of a highly technical nature. Other examples in the social field include a seminar on social defense (concerned with crime, prison organization, etc.) organized in 1953 by the United Nations with the collaboration of the Arab League and the Egyptian government, and in 1959 a seminar on cooperatives in the Middle East, sponsored jointly by the ILO, the FAO, the Arab League, and the government of the UAR. A seminar on the development of society in the Arab world, held in Cairo in November 1963, drew representatives from eleven Arab states and observers from FAO, WHO, ILO, and UNICEF.

The seminar approach has also been extended to other fields that are of interest to the Arab League. In 1960, the Secretariat was reportedly planning a series of Arab Health Seminars similar to the successful Social Welfare Seminars. In the cultural field, the seminar approach has been used for teacher training, to investigate the exchange of publications, and other technical problems. The third joint UNESCO-Arab League seminar on university education in the Arab states, held in September 1963 in Beirut, discussed a proposal to establish a federation of Arab universities. Conversely, as in the case of conferences, members of the League Secretariat staff and Arab "experts" attend seminars conducted by the United Nations and the Specialized Agencies when these seminars touch on subjects of interest to the Arab League. The net effect of this type of activity is to extend the limits of knowledge and practice to encompass all those League states that desire social and cultural progress.

A significant portion of the League's social program has been devoted to the development of youth activities. An "Arab Olympics" has been established on a four-year cycle and so-called Pan-Arab Games were held in 1953, 1957, and 1961. The Arab League was also instrumental in establishing annual training programs for athletic trainers and coaches, beginning in 1955. Also in the youth field, the League has sponsored Arab Boy Scout Jamborees every two years since 1954. More than 3,000 Boy Scouts from twelve Arab League member states (only Iraq was not represented) participated in the Fifth Arab Jamboree in Rabat, Morocco, in August 1962. Although this type of activity may seem innocuous, it is worth remembering that the traditional Arab patriarchal society normally has failed to encourage either individual or team sports as they are known in the West, or voluntary social service organizations like the Boy Scouts. The effect of the League's program has not been to introduce such activities—the Scouting movement in the Middle East is about 50 years old, for example—but to extend the scope of voluntary social organization, to help develop desirable leadership qualities, and to encourage popular participation in organized athletics among the younger generation as it breaks away from the traditional society.

The encouragement of professional writing is another type of cultural activity carried out by the Arab League Secretariat. Prizes have been offered for several years for outstanding Arabic works in the fields of political science, economics, sociology, and literature. In some cases the publication of significant works have been subsidized by the League Secretariat. The League is also the occasional publisher of collections of papers read at the various conferences and supports an active translation program covering both standard works and recent studies of social problems produced by the United Nations. The Secretariat has taken steps to extend copyright protection and to accumulate a systematic bibliography of all published works produced in Arab countries.

Like the secretariats of most international organizations, the Secretariat of the Arab League performs statistical services in several fields, notably in the collection and publication of statistics on education in the Arab states. The significance of this type of activity can hardly be overemphasized, in view of the dearth of statistical data in most countries of the Arab world prior to 1945.

Finally, the League Secretariat has under its supervision a number of operating agencies designed to implement programs or to provide continuing services of one form or another. Directly affiliated with, and under the control of, the Secretariat are the Arab Narcotics Bureau; the Arab Manuscript Institute; the Cultural Museum; a series of demonstration Social Service Centers in Iraq, Lebanon, Yemen, Jordan, and Syria; a Cooperative Training Center; an Institute of Advanced Arab Studies (designed to encourage the study of Arab culture and civilization); and several residence halls for Arab students in Cairo (including one for women). In addition, the League provides scholarships to each member state to cover the expenses of candidates selected to attend the Zeitun Demonstration Center for the Blind, the School of Social Work (Cairo), and the Institute of Physical Culture (Cairo).

A detailed discussion and evaluation of the Arab League's activities and programs in the social and cultural fields is beyond the scope of this chapter. It can be said, however, that the social and cultural activities carried on by the League since 1945 have earned the organization well-deserved credit. Nevertheless, progress has often been somewhat uneven because of the opposition of some local authorities to social change and cultural identity. Quantitative measurement of the results of the League's programs in health, education, social welfare, and related fields is impossible. In qualitative terms, however, there is little doubt but that the energy expended by the Secretariat and by member states of the Arab League in the cultural and social fields has helped accelerate developments in these fields. Moreover, the League's efforts have contributed to the development of higher standards of achievement, to a beneficial standardization of techniques and methods, and to the formation of better qualified professional and semiprofessional cadres.

If Arab League programs have fallen short of planned objectives, as is undoubtedly the case in some instances, the fault would seem to lie less with the League as a functioning agency than with the officials of member states who fail or refuse to carry out the programs. Although the League has at its disposal increasing numbers of "experts" who can be loaned to member governments, the decentralized operations of the League require that the member states take the initiative and furnish operating personnel to carry out programs and projects of mutual interest. The League has virtually no enforcement authority in the functional fields, and the limited staff of the Secretariat can hardly support large-scale regional programs of technical assistance such as those implemented by the United Nations and several of its Specialized Agencies. The best that the departmental staffs in the League Secretariat can hope to do under present circumstances is to maintain contact with the appropriate officials of member governments, remind them of the mutually determined joint objectives, and request progress reports. Only in the institutions operated by the League Secretariat do the departmental staffs have any executive authority.

It is, therefore, of considerable significance that one of the results of the Secretariat's activities in the social and cultural fields has been the formation of a variety of autonomous professional societies. These "associational interest groups," as Gabriel Almond has called them, operate on a regional basis, cutting across national boundaries to appeal over the heads of government and "official" society to diverse interest groups.[2] They have done much to expand the scope of active political and social participation by individual Arab citizens in member states of the Arab League. The development of the Arab League professional conference into what Almond terms a "specialized structure for interest articulation" is well illustrated in the medical field.

The tenth Arab League medical conference, held in Baghdad in March 1962, was also the first congress of the Federation of Arab Physicians (or, Arab Physicians' Union). The newly formed federation, complete with its own secretary general and a permanent secretariat, was an outgrowth of the several previous medical conferences sponsored by the League Secretariat. In 1962, now autonomous, it assumed the burden of organizing and conducting the regional program; in addition to the usual sessions on diseases, the conference at Baghdad set up committees to study the problem of unifying Arabic medical terminology and produced a panel discussion on ways to raise the standards of physicians in the Arab world. More important, however, the 800 participants decided "in principle" to form an Arab health organization similar to the Pan-American Health Organization affiliated with the Organization of American States. This proposal, if carried out, would add another Arab region "specialized agency" and could serve to increase the

[2] See Gabriel Almond's introduction to Almond and Coleman, *The Politics of the Developing Areas* (Princeton, N.J.: Princeton University Press, 1960).

effectiveness of the regional health program without adding to the staff (or power) of the League Secretariat. Such an organization could also justifiably coordinate or absorb some of the programs and activities of the Arab Dental Federation, Arab Veterinary Federation, and Arab Pharmaceutical Federation and take over such functions from the Arab League Secretariat as the operation of the Arab Narcotics Bureau. Eventually such an organization could become the focal point for Arab regional cooperation with the World Health Organization.

The considerable political potential characteristic of the rapidly increasing roster of "associational interest groups" in the Arab world is not always an asset to Arab League programs. The Arab Lawyers Federation, for example, was originally sponsored in 1956 by the League Secretariat for the purposes of standardizing legal terminology, improving professional standards, and unifying Arab legal codes and procedures. In the process, the permanent secretariat of the Lawyers Federation allegedly came under the influence of Egyptian "agents" who were said to be more concerned with furthering President Nasser's foreign policy than in legal reforms. In 1962, a particularly vicious propaganda battle between Cairo and Damascus broke out as a result of alleged pro-Egyptian activities of the Federation after Syria withdrew from the United Arab Republic.

The International Confederation of Arab Trade Unions (ICATU) is another controversial organization with a highly political program. It is closely associated with the Arab League Secretariat, though it was not established as a direct result of League activity. Established at a 1956 Arab Labor Congress in Damascus, the organization soon came under Egyptian influence and is widely believed by non-Egyptian Arabs to be an instrument of

Egyptian policy.[3] These charges stem to some extent from its attempts to foster non-alignment in the international labor arena, offering itself as an alternative to both the Communist-dominated World Federation of Trade Unions and the Western-oriented International Confederation of Free Trade Unions.

ICATU has long associated itself with the Arab League as its unofficial regional labor arm. In March 1964, the League Council was reported to be considering an annual subsidy of $5,000 to assist ICATU to establish an office in New York.[4] Moreover, ICATU has won recognition by the International Labor Organization as a regional labor organization, and it offers to Arab labor the opportunity for centralized programs of labor organization. By 1964, labor unions in seven Arab League states had associated with ICATU.[5] Whereas the Arab League Secretariat collaborates with the ILO in the standardization of labor codes and practices in member states, ICATU's primary concern is to organize workers in areas where trade union activity has been minimal and where organizational activities may still be illegal. Obviously, ICATU is not very popular in some Arab quarters, or among some foreign businessmen in the area.

The high political content of the new professional societies and of such organizations as ICATU, however, seems to be symptomatic of a phase in social organiza-

[3] Willard A. Beling, *Pan-Arabism and Labor* (Cambridge: Harvard University Press, 1961), Chap. II and pp. 22-24.

[4] *Arab World* [Beirut] (March 24, 1964).

[5] Egypt, Iraq, Jordan, Lebanon, Libya, Syria, and Sudan; the Aden Trade Union Federation also belongs to ICATU. The expulsion of the Federation of Syrian Trade Unions by ICATU in April 1964 was seen by some observers as an outgrowth of the UAR campaign against the Ba'th government in Syria. The official reason for the action was that a new Syrian labor law emasculated the Syrian labor movement and put it squarely under government control.

tion. To some extent the political objectives may impede progress toward social goals, but, in the long run, most of these organizations appear to channel national interests into useful programs of regional modernization and will play increasingly important roles in breaking down or moderating national particularisms.

SCIENTIFIC AND TECHNICAL COOPERATION

Activities carried out in the general field of scientific and technological cooperation are, in reality, correlative with those in the social and cultural fields. The 1947 Cultural Treaty encouraged cooperation between scientists, promotion of scientific conferences, the development of research laboratories and institutes, and publication of scientific papers and studies. The Cultural Department of the League Secretariat is charged with implementing these provisions. For purposes of discussion, however, the various aspects of scientific and technical cooperation have been combined here.

To the Westerner, it is apparent in this scientific age that science and technology are the keys to economic and social development. In the Middle East, however, the principal concern since the early 19th century has been to exploit the scientific advances and technological know-how of the West for the military and economic advantages to be expected, but at the same time to preserve the best features of the prevailing regional culture and civilization. Considering the essentially secularistic, asocial character of science and technology, however, it is a moot question whether the 19th century objective of a modernized Islamic civilization bolstered by contemporary scientific know-how is attainable. After a century and a half of endeavor toward this elusive goal, it appears that the scientific and technological elite has merely become demonstrably secularist while the overwhelming mass of people, clinging to a large extent to their Islamic heritage, remains demonstrably unscientific. In any event, little real progress had been made in the Arab areas in science and technology through the first half of the 20th century.

It is to the credit of the Arab League that a considerable increase in scientific activity has occurred in a number of Arab states. The Arab League has undoubtedly played a major role in stimulating scientific and technological developments in the area, although this credit must be shared with operating agencies of the United Nations, the Specialized Agencies, and foreign government and private programs (e.g., A.I.D. and Ford Foundation programs, in the case of the United States).

The conference technique has been used to good advantage by the League Secretariat. Several Arab conferences on science had been held by the end of 1964, along with nine Arab Engineers' Congresses. As a result of the first Scientific Conference, held in 1953, the League was instrumental in organizing a regional Arab Scientific Federation.

The scientific conferences and congresses resemble the typical professional society meetings: original research papers are presented, lectures are presented by distinguished scientists (some from outside the Arab world), and discussion groups and panels wrestle with problems of topical interest. Technical displays at recent Engineers' Congresses have depicted development projects and the progress of industrialization in the Arab states. The noteworthy distinction between the Arab League conferences and those of international professional associations, however, is that the League Secretariat has played a conspicuous role in the initial arrangements, programs, and exhibitions. The conferences themselves have a quasi-official status, and resolutions may be referred through League channels to the League Council for approval.

The organization of the Arab Scientific Federation

illustrates the role and techniques of the Arab League Secretariat.[6] The first Scientific Conference, held in Alexandria in 1953, proposed the establishment of a permanent Arab Scientific Federation. The appropriate resolution was forwarded to the meeting of ministers of education of the Arab League countries, convened in Cairo in December 1953. This group reviewed the proposal and approved the concept of the Federation. The project was then submitted to the League Council in January 1954. Following review and approval by the League Council, the Cultural Department in the League Secretariat established a preparatory committee of professors of science in Cairo for the purpose of drawing up a constitution for the organization. The proposed constitution was subsequently submitted to scholars in the Arab states and, finally, to the Cultural Department. The approved text of the constitution was resubmitted to the preparatory committee at a meeting held in Lebanon in September 1954; it was subsequently adopted by founding members of the Federation at a general meeting.

The Arab Scientific Federation was finally established as an independent organization, although cooperation with the League is assumed. The constitution of the Federation provided for a principal headquarters in Cairo and affiliated national sections in each Arab country. Its functions are essentially those of any international professional association: to arrange for periodic scientific congresses; to maintain relations with foreign (i.e., non-Arab) scientific organizations for exchange of reports, research, and scholars; to publish a scientific review, including information of foreign scientific activities; to provide financial assistance to scholars for research and publications; and to encourage cooperation between scientific institutes and organizations in the region. The

[6] Discussion based on *Aperçu general de l'activité culturelle de la Ligue des Etats Arabs, 1946-56* (Cairo: League of Arab States, no date), pp. 36-37.

Federation's national sections are charged with organizing meetings and conferences, encouraging scientific research, and stimulating publications in their respective countries.

The scientific and engineering conferences have developed into useful affairs over a period of a decade or so. The 1959 Congress of Arab Engineers, for example, drew 1,500 participants from all over the Arab world, although 700 to 800 participants is more usual. The papers and proceedings of the conferences are published and given wide distribution; the scientific congresses have published their proceedings in both Arabic and English. In this connection, incidentally, one of the important tasks undertaken by the Arab Scientific Federation has been its program of standardizing scientific terminology in Arabic. The conferences also have other long-range concerns. For example, the agenda of the ninth Arab Engineers' Congress (Baghdad, December 1964) included discussions of (1) engineering and technical education in the Arab League states, (2) the exploitation of mineral resources in the Arab world, and (3) the engineer's role in agricultural planning and land reclamation.[7]

The Arab League has not established operational training and research facilities in the sciences and technology as it has in the fields of social and cultural affairs. With the encouragement of the Arab Scientific Federation, however, the scope of pure and applied scientific research is being extended under the sponsorship of the universities of the region and, more recently, by national research institutes. There would seem to be little point to the League's establishment of expensive research facilities; its function of promoting coordination and cooperation in the sciences seems to be adequate for such an international organization. The League Secretariat has participated in regional scientific programs such as those

[7] Reported by *al-Manar* [Baghdad], June 20, 1964.

sponsored by the UNESCO Science Cooperation Office in Cairo, and the IAEA regional isotope training center in Cairo is intended for the Arab states.

Two closely related Arab League technical organizations, the Arab Telecommunications Union and the Arab Postal Union, are worth mentioning here, since they maintain permanent bureaus affiliated with the League Secretariat in Cairo. Both organizations were established by international treaties and are linked with the Arab League by formal conventions. The concept of an Arab Postal Union was approved by the League Council in 1946, but problems arising during the drafting of a suitable convention delayed the establishment of the Union until 1956. The Arab Telecommunications Union convention was signed in February 1953. Texts of both treaties have been published in English in the League's *Treaty Series*.

The function of these two "specialized agencies" is to provide technical information and consulting services to member states, to exchange technicians between Arab states, to unify operating programs between member states, and to standardize equipment, operating techniques, and rates. Periodic plenary congresses are held. The bureaus or permanent offices of the two organizations are subject to the control of these congresses; they are, in fact, the secretariats of the congresses. Although the bureaus are located in Cairo and cooperate closely with the League Secretariat, their operating budgets are approved by the plenary congresses. Operating funds are provided directly by participating governments. The congresses also elect the directors of the two bureaus.

The Arab Telecommunications Union has designed several telecommunications projects which contemplate the development of international micro-wave radio circuits between various key Arab centers, with links to Europe, as part of a larger program developed by the

International Telecommunications Union These projects have been proposed for Arab League support. The Director of the Arab Telecommunications Union until 1964, Dr. Mahmud Riad, was also the Director General of the UAR Telecommunications Organization.

The Arab Postal Union is a member of the Universal Postal Union in accordance with Article 8 of the Universal Postal Convention, which regulates cooperation between the UPU and other "restricted" postal unions. Its plenary congress meets every three years; meanwhile an executive committee transacts essential business not suitable for the permanent office in Cairo. In 1962, the APU had an annual budget of about $41,000. In addition to the Cairo office, the APU has operated since 1958 an Institute for Advanced Postal Training in Khartoum. It regularly publishes a newsletter, a technical review, and a directory of post offices in the Arab states.[8]

Other technical agencies with regulatory functions approved in principle by the League Council but not yet operational in 1964 included an Arab Broadcasting Union and an Arab Civil Aviation Council.

A 1953 meeting of the League's Communications Committee also approved the concept of a Pan-Arab transportation network, including rail, highway, air, and marine routes. Approval in principle of the series of projects developed by the Communications Committee was granted by the League Council on April 9, 1963.[9] All these proposals, while potentially useful to the region, require vast technical and financial resources not readily

[8] *Yearbook of International Organizations, 1962-63* (Brussels: Union of International Associations, 1962), p. 186.

[9] In April 1953, the following League Council resolutions concerned regional communications: 551 (integration of land and air communications on a regional basis), 552 (League support for the Hejaz railway), 554 (establishment of an Arab shipping company), and 555 (a project on inter-Arab river navigation). Cf. Butros-Ghali, *op.cit.*, p. 434.

available to the Arab League. For, so far the Arab League has no coordinated technical assistance program nor any functioning agency comparable to either the World Bank or the United Nations Special Fund. Consequently most of these projects must be postponed unless support can be obtained from one of the UN agencies or a foreign government. Because of the regional character of most of these projects, however, a coordinated Arab League program of technical assistance may be feasible in connection with the Arab Development Bank, once it starts operations.

CONCLUSIONS

This brief analysis of activities in the fields of social and cultural integration and the allied fields of scientific and technological cooperation points to two significant developments. First, in order to coordinate and administer programs which are, by their very nature, becoming more ambitious and more technical, increasing consideration is being given to the establishment of autonomous Arab League "specialized agencies" similar to those affiliated with the United Nations. Such organizations should free the overworked League Secretariat staff for essential tasks concerned with over-all coordination of League activities and, at the same time, contribute to regularizing administration of highly technical programs under duly constituted staffs better able to minimize the political implications of programs now directed by the Secretariat itself.

Second, the League Secretariat has systematically encouraged the formation of numerous non-governmental "associational interest groups," particularly among Arab professionals, which transcend national boundaries and help to develop collective agreement on pertinent problems. Although some of these groups seem to be preoccupied with political problems, to the possible detriment of functional programs, the majority of them are accomplishing at least limited objectives in a long-range drive to articulate and realize regional goals in the cultural, social, and scientific fields.

National particularisms and regional rivalries obviously can limit the effectiveness of functional programs or perhaps cripple them, even in the relatively innocuous realm of social and cultural affairs. Saudi Arabia (and Yemen), for example, accepted the 1947 Cultural Treaty with the following reservation: "The government of Saudi Arabia agrees to the terms of this Treaty, except to what it does contradictory to Islamic faith or is inconsistent with its local organization and situation."[10]

The question of the exchange of teachers or the supply of teachers to countries whose educational facilities are minimal, moreover, has become a political issue. Young teachers trained in modern educational methods tend to be secular missionaries. When this fact is exploited for political ends, as it allegedly has been by Egypt, the effects can be explosive. Little progress has been made on standardizing the teaching of Arabic—the great unifying language of the region—in the public schools, partly because of the irreconcilable points of view of Arabic scholars on what constitutes good Arabic and partly because of the potential for undesirable political indoctrination posed by uniform language texts. The question that remains, therefore, is how to improve the efficiency of League-sponsored programs within the context of a membership composed of sovereign states jealous of their independence and freedom of action.

A project for an Arab UNESCO (the Arab Economic, Scientific, and Cultural Organization, ARESCO), approved by most member states in 1964 may go a long way to clarify the air and solve some of these problems. When it is implemented, the Arab Cultural Unity Treaty that

[10] *Treaty Series*, nl d, p. 5.

created ARESCO will replace the 1947 Cultural Treaty. ARESCO will presumably operate much like UNESCO, but on a more restricted regional basis. It could be the center for coordinating such diverse non-governmental associational interest groups as the Arab Tourist Federation, the proposed Federation of Arab Universities, and the Arab Journalists Federation. It could assume some of the burdens of the League Secretariat in the social field, and it could serve as the regional coordinating agency for joint programs sponsored by UNESCO and the Arab League. At the same time, ARESCO will presumably work toward the formation of national organizations of private citizens in member Arab states to support its programs.

Another prerequisite to the more efficient implementation of regional functional programs would seem to be the establishment of an Arab League technical assistance bureau, probably within the Secretariat, which could effectively coordinate regional programs such as those suggested in the field of inter-Arab communications. Such an activity would, of course, work closely with the United Nations and other international agencies as well as with its own Arab region specialized agencies.

Despite the conflict between particularistic national goals and regional functional integration, considerable progress has been made in the cultural, scientific, and social fields by the Arab League. Not everything proposed by the League has been accomplished, but it is an inevitable fact of life that the translation of objectives into concrete programs and, finally, into achievements is difficult at best. If a criticism is warranted, it is probably not that the League has accomplished so little but that it has attempted so much.

CHAPTER 9 FUNCTIONAL ACTIVITIES AND PROGRAMS II: REGIONAL ECONOMIC DEVELOPMENT

FACTORS INFLUENCING REGIONAL ECONOMIC INTEGRATION

REGIONAL economic development has always had a high priority in Arab League plans and was presumably one of the principal motivating factors in the establishment of the League, but actual progress toward this goal by the League has been limited. It is precisely in the area of economic development that particularistic national policies and objectives come into open conflict with the policies and goals of the regional organization to confound the proponents of "functionalism." Little headway has been made so far, despite the urgings of technicians and economists, toward reshaping national goals and bringing them into harmony with the presumably higher level objectives of economic cooperation within the region. To a large extent the problem is rooted in historical experience, particularly during the period of Western control and the League of Nations' mandate system prior to the Second World War.

French influence in Syria, Lebanon, Morocco, Algeria, and Tunisia left these states with French political institutions, customs regulations, fiscal and financial structures, legal apparatuses, and educational systems. In other words, most of the paraphernalia of the modern state—on the French model—were placed on top of the basically unchanged traditional society like a thin, plastic coating. Iraq, Jordan, Egypt, and the Sudan were similarly influenced to varying degrees by British advisors. In the Yemen, Libya, Kuwait, and Saudi Arabia, however, traditional Muslim institutions have remained strongly entrenched, with the result that the necessary institutions for modern economic and political life are almost completely lacking or have been developed only over the past fifteen years.

Two economic characteristics of the area which serve to retard economic integration developed largely as an outgrowth of European and British control of strategic regions in the Middle East and North Africa during the last century. The first is the hardening of former administrative boundaries into political and economic frontiers, with all the attendant institutions: customs regulations, import and export duties, currency regulations, and foreign exchange problems. The other is the solidification of patterns of trade, to a large extent in accordance with the trading patterns of the once dominant Western power.

A third economic characteristic is the region's general reliance on agriculture, the processing of agricultural products, and extractive industry. In the classic pattern, Arab countries have exported raw materials and processed agricultural products in return for imported finished goods. Intra-regional trade, therefore, has always been less important than extra-regional trade. Geographic patterns of trade for most of the Arab states emphasize trade with Continental Europe and Great Britain. In 1960 the Middle East trade with these two markets accounted for about 46 per cent of the area total, both export and import, compared to intra-regional trade of about 10 per cent in each direction.[1] In North Africa, the established patterns of trade for Libya and the former French territories of Algeria, Morocco, and Tunisia are

[1] Based on data in Table IV-3, *Economic Developments in the Middle East, 1959-61* (New York: United Nations, 1962).

even more heavily dependent on the European market, principally France. Furthermore, for the area as a whole, intra-regional trade declined steadily during the period 1957-60, although the value of commodities exchanged remained about the same. These few facts help explain the Arab League's concern over the external policies of the European Common Market and the intense interest of the Arab states in the United Nations Conference on Trade and Development held at Geneva in the spring of 1964.

Fourth, closely allied to the third factor, is the slow, uneven capital formation in most of the area. Such surplus capital as has been generated within the framework of traditional economic pursuits has largely been reinvested in real estate. Industrial investments made before industrialization became a universal objective were predominantly in processing industries (e.g., vegetable oils, soaps, textiles, tanneries, food processing). In the non-petroleum producing Arab League states capital needed for economic and social development must come from foreign aid programs and commodity exports. Foreign assistance of various types is said to account for about half of all new capital invested each year in Syria, and for about 75 per cent in Jordan and the United Arab Republic (Egypt).

Petroleum royalties to Arab League members, amounting to more than a billion dollars annually since 1960, are highly localized in three states: Iraq, Kuwait, and Saudi Arabia. The development of major oil fields in North Africa will soon result in vastly increased revenues for Algeria and Libya. The fact is, however, that revenues from the exploitation of the huge oil reserves in the Arab world have been significant for only about a decade. Four other Arab League members derive some income from oil transport. Transit agreements involving pipelines across Jordan, Lebanon, and Syria bring these states about $35 million each year; and since 1960, the UAR's receipts from tankers transiting the Suez Canal have amounted to more than $100 million a year.

The huge revenues enjoyed by the few petroleum producing states have not always been available for constructive capital investment. This is particularly true in Kuwait, Saudi Arabia, and the Persian Gulf sheikhdoms (Qatar and Bahrain, for example, which are not members of the Arab League but which have annual oil revenues of $70 to $80 million). In these areas, oil royalties have normally accrued to the sole benefit of a patriarchal ruler and whatever use is made of the money depends to a great extent upon the pleasure of the ruler. In Kuwait, constructive uses have been found. In Iraq, of course, a state development agency was established fairly early in the petroleum era in an effort to channel at least a portion of the royalties into a broadbased national social and economic development program.

In 1961 Kuwait established an "Arab Economic Development Fund," now a $280 million fund designed to serve as a source of much needed low-interest hard-currency loans to other (non-producing) Arab states. Much has been made of the Kuwait scheme since it seems to illustrate the now widely advocated principle that the oil-rich Arab states should share their wealth with their less fortunate Arab neighbors. Kuwait has, in fact, long carried on an economic assistance program for some of the other Persian Gulf sheikhdoms—particularly in the educational and social fields. Since the fund was established, Kuwait has extended assistance to the UAR, Algeria, Jordan, Yemen, the Sudan, and the municipality of Beirut for various special development programs. The success of the Kuwaiti program, and the acceptance of its basic premise of mutual assistance by other oil-producing Arab states, remains to be seen.

A fifth major factor influencing regional economic development is the presence of Israel in the midst of the Fertile Crescent trading area. The economic impact of the establishment of Israel has been to interrupt normal overland communication within the area (including communication with Egypt), to cut off the Arab interior from some of its traditional Mediterranean ports, to disrupt traditional patterns of trade within the Fertile Crescent area, and to limit the possibility of future development of the Jordan River Valley for the benefit of the entire region. The emphasis on regional military preparations since 1947 and the purchase of arms (both by the Arab states and by Israel) out of all proportion to the ability of the economies to support such activities is another unfortunate reality associated with the establishment of Israel.

Under the circumstances, the interaction of economic and political factors encourages particularistic economic development, with tendencies toward autarky, which mitigates against constructive plans for regional economic development or cooperation. Paradoxically, the political experiences of the newly independent Arab states since 1945 have tended to confirm particularism rather than unification. Largely as a result of this fact, the Arab League has so far been relatively unsuccessful in the field of regional economic development.

Regional economic integration, nevertheless, has been a constant concern of the Arab League and some progress has been made despite seemingly overwhelming political obstacles. The various aspects of the problem have been approached at three different levels: (1) general conventions designed to facilitate intra-regional trade, transit trade, and movements of capital, including payments for goods, (2) joint Arab development projects, capped by an industrial development institution supported by the member states of the League, and (3) a movement to establish an independent economic union—resembling the European Economic Community—and an Arab Common Market. The prospects for at least a limited economic union were measurably improved in 1964 as a result of the political détente growing out of the Arab summit conference held in Cairo in January.

REGIONAL TRADE AND PAYMENTS CONVENTIONS

Two formal economic treaties drawn up by the Arab League in 1953 illustrate the first level of approach to regional economic integration. The "Convention for Facilitating Trade Exchange and the Regulation of Transit Trade Between States of the Arab League" provided for exemption from customs duties of almost all the raw materials produced in the region (neatly referenced in an annex to the treaty), and a 25 per cent reduction of customs duties on a most-favored-nation basis for most industrial products, largely processed agricultural products such as textiles, flour, vegetable oils, and canned foods (also listed in the annex).[2] A "Convention for the Settlement of Payments of Current Transactions and the Movements of Capital Between States of the Arab League" provided for "the utmost of favoured treatment" in the transfer of payments and movement of capital between contracting countries.[3] An appended list of transfers subject to the treaty included: transactions covering payment for goods; transfers of commercial profits and dividends; official government expenses; expenses of tourists, pilgrims, and commercial travelers; educational and professional expenses; payments for communications and transportation services; premiums and surrender values of insurance policies; royalties from patents and copyrights; and the proceeds from sales or subscriptions of movie films, newspapers, and magazines.

[2] English text in the Arab League's *Treaty Series*, pp. 53-66. A supplemental schedule in 1957 provided for reductions of 50% on some industrial products.

[3] English text in *ibid.*, pp. 67-71.

Each of these conventions, however, depends on whole-hearted cooperation; no enforcement is envisaged. And each convention contains broad escape clauses which seem to be designed to ensure that it will have little or no real effect on regional trade. Article 2 of the Trade Exchange convention declares that "the provisions of this convention shall not be applicable to articles subject to government monopoly." Article 3 further excludes from the purview of the convention all goods "the import of which is prohibited or *to be prohibited* into the territories of one of the Contracting parties, according to binding regulations in that country." Considering the broad impact of these two provisions, it seems doubtful that this convention could actually have stimulated trade between the member states of the Arab League and, in fact, intra-regional trade declined as a per cent of total trade during the period that it has been in effect, though the value of trade remained reasonably constant.

The 1953 payments and capital movements convention also has escape clauses which serve to limit its effect. In paragraph 2 of Article 1, the convention recognizes the existence of national restrictions on transfers of payments and merely requires that each contracting country permit its residents to utilize existing credit accounts outside the country to settle just debts. According to Article 2, movements of capital transfers are to be permitted "within the limits of regulations laid down by each state." In effect, then, the convention would seem to be subject to the vagaries of national policy and only marginally useful.

Despite the limitations inherent in the two trade and payments conventions, they have helped expand and regularize trade within the Arab area. The trade convention has provided the basis for a series of bilateral agreements between Arab trading partners in which "most-favored nation" treatment is confirmed. Exemptions from existing trade restrictions (e.g., import and export licensing) have been written into many of these agreements.[4] For example bilateral trade and payments agreements between Iraq and several Arab League member states (Jordan, Lebanon, Saudi Arabia, Syria, and the UAR) within the context of the two Arab League conventions regulate capital movements, labor permits for nationals of the signatories, credit ceilings, and special schedules of agricultural and industrial products which either exempt such products from customs duties or favor them with reductions of 50 to 75 per cent.[5]

A supplementary agreement on inter-Arab transit trade was negotiated in the winter of 1959-60, partly as a result of the damage caused to the Lebanese economy by regional political tension after mid-1958. The agreement, concluded in December 1959 between Lebanon, Jordan, Saudi Arabia, and the UAR (in the interests of the Syrian region), extended to the transit rights of the signatories in Lebanon, Syria, Jordan, Saudi Arabia, and Kuwait for motor trucks belonging to their nationals without hindrance, customs procedure, or transit fees.[6] Quotas were also established for rail traffic between Damascus and Beirut, and a proviso was added that 40 per cent of the transit trade through Syria must be carried in UAR-owned vehicles.

The signatories agreed to the establishment of a supervisory commission composed of members from each of the adhering states. Significantly, they agreed to be bound by the agreement after it had been ratified by three states and *it had been reported to the Arab League Council.* Following the implementation of the agreement, in August 1960, the League's Economic Council urged that other Council members adhere to the agreement. Iraq, at odds with most of the signatories, agreed to

[4] *Economic Developments in the Middle East, 1959-61,* p. 90.
[5] *Ibid.,* p. 92.
[6] *al-Hayat* [Beirut], January 22, 1960.

study the agreement in late 1960. The development of the transit agreement provides an encouraging example of intra-regional cooperation, cutting across political obstacles, that probably would not have been possible without the influence of the earlier Arab League trade and payments conventions.

The prospects for greatly increased intra-regional trade appear to be slight in spite of recent moves to industrialize Arab economies. The reasons are only partly economic, however. Deep-seated Arab political rivalries and regional tensions (particularly the Arab-Israeli dispute) encourage the development of self-sufficient or autarkic economies. For example, the United Arab Republic (Egypt) has embarked on an economic development program emphasizing domestic production of "import substitutes" and a corresponding increase in industrialization, extending to a wide range of end products, from steel and basic chemicals to frozen foods and dairy products. During the phase of industrial development, the Egyptians exclude competing foreign imports in favor of domestic products. Once production has progressed to the point of satisfying domestic demand, however, the Egyptians presumably expect to export their industrial surpluses within the area of the Middle East and North Africa.

Before the breakup of the UAR in the fall of 1961, for example, Syria had already been required to import Egyptian industrial goods almost to the exclusion of others (see Figure IV). In 1960, trade between Lebanon and Syria—traditional trading partners—was virtually stopped, and exports of goods from Lebanon to Egypt were sharply curtailed. An acute shortage of foreign exchange in the UAR influenced these moves, but the impact on Lebanon was serious. As a commercial country, Lebanon depends heavily on transhipping goods between Europe and the Arab states or within the Arab region.

FIGURE IV

SYRIA: COMMODITY TRADE WITH EGYPT, 1953-1961[a]

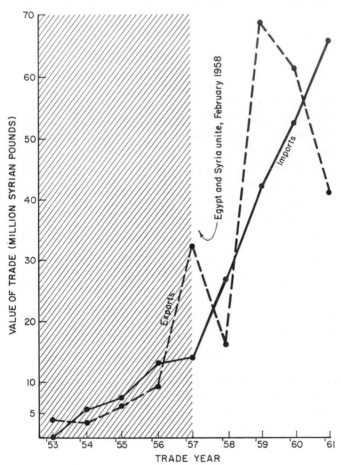

a Source: Table IV-4, *Economic Developments in the Middle East, 1959-61*, United Nations, 1962.

The situation was instructive to free-wheeling Lebanese and Syrian businessmen, who interpreted the virtual Egyptian domination of Syrian trade and the resulting distortion of economic relations in the Fertile Crescent states as symptomatic of "Arab unity." Moreover, the apparent Egyptian assumption that the UAR is destined to become (or already is) the industrial center of the Arab world—and that it will thereby naturally win Arab regional markets formerly dominated by the West—is not particularly appealing to some other Arab League members. The fear that Iraq and Syria would be limited in the future to the role of raw material suppliers for Egyptian industry was openly expressed in the spring of 1963 when union between the three Arab states seemed imminent. Aside from the political overtones, moreover, Egyptian products tend to be expensive as a result of the government's policy of protecting new industry in order to conserve foreign exchange, sometimes without regard to the effect on unit production costs. And, since other Arab countries are following similar policies in their own economic development programs, it is hardly necessary to add that the range of import restrictions and government monopolies in the Arab world may just as readily increase as decrease in the future. Something more fundamental than the existing Arab League trade and payments conventions therefore seems essential.

JOINT ARAB DEVELOPMENT PROGRAMS

Proposals for some form of economic development organization have been in the air at least since 1952. The idea was first given official notice by a meeting of ministers of finance and economy of the Arab League states in May 1953, which referred the notion to the League Secretariat for study and evaluation. In the course of this study, the League worked closely with the World Bank. A draft project was presented to the first meeting of the League Economic Council in December 1953. The final decision by the Economic Council, however, was not reached until June 1957.

The agreement concerning the establishment of the Arab Financial Institution for Economic Development or, as it is generally called, the Arab Development Bank, presents as its purpose the encouragement of "the steady growth of productive projects undertaken by governments, organizations, and individuals." The agency combines the functions of the World Bank, the International Finance Corporation, and the International Development Association, all affiliated with the United Nations. Support for worthwhile projects may take the form of project loans, loan guarantees, or participation (equity); the agency may also provide funds for the requisite technical studies.[7]

The capital of the Arab Development Bank was established initially as 20 million Egyptian pounds ($57,400,-000), divided into 2,000 shares; this limit was later raised to 25 million pounds to accommodate Kuwait. Member states of the Arab League join the Bank by subscribing to shares of a value proportional to their percentage contribution to the League's annual budget. The Bank was formally inaugurated on January 12, 1959, when the requisite 75 per cent of the initial capital had been pledged. No activity had been reported, however, as of the end of 1964, although the project was revived following the January 1964 summit meeting.

In retrospect, it appears that the establishment of the Arab Development Bank has failed to capture the imagination of Arab political leaders. And, considering the prolonged gestation period, it would appear that one of the motives for establishing the Bank in the period may have been to provide a show of Arab solidarity in the face of President Eisenhower's 1958 scheme for a UN-supervised Arab development institution on a regional basis, proposed in a speech to the UN General Assembly on Au-

[7] Text of agreement in "The Arab Financial Institution for Economic Development" (mimeo.), Arab Information Center, N.Y., 1958.

gust 13, 1958. At the economic level, the problems connected with establishing an effective regional development institution start with the basic fact that most of the states of the area have inadequate investment (surplus) capital to start with. Because of the fact that industrial development requires unusually large expenditures of "hard currencies"—primarily to import capital equipment—Article 6 of the Bank charter requires that 75 per cent of the value of the shares subscribed by each member be paid in gold or in a currency convertible to gold. Since most of the countries in the Arab world are chronically short of hard currencies, this condition is particularly difficult to meet.[8]

Many Arabs have suggested that a large proportion of the hard currency required for regional development could come from the three oil-producing Arab League states of Iraq, Kuwait, and Saudi Arabia—and eventually, from other Persian Gulf sheikhdoms, as well as Libya and Algeria. More detailed studies of the incomes of oil-producing Arab states, as compared to incomes of other Arab states, led the late Émile Bustani, of Lebanon, to propose the formation of a development association to which the oil-producers would contribute 5 per cent of their oil receipts for the benefit of the region. Unfortunately, however, political rivalries—among other factors—virtually rule out the practicality of such a plan, and it is essentially a dead issue. The sixth conference of the Arab League Economic Council, in March 1960, shelved the Bustani plan after it was rejected by Saudi Arabia.[9]

[8] Beyond the problem of collecting pledged shares has been the problem of future political control over the organization. Lebanon demanded that each member be limited to one vote on the Board of Governors, for example, thus opposing the provision of Art. 21 of the Bank charter of one vote for each share held. See interview with Philip Takla, then Lebanon's Minister of Economy, in *Arab World Affairs* [Cairo], March 24, 1960, p. 17.

[9] *Middle East Journal*, xiv (1960), 175.

The Arab Development Bank appears to have an important role in industrial development within the Arab League's area of interest, at least potentially, but it cannot be expected to solve the basic problems of the area. According to the Bank's charter, it is to support "productive projects undertaken by governments, organizations, and individuals." A carefully coordinated program of regional industrial development certainly would be more effective than the present pattern of random development, and the experience (and, to some extent, the resources) of the World Bank and its affiliated agencies should be available once the Arab Development Bank begins its operations. In principle, the plan provides the bank regional autonomy—and responsibility—within the framework of a rapidly developing universal economy. In practice, however, the utility of the plan is questionable insofar as *regional* development is concerned.[10]

What appears to be required over the long term is a regional authority capable of financing and directing major social overhead projects in the fields of water resources, health and sanitation, transportation, telecommunications, and agriculture. It was presumably this type of regional development that the British and the Americans seemed most prepared to support in 1944 and 1945 when they encouraged the formation of the Arab League. And this was presumably the import of President Eisenhower's proposal to the United Nations a decade or so later. Meanwhile, of course, the fundamental reorientation of the Great Power structure in the wake of the Second World War had resulted in the collapse of the wartime Middle East Supply Center, the virtual withdrawal of the British from a decisive role in the region (flagged by the 1947 Truman Doctrine and confirmed by the 1956

[10] For some recent insights into the problems of economic integration, see Lincoln Gordon, "Economic Regionalism Reconsidered," *World Politics*, xiii (January 1961), 230-253.

Suez crisis), and the remarkable development of the American program of military and foreign aid during the Dulles era of the Cold War. The built-in policy bias of the aid program that sought to "reward our friends and punish our enemies" and its absolute insistence on bilateral agreements effectively destroyed any remaining hope that the United States would assist the Arab states with meaningful regional development.[11] Under these circumstances, the best hope for regional economic integration probably now lies with the United Nations, and there are some indications that the UN is itself moving away from bilateralism to promote fundamental regional development programs under the general terms of the UN technical assistance program (see Chapter XI).

The Arab Development Bank could perform valuable services within its regional framework—after a change in its charter—as a regional planning and development authority. Its funds could be beefed up by the World Bank and other sources to support *non-productive* regional social overhead projects undertaken by two or more Arab member states. A special fund might even be established for such projects from which funds could be made available on a basis similar to that developed in the United States, where Federal funds are made available to the states on a matching basis for certain public works projects. In any event, however, the Arab Development Bank will undoubtedly have to develop sources of long-term grants, investments, or loans outside the region. The suc-

---

[11] On the face of it, Pres. Eisenhower's proposal for a regional development authority was clearly too late. It followed the two other attempts at "regional planning" by the U.S., namely, the Johnston Plan for the Jordan River valley (which the Arabs interpreted as a bribe for recognizing Israel) and the Baghdad Pact (now CENTO) which was resisted as an attempt to split the Arab world. (The U.S. experience with CENTO, however, has established a precedent for U.S. support to genuine regional development in the fields of communications and transportation.)

cess of the Inter-American Development Bank in 1964 in floating its bonds in the European money market suggests that a similar procedure is worth investigating for the future Arab Development Bank.

The proliferating Arab League projects for joint Arab commercial ventures, however, seem to have little real merit. Specifically, they seem to have little real connection with the work of the Arab League as a regional organization under the terms of its own charter. The proposals, most of which concern transportation enterprises, include the formation of an "Arab Tanker Company," an "Arab Pipeline Company," an "Arab Shipping Company," and an "Arab Airline." Each "company" is intended to be a stock corporation owned jointly by Arab League governments. These projects were broached during the 1950's and spurred to some extent by the Suez crisis of 1956, but none had gone beyond the planning stage by mid-1964 despite the attempt to resurrect them following the January 1964 Arab summit conference.[12]

The only proposed joint venture of this type to show any sign of transcending the planning phase is the Arab Potash Company, a joint undertaking of the governments of Jordan, Syria, Saudi Arabia, Lebanon, and the United Arab Republic with the participation of the privately owned Arab Bank. The Arab Potash Company was proposed in 1953, chartered in 1956, and confident that it would soon be in large-scale commercial production in 1964.

There is some merit to the idea of consolidating Arab airlines, most of which are already owned and operated as government agencies. The European Economic Community has had under discussion since 1959 a similar plan to merge the airlines of its six member states. But the

[12] The three joint ventures promoted after the 1964 Arab summit were to be capitalized as follows: Arab Tanker Co., $98 million; Arab Airline Co., $47.6 million; Arab Shipping Co., $12.2 million.

proposals for tanker fleets, oil pipelines, and a steamship line appear to stem from a vague urge for regional political control over the exploitation and allocation of the area's principal economic resources and not from the demonstrated need for an economic enterprise where none exists. Deliberate steps to commit scarce financial, technical, and manpower resources to highly dubious ventures seem frivolous to the outside observer. Furthermore, one is tempted to speculate that the proposals for at least some of the Arab joint ventures are associated with the success of Israel in the same fields. The apparent success of Israel's ZIM shipping line and El Al Israel airline could presumably excite some Arab envy. And, since Israel long ago took over the operations of the original Dead Sea potash company in a modestly successful fashion, it may be less than a coincidence that the first venture by the Arab states is a potash extraction plant on the Jordanian side of the Dead Sea. The first question that needs asking, however, is: are these projects economically feasible?

Politics, on the other hand, is admittedly the reason for Arab reluctance to engage in a constructive program of development oriented to the Jordan River valley. The inclusion of Israel in Eric Johnston's regional water development scheme for the Jordan River—a sort of Middle Eastern TVA—is the principal reason given for the refusal of the Arab League Council to agree to the plan in 1954, despite at least tacit approval of the scheme on technical grounds. Even if, from a juridical point of view, one were to agree with Arab spokesmen that Israel exists only as a hostile force illegally occupying Arab territory —and therefore not entitled under international law to any of the water from the Jordan River—it was difficult to argue away the fact in 1964 that Israel was ready, willing, and able to pump Jordan River waters to the Negev Desert while Arab leaders debated the consequences. Those sympathetic to the Arab side of the dispute can only wonder why Arab leaders refused to acknowledge over a period of ten years that the Johnston plan was capable of being implemented piecemeal, without the necessity of recognizing Israel.

Once again, however, the negative influence of politics appears to have dictated Arab League policy with respect to regional economic development. The Arab proposals at the Cairo summit conference in January 1964 to "divert" the Jordan River were essentially the Arab League's proposals for the implementation of the Johnston plan in 1954-1955, developed by a special technical committee of the Arab League Secretariat but rejected by the League council for political reasons. Of course, hindsight is better than foresight. In 1954 and 1955, the Arab League was rent by the controversy over the Baghdad Pact, Egypt was still trying desperately to eject the British from the Suez Canal Zone, and few observers would have accepted the fact that the United States or any other Western power would assist the Arab League in the development of the Jordan Valley, with or without Israel.

PLANNING FOR THE FUTURE: THE ARAB COMMON MARKET

Although regional economic integration has been hindered by political obstacles, it seems equally true that political expediency has played a large role in shaping Arab League economic programs and policies. The basic economic problems confronting the region are not so much unknown to the Arabs as they are apt to be ignored or misunderstood within the context of a deep-seated urge toward regional independence and political unification. The activities of the League's Economic Council and, since 1959, the Arab Petroleum Congresses illustrate this situation. More significant, perhaps, is the tendency toward purer economic solutions suggested by the move toward an Arab Common Market.

For the past decade, the Arab League Economic Council has been nominally, at least, the principal policy-making body in the field of regional economic integration. The Council's primary orientation has been political, however. The Economic Council was established by the 1950 Collective Security Pact for the purpose of bringing about "security and prosperity in the Arab countries."[13] Its activities were to be closely related to those of the Permanent Military Commission, and close cooperation between the two bodies was envisaged "for the exploitation of natural, agricultural, industrial, and other resources of all Contracting States in favor of the inter-Arab military effort and joint defense." The Economic Council, itself, was to be composed of the ministers of economy of the contracting states, or their representatives. Further emphasizing the connection of the Economic Council with security matters was the fact that until 1960 membership in the council remained limited to those states which adhered to the 1950 treaty.

The virtual failure of the military provisions of the 1950 Collective Security Pact left the Economic Council in an anomalous position. While the membership of the Economic Council was legally restricted to the states adhering to the collective security agreement, the membership of the Arab League increased. And, because of its essentially political orientation, the Economic Council has occupied itself with such political questions as the boycott of Israel, proposals for economic sanctions against France to protest its activities in Algeria, and relations with West Germany arising from Germany's payment of World War II "reparations" to Israel. Far from being a regional economic coordinating body, the Economic Council failed even to convene until December 1953; and during the

[13] Article 7 (text in Appendix C). The close relation between regional security and economic mobilization established by the treaty is a reaction to the Palestine "disaster" of 1948.

1955-58 hiatus in inter-Arab political relations caused by Iraq's adherence to the Baghdad Pact, the Economic Council was largely inactive. Only since May 1957 has the council taken on some of the functions of promoting regional economic integration.

During the first fifteen years of its existence, therefore, the Arab League operated in the main without an authoritative or consistent economic coordinating agency. The original Permanent Economic Committee—displaced by the Economic Council—was largely responsible for the 1953 treaties on trade and payments. The Economic Committee was also instrumental in initiating a number of projects, including the Arab Development Bank, the proposal for an Arab shipping company, the study of a customs union, and others. The role of the League Secretariat is, of course, assumed in support of the Permanent Economic Committee and, later, of the Economic Council.

Under the circumstances, an important autonomous agency in the field of regional economic activities had a great deal to do with the development of whatever programs the Arab League has instituted. This was the Federation of Arab Chambers of Commerce, Industry, and Agriculture, an independent organization originally sponsored by the Economic Committee. The Federation has often acted as a forum for proposals before they are referred to the Arab League, and in 1953 it was instrumental in bringing about the first meeting of the Economic Council.[14]

After 1957, the Federation consistently demanded the expansion of the Economic Council to include all members of the Arab League. At a meeting in January 1958,

[14] The Federation, now independent of the Arab League, maintains its permanent secretariat in Beirut, under Executive Secretary Burhan Dajani, a Jordanian economist. In October 1953, the group petitioned the League and its member governments to expedite the formation of the long-delayed Economic Council, *Middle East Journal*, VIII (Winter 1954), 72.

the Federation requested the League Secretary General to find a legal formula by which non-member states could become full members of the Economic Council. In March 1959, the Federation proposed that the Economic Council be made independent of military considerations and re-designated as a semiautonomous body composed of members from all Arab states and territories. Finally, in June 1960, an annex to the Collective Security Pact of 1950 was promulgated that provided that all members of the Arab League and all other Arab states could join the Economic Council; Morocco and Libya subsequently became members. One of the other functions of the Federation has been that of demonstrating to Arab governments the soundness of economic cooperation. In 1957, the organization originated a proposal for an Arab Economic Union similar to the European Economic Community.[15]

A somewhat different approach to the problems of the Arab world has been taken by those who see Arab petroleum as the main issue. These young Arab technocrats, Saudi Arabia's fiery Texas-trained former Minister of Oil Affairs, Abdulla al-Tariki, for example, advocate increasing control by the Arab states over the exploitation of the Arab world's most abundant resource. While they shy away from advocating outright nationalization of foreign-owned enterprises, the Arab oil men envisage a shift from the export of crude oil to export of refined petroleum products, including petrochemicals, in cooperation with the oil companies. The concept is of an integrated regional petroleum economy in which the processing of Arab crudes would play a large role in the economic development of the region. In addition, the Arab oil experts have visions of an Arab-owned pipeline parallel to the Suez Canal and an Arab tanker fleet—jointly ensuring

[15] See Burhan Dajani, *Middle East Forum* [Beirut] (February 1958), 3.

that transit revenues redound to the advantage of the region. While these ideas captured the imagination of many men in oil-producing regions and were discussed at the four Arab Petroleum Congresses sponsored by the Arab League since 1959, there is little reason to expect any dramatic action. Tariki and other outspoken Arab oil men have been less influential since the North African oil discoveries and since the Soviet Union began to dump cheap oil on Western markets. Nevertheless, the "Arab oil" issue was revived in 1964 as a part of the Arab-Israeli problem, with vague threats of denying oil to Western Europe.[16]

On the other hand, a gradually increasing role for the oil-producing states in the petroleum and petroleum-related fields is almost certain under any circumstances. Refineries are being built closer to the producing fields, and petrochemical industries are developing in Saudi Arabia, Egypt, Kuwait, and Iraq in the East and in North Africa. Arab technicians, engineers, lawyers, and management officials more and more share the work and responsibility of managing the huge petroleum operations. Better uses are being found for oil revenues. But the worldwide glut of petroleum means that the simple answer to regional economic development is not likely to lie where the Arab oil experts have hoped it would. Furthermore, the problems of interstate cooperation are too well known to make the establishment of joint Arab tanker fleets and pipelines much more than optimistic plans any time in the near future.

In the context of the political frustration of regional economic integration, from which the panaceas of the

[16] More or less dormant for two years, the idea of a "permanent Arab petroleum organization" was revived by influential UAR editor Mohammed Hassanain Haikal in *al-Ahram* [Cairo], June 19, 1964. Haikal called for a unified "Arab oil policy" to apply "moral pressure" on the West in order to solve Arab world problems; he did not, however, recommend stopping the flow of oil to the West.

oil-technocrats have grown, new solutions are being advanced. The remarkable success of the European Common Market, in particular, has not escaped the Arabs. Studies of its organization and operations have been in progress since at least 1957. And in January 1958, the Arab League Economic Council approved in principle the concept of a Council of Economic Union with objectives modeled on those of the European Common Market: (1) freedom of movement, work, and capital for all Arabs within all member Arab states, (2) unconditional freedom for transit trade, (3) reduction of restrictions on trade within the region, and (4) freedom to establish economic projects anywhere within the region.[17] One of the major purposes of the Council of Economic Union will be to preside over a proposed Arab Common Market.

Although internal and external economic pressures seem to make a decision on regional economic integration essential, the prospects for the formation of the much-studied Arab Common Market depend essentially upon political decisions. Vested political interests, dedicated to maintaining and developing *national* economies, have not easily been convinced of the efficacy of regional economic cooperation for the long term. The oil-producing states seemed to be pushing in one direction, commercially minded states like Lebanon in another, and industrially oriented states like Egypt in still another. The adherence of Algeria, Morocco, and Tunisia to the League, with their ties to the franc bloc, introduced another complicating factor. After 1962, the debate over Nasser's Arab socialism added still another.

In 1962, the League's seemingly ineffectual Economic Council came close to legislating itself out of existence. On June 6, 1962, at the conclusion of the eighth session of the Economic Council, five Arab League members

[17] Burhan Dajani, The Arab Economic Council," *Middle East Forum* [Beirut] (March 1959), 11.

signed an agreement providing for the establishment of a Council for Arab Economic Union: Jordan, Kuwait, Morocco, Syria, and the United Arab Republic. The agreement undertook to provide for the signatory states (and any later adherents):

1. freedom of travel and of transfer of capital;
2. freedom of exchange of goods;
3. freedom of residence, work, and economic activity;
4. freedom of transit and of the use of harbors and airports; and
5. rights of ownership and inheritance.[18]

Article Two of the agreement defined a series of steps by which the objectives would be reached. In effect, the result was to be the establishment of the much-discussed Arab Common Market. The article envisaged a single Arab customs area under one administration; legislation pertaining to tariffs and customs was to be unified as were all legislation and regulations relating to import and export procedures. Transport and transit laws were to be reviewed and unified as required. The conclusion of trade and payments agreements between foreign states and the Arab members of the agreement was expected. Uniform policies relating to agriculture, industry, real estate, and monetary activities were envisaged. And, finally, provision was made for the coordination of labor laws and legislation relating to social security. The executive agent for this program was to be the Council of Arab Economic Union.

This Council was to comprise one full-time representative from each of the member states. According to the agreement, the Council would have its headquarters in Cairo, but it could meet in any Arab city. It would have its own budget, contributed by member states, and oper-

[18] *Arab News and Views* (New York), June 15, 1962. Yemen and Iraq adhered to the agreement in the winter of 1963-64.

ate as an independent entity. The presidency was to be held by each country in turn, for a one-year period, and decisions were to be adopted by a two-thirds majority vote. In addition to special economic and administrative committees, the Council was provided a technical advisory office and a statistical section.

The agreement, ratified by the required three signatories by the end of January 1964, took effect sometime in April 1964. Kuwait was the first to ratify (1962), followed by the UAR, Syria, Iraq, and Jordan in 1963-64. Other Arab states are eligible to join the Council; their adherence becomes effective one month after their signature of the agreement.

At Cairo in December 1963 the ninth Economic Council session set about to pave the way for implementation of the Arab Economic Union Agreement. In addition to establishing working committees to prepare for the conversion to the new system, it ordered that a full-scale proposal for the future Arab Common Market be drawn up and submitted to the tenth meeting of the Economic Council. In rough outline, the proposal was to cover the establishment of the Arab Common Market over a ten-year period by the gradual reduction of customs duties, until all commodities traded between members are duty free.

Meanwhile, the first session of the Council of Arab Economic Union met at Arab League Headquarters in Cairo in June 1964 to put itself in business. The five members of the Council (Iraq, Jordan, Kuwait, Syria, and the UAR) were joined by five other Arab League member states: Algeria, Morocco, Sudan, Tunisia, and Yemen. Lebanon, Saudi Arabia, and Libya were not represented. At the conclusion of the meeting, it was announced that the Economic Union Council had studied a proposal for an Arab Common Market and would report its findings to the Arab League Council. The members of the Economic Union Council reportedly agreed that membership in the proposed common market would be open only to those Arab states adhering to the 1962 Arab Economic Union Agreement.[19] The Council also established three permanent committees, approved a budget of about $215,-000 for the first year (payable in proportion to member shares in the League budget), and agreed to hold regular meetings every three months. The President of the council for the first year was a Jordanian, Dr. Mohammed al-Fara.

It is possible to postulate a common market arrangement which could shelter many of the separate development projects already discussed by the League. Some sort of autonomous "Arab Petroleum Authority," for example, could play a role similar to that of the European Coal and Steel Community of the European Common Market area. Such an authority might, for example, operate or coordinate the operations of the proposed Arab tanker fleet and the pipelines, supervise production quotas, set up training programs, and coordinate a joint Arab oil policy in cooperation with the regional petroleum concessionaires. The international oil companies will undoubtedly resist any such development, but it appears to be inevitable that the Arab states will attempt to exercise increasingly close control over the exploitation of Arab oil. From the point of view of the concessionaires, it would seem preferable to deal with one responsible regional authority than with half a dozen competing claimants.

A similar authority could conceivably rationalize mutually competing activities in the agricultural fields, per-

[19] *Arab World* [Beirut] (June 12, 1964). On August 13, 1964, representatives of the UAR, Iraq, Syria, Jordan, and Kuwait signed a treaty establishing the Arab Common Market, effective on January 1, 1965. The agreement provided for reductions on agricultural products of 20% annually; tariffs on manufactured goods were to be reduced 10% annually. See *al-Ahram* [Cairo], August 14, 1964.

haps by establishing regional production quotas for such commodities as wheat, cotton, oil-seeds, and livestock so as to insure stable markets and prices and to provide for some complementarity in regional development. Such an agency could well devote considerable attention to improved methods of agriculture, expansion of agricultural credit, improved seed stock, introduction of modern livestock breeding techniques, and the development of new commercial crops in the region. The League's Economic Council has already taken several steps in the direction of regional agricultural policy by encouraging agricultural cooperatives, by the establishment of a permanent committee to coordinate Arab agricultural policies, by the establishment of a permanent veterinary office to improve livestock, and appointing an observer to the European Economic Community in Brussels.

Coordinated social overhead development at the regional level and the coordination of financial support for approved basic industrial projects could become the function of the already established Arab Development Bank, as already suggested, working in close cooperation with the World Bank and its affiliated agencies.

Over-all supervision of such autonomous "authorities" by the Arab Economic Union Council—with the much-discussed Arab Court as an adjunct—would serve to integrate production and marketing policies for the benefit of the entire region. Any real progress toward settling the political differences which now impede regional economic integration should lead to increased private investment, including investment of foreign capital, in secondary industrial projects of significance to the future development of the region. Close ties with the European Common Market and other trade blocs are assumed, of course.

Over a period of twenty years, some of the basic steps toward Arab regional economic integration have been taken despite the simultaneous solidification of disintegrative nationalistic political trends. But the Arabs, like most observers, know that there is no easy road to an Arab Common Market: the plans wisely call for a ten-year transition period. But even ten years is a short time in which to achieve realistic regional economic integration. The Arab world lacks the interdependence that characterized Europe for fifty years or more before the establishment of the European Economic Community. The sectoral imbalances that emphasize agricultural raw materials and unprocessed minerals and petroleum will continue to tie the area to distant commodity centers. The lack of efficient regional transportation and communications networks will continue to hamper the development of internal markets. And this, after all, is the basic requirement of a "common market" scheme.

The development of industry, hand-in-hand with improvements in agriculture and the efficient exploitation of available mineral resources, and, presumably, including the establishment of sophisticated processing industries, requires the development of a regional market that simply does not exist. Moreover, this regional market must be coordinated with other existing market areas of the world. These requirements presuppose the efficient management of regional resources and the coordinated development of regional industry. The proposed schemes for an Arab shipping line and a tanker fleet, ironically, will only confirm the dependence of the Arab states on exports of unprocessed raw materials to distant markets. It is for this reason that it seems essential to give first priority to intra-regional communications. The present pattern of autarkic economic development, finally, discriminates heavily against regional integration.

Only partially submerged in any plan for an Arab Common Market is the question of the future of the Arab League itself. Two possible courses exist. The first, involves the Arab League as the regional organization which maintains political control over the essentially technical operations of the Economic Union Council by means of broad policy guidance and which continues its other programs in close coordination with the United Nations, adjacent regional organizations, and other international agencies.

The second course of action involves the gradual development of the Council of Economic Union from a regional economic development authority to a political body with the characteristics of a regional federal government. This is the course upon which the European Economic Community has embarked; gradual erosion of national sovereignty by extension of "economic" activities into the realm of political decisions is already well advanced. It is perhaps this course of action that both the proponents and opponents of the Arab Common Market plan envisage, with mixed reactions.[20]

Opposition to the Arab Common Market projects thus continues to be related to political interests; and, despite the urging of economic experts and regionally oriented businessmen, the decision will be made on political grounds. It is a paradox that the exigencies of the situation may force a reluctant decision for Arab unity as an economic and social necessity by politicians who have consistently failed to agree on unity as a politically desirable objective.

[20] Although little more than a straw in the wind, the UAR National Assembly debated in June 1964, an "Arab parliamentary convention" that would discuss such matters as the establishment of the Arab Common Market, the Arab Development Bank, and the Arab Monetary Fund.

CHAPTER 10 COLLECTIVE SECURITY AND THE PEACEFUL SETTLEMENT OF DISPUTES

REGIONAL SECURITY AND THE UNITED NATIONS CHARTER

ARTICLE 52 of the United Nations Charter, the first in Chapter VIII on "Regional Arrangements," appears to imply that regional organizations must have, as a minimum, effective means "for dealing with such matters relating to the maintenance of international peace and security as are appropriate for regional action." According to the Charter, regional "arrangements" include reciprocal responsibilities of attempting to settle regional disputes before referring them to the Security Council and, as directed by the Security Council, of acting as a local agency of the United Nations in effecting peaceful settlement of disputes. American commentators in particular are therefore prone to insist that Article 52 means that a regional arrangement must deal primarily with security matters, and deal with them effectively. Indeed, one American authority insists that any "arrangement dealing with other matters is not a regional arrangement within the meaning of Chapter VIII."[1]

While the latter view is not widely accepted, the circumstances of UNCIO in 1945 do seem to support the conclusion that only an organization with an effective mechanism for dealing with regional disputes, that is, with a collective security agency, can qualify for recog-

[1] See Kelsen, *op.cit.* (1951 Supplement), p. 919.

nition as a regional organization. Conversely, the Security Council was given ultimate authority over the regional organizations in the matter of actions to enforce the peace, in accordance with Article 53/1. It is this latter provision of the UN Charter which has led to the confusion between regional organizations within the meaning of Chapter VIII and the agencies formed for "collective self-defense" under the provisions of Article 51.

Largely in an effort to maintain the traditional freedom of action of the Americas, and particularly to render effective the Act of Chapultepec, the United States' delegation to UNCIO proposed an amendment to the Dumbarton Oaks Proposals "so as to give countries with a tradition of collective action . . . the right to defend themselves in case the Security Council failed to maintain peace."[2] Both the Latin American delegates and the Arab delegates at UNCIO supported the amendment in the expectation that their respective regional organizations would be named in the final version of the UN Charter —thereby acquiring special status as recognized "regional arrangements." For various reasons, however, neither organization was mentioned in the Charter; and the amendment became Article 51, outside the chapter on regional arrangements.

Inexplicably, the result of the maneuver has been that the original regional organizations (the Organization of American States and the Arab League) and the newer collective-defense organizations (such as NATO) both invoked Article 51 and not Article 52 when they drafted their security treaties. While it is not the task here to attempt to untangle this knot of confusion, an effort should be made to establish the critical framework within which to evaluate the collective security program of the Arab League.

[2] Majid Khadduri, "The Arab League as a Regional Arrangement," *American Journal of International Law*, 46 (October 1946), 773.

In his discussion of collective security, Julius Stone has taken pains to show that "the invocation of 'collective self-defense' as a residual *obligation* of Members under Article 1, paragraph 1, cannot conceal the fact that 'collective self-defense' comes not to fulfill the Charter, but because, alas, the Charter remains unfulfilled."[3] In effect, says Stone, Article 51 was designed as an escape clause, in anticipation of the inability of the international community to act in the cause of peace. In the opinion of another observer, regional organizations rightfully "should be considered as agencies for dealing with special problems of local interest and not as institutions usurping the security functions of the world organization."[4] They should, properly, strive to eliminate the causes of conflict, initiate the machinery of negotiation, and bring world opinion to bear on issues so as to prevent aggression.

The distinctive role attributed to the regional organization in the maintenance of regional security by Article 52 of the United Nations also implies that the source of danger is normally to be sought within the region. By contrast, collective defense agencies established in accordance with Article 51 have as their primary purpose countermeasures directed against external aggression or the threat of aggression. This fundamental distinction, of course, does not rule out the possibility that a regional collective security organization may have to face external aggression.

Discussion of the general nature of regional organizations in Chapter I concluded that collective security is not the primary or exclusive concern of the regional organization. The original proponents of regionalism in-

[3] Stone, *op.cit.*, p. 264.
[4] Panikkar, *op.cit.*, p. 6. But, see Kelsen, *op.cit.*, p. 923, where he alleges that "the original idea was that regional arrangements will be concluded against former enemy states."

sisted that the primary purpose of the regional organization is to facilitate functional integration. The position that only a security-oriented arrangement can qualify as a regional organization under the terms of Chapter VIII of the UN Charter is patently untenable within the context of the development of the principles and practice of regional organization and, furthermore, seems to have little legal validity. The conflicting provisions of the Charter have, however, distorted the collective security functions of the regional organization. Hence, since the discussion here is of the Arab League as a regional organization and not as a "collective self-defense" arrangement, it is important that the terms of reference be those of Article 52 and not of Article 51: i.e., the question is that of the capacity and efficiency of the Arab League to deal with internal disputes and bring them to peaceful settlements.

From this point of view, the two aspects of regional collective security to be emphasized in this chapter are (1) the formation and functioning of the Arab League collective security mechanism, and (2) the League's procedures for peaceful settlement of disputes by means short of military action. At the same time, however, it is impossible to discuss the collective security problems of the Arab League without reference to the "collective self-defense" provisions of Article 51. The role of the Middle East in the Cold War strategy of the West and the implacable dispute between Israel and the Arab states have added unexpected dimensions to otherwise simple problems.

THE 1950 ARAB COLLECTIVE SECURITY PACT

The Pact of the League of Arab States contained no provisions for an institutionalized security organization. Article 5 of the Pact, however, prohibited signatories from using force to settle disputes. It also empowered the League Council to mediate disputes which threatened to lead' to war, including those between member states and a third state, and provided for arbitration by the League Council in certain other cases. Article 6 of the Pact established the role of the League Council as the agency concerned with repelling aggression, primarily but not exclusively that originating from within the membership.

The discussions and negotiations at San Francisco in 1945 had clearly indicated that in order to qualify as a regional organization under the UN Charter, such an organization must provide an institutionalized mechanism for settling regional disputes.[5] The Arab delegates thus came away from UNCIO with the certain knowledge that their primary objective, that of acceptance by the United Nations as a bona fide regional organization, could only be achieved upon the establishment of a more formal security mechanism. For the Arabs, the turn of events at San Francisco was more a cause for disappointment than a goad to action. Aggressions from within the Arab community were considered unlikely, and the general provisions for peaceful settlement of disputes already contained in the Pact were considered to be adequate. No significant intra-Arab dispute had occurred since 1936, following the Treaty of Arab Brotherhood between Saudi Arabia and Yemen, and no Arab state had any significant military force prior to 1945. Nor was there any apparent external threat, particularly in view of the initial support promised the Arab League by Great Britain and the United States.

Perhaps the first evidence of a change of position in Arab thinking was the reported Lebanese proposal for an Arab mutual security pact in 1948, which would have prohibited military pacts with the Big Four.[6] Serious consideration of such a proposal, however, was delayed by

[5] See G. Bebr, "Regional Organizations, a United Nations' Problem," *American Journal of International Law*, 49 (1955), 169.

[6] Reported by *al-Ahram* [Cairo], January 25, 1948.

the protracted negotiations and eventual conflict over the status of Arab Palestine. Paradoxically the disastrous lack of coordination of the Arab military effort during the Arab-Israeli War made the principle of organized collective security more significant. In 1945, the Arab League had provisionally included Palestine, though it was still a British mandate, and the Arabs confidently expected the homogeneity of the Arab Middle East to continue undisturbed. After 1948 the Arabs were confronted by a potential non-Arab source of disputes—and, possibly, of aggression—from within the formerly all-Arab region.

The Arab League Council formally adopted the principle of collective security in October 1949, at its first session since the war over Palestine. By this time a movement was under way in the West to bring the Middle East into some form of "collective defense" arrangement in extension of the newly formed North Atlantic Treaty Organization. For the Arabs, nevertheless, the question of UN recognition of the Arab League as a regional organization remained the important consideration, especially since the original provisions of the Arab League Pact had been proven inadequate. It is therefore significant that the Arab League was invited by the General Assembly in November 1950 to send an observer to the UN General Assembly, barely six months after the signature of the Arab League Collective Security Pact. Arab League officials consider *de facto* recognition of the League's status as a regional organization to stem from this fact.

The conditions under which the Arab Collective Security Pact (actually, "Joint Defense and Economic Cooperation Treaty between the States of the Arab League") was established were anything but auspicious. The failure of the Arab League in Palestine had led to mutual recriminations. Egypt and Iraq were at each other's throats, and Transjordan had unilaterally incorporated the remaining Arab districts of Palestine into the new Kingdom of Jordan.[7] The establishment of Israel, officially unrecognized by the Arab states, had complicated the security problems of the region. And, finally, Western pressure was building up to weld some of the Arab states and other Middle Eastern countries into a defensive alliance against potential Soviet expansion into the Mediterranean.

The provisions of the Collective Security Pact (see Appendix C) are not particularly remarkable. The treaty invoked Article 51 of the UN Charter as its basis but was framed as an extension of Article 6 of the Pact of the Arab League. The treaty established a Joint Defense Council (consisting of the foreign ministers and the defense ministers of the contracting parties) and a Permanent Military Commission composed of "representatives of the general staffs of the armies of the contracting states." The principal effect of several Iraqi proposals of 1950, incorporated in a protocol of February 2, 1951, was to add an advisory body composed of the chiefs of staff of each of the contracting parties. A Military Annex provided for the appointment of a joint Arab commander in chief in the event of war, but no permanent military command was envisaged. This fact would seem to undermine criticism that the Arab Collective Security Pact was aggressive in design but, at the same time, it limits the defensive efficiency of the Pact as far as external threats are concerned. The principal function of the Permanent Military Commission was to carry out contingency planning, including organizational plans, for various unspecified situations.

In general terms, the Arab Collective Security Pact is closer in principle to Articles 45 to 50 of the UN Charter than it is to the typical "regional defense treaty," such as

[7] Under the circumstances, Iraq refused to sign the draft treaty (June 17, 1950) pending acceptance of proposed revisions, and Jordan was absent from the ceremony. Iraq, however, adhered to the revised text on February 2, 1951. See *Oriente Moderno*, XXXI (1954), 5.

NATO, developed in accordance with Article 51. Like the United Nations, the Arab League disposes of no permanent body of troops, and not until 1964 was a serious effort made to allocate national contingents to a "Joint Arab Command." Before 1964 the Arab League had no permanent military staff, and a "joint commander in chief" was provided only in case of war. In 1964, the designation of UAR General 'Ali Amer as "Joint Commander," the formation of a permanent joint Arab military planning staff at the Secretariat, and plans for joint maneuvers suggested a firmer resolve to coordinate regional security requirements. However, there seemed little likelihood that any Arab member state would permit the establishment of a permanent "Joint Arab Command" of any importance on its soil. The emphasis remained on such problems as the standardization of doctrine, training, and weapons and equipment, and on joint contingency planning (reportedly defensive plans against an Israeli attack).

Although the Pact was signed in June 1950, it was not implemented until mid-1953 when the chiefs of staff of the Arab states met in Cairo to draw up final plans—duly passed on to an Arab Defense Council meeting in September. In October 1953, the Permanent Military Commission met in Cairo for a week. In November a joint meeting of the Military Commission and the League Secretariat reportedly worked on the problems of implementing the provisions of the Pact. Little came of these meetings except a recommendation for "unifying the efforts of the Arab states in defense and the maintenance of peace and security."[8] Plans for a joint Arab defense fund were discussed in February 1954 by the League's Economic Council. In May of the same year, the

---

[8] *Middle Eastern Affairs*, IV (1953), 345. According to a subsequent report, however, the Joint Defense Council approved a plan for a 150,000-man joint Arab army. *Ibid.* V (1954), 5.

chiefs of staff met to discuss standardization of officer schools and problems of coordinating defenses against Israel. These discussions led to no practical results.

The adherence of Iraq to the Baghdad Pact in 1955, a matter for Arab League debate during most of 1954, effectively paralyzed the Arab Collective Security Pact. For several years perhaps the only tangible influence of the Pact was as a bargaining point between the British and the Egyptians in the negotiations which led to British withdrawal from the Suez Canal Zone in 1956. Paragraph 4/1 of the agreement, dated July 27, 1954, provided that: "In the event of an armed attack by an outside power on Egypt, or on any country which at date of signature of the present agreement is a party to the Treaty of Joint Defense between the Arab League States or on Turkey, Egypt will afford to the United Kingdom such facilities as may be necessary in order to place the base on a war footing and operate it effectively."[9] Meanwhile, Western pressures for an effective regional security arrangement split the Arab ranks. For all practical purposes, the Arab League's collective security preparations collapsed. In November 1956, however, in the aftermath of the Israeli campaign in the Sinai and the joint Franco-British attacks on the Suez Canal Zone, a meeting of the Arab heads of state in Beirut threatened to invoke the 1950 Collective Security Pact if the UN resolutions on a cease fire were not respected.[10] This was an astute political gesture designed to convey the impression of Arab solidarity in the face of aggression, but the threat could hardly have been carried out because of the complete failure to coordinate Arab League forces under the terms of the 1950 treaty.

REGIONAL SECURITY AND THE COLD WAR

The development of the Cold War and the resulting bi-

[9] Text of agreement in *Middle East Journal*, VIII (1954), 460.
[10] See *Oriente Moderno*, XXXVI (1956), 686.

polarization of the world in the aftermath of the Second World War has complicated the problem of Arab regional collective security.[11] Tentative discussions between the British and Egyptian governments on a plan for a Middle East alliance to support the West in event of conflict with the Soviet Union took place in Cairo as early as the fall of 1948.[12] In discussions with the British ambassador to Cairo, the Egyptian Prime Minister, Nokrashi Pasha, reportedly asserted the neutrality of Egypt and the Arab states in the event of an East-West conflict. In the early months of 1949, Tsaldaris, the Greek Foreign Minister, offered a plan for a Mediterranean security pact to Britain's Ernest Bevin.[13] This plan was to be effected in two stages: (1) the alliance of the countries of the Mediterranean, from France to Turkey, and, (2) the integration of the Middle Eastern countries, extending as far east as Pakistan. Since it was at about this time that the Arab League was beginning to take a serious look at the concept of collective security, the conclusion of some Western observers has been that the idea promoted within the League, particularly by Egypt, was for an Arab Collective Security Pact as a countermeasure to growing Western pressures.[14]

By the time the West developed its famous plan for a Middle East Defense Command, the Arab League states

[11] For comprehensive general discussions of the situation, see John C. Campbell, *Defense of the Middle East* (New York: Harper, 1960); Walter Z. Laqueur, *The Soviet Union and the Middle East* (New York: Praeger, 1959); and Elizabeth Monroe, *Britain's Moment in the Middle East 1914-1956* (Baltimore: Johns Hopkins Press, 1963), especially Chaps. 7 and 8.

[12] *Oriente Moderno*, xxviii (1948), 174, from an Egyptian Government report. This was three years before the abortive proposal for a Middle East Defense Command.

[13] *Oriente Moderno*, xxix (1949), 12. Tsaldaris is also reported to have discussed his plan with the Egyptian foreign minister in the early fall of 1948. See *Oriente Moderno*, xxviii (1948), 174.

[14] See James W. Spain, "Middle East Defense: A New Approach," *Middle East Journal*, viii (1954), 257.

had long since drawn up and signed their own Collective Security Pact. The proposed Middle East Defense Command, revealed on October 13, 1951, by the United States, Great Britain, France, and Turkey, required the establishment of a joint headquarters in Egypt.[15] In return for contributing bases, military facilities, staff officers, and supporting armed forces, Egypt was offered concessions with respect to the 1936 Anglo-Egyptian Treaty and the administrative regime in the Sudan. The West assumed, moreover, that the adherence of Egypt to the plan would automatically insure the accession of other Arab states, though the original proposal was extended only to the Egyptian Government. When Egypt promptly rejected the plan, the U.S. State Department announced that it would proceed without the Egyptians and undertook discussions with other Arab states and Israel.[16]

In the following weeks, both the Egyptians and the Iraqis advanced alternative plans in an effort to gain acceptance of the Arab League's Joint Defense Treaty as a substitute for the Western sponsored Middle East Defense Command. The basic orientation of the Arab League states—i.e., no compromise with the West until local grievances were satisfied—prevented the Arabs from accepting a direct alliance with the West in a conflict which they generally regarded as outside their sphere of interest. But the Egyptians had already hit on the idea of extending the bilateral Anglo-Egyptian discussions on the future of the Suez Canal Zone to a general regional conference with the Arab League on one side and the British and Americans on the other.[17] On No-

[15] Text of the proposal for a Middle East Defense Command is in *Middle Eastern Affairs*, II (1951), 367-69.

[16] On October 31, 1951, the State Department announced that discussions had been held with the other Arab League states and Israel. *Middle Eastern Affairs*, II (1951), 373.

[17] Reported on January 1, 1951, by *al-Musawwar* [Cairo] according to *Middle East Journal*, V (1951), 200.

vember 17, 1951, a month after the Western proposal, Iraq's Nuri as-Sa'id submitted a compromise plan to Anthony Eden, in London. It called for evacuation of the Suez Canal Zone, a plebiscite on the future of the Sudan, evacuation of British forces from Iraq, and the provision of Western arms and training for a proposed Arab League defense force. The plan envisaged an Arab alliance with the West, but without the physical presence of Western military forces.[18] Despite a Soviet warning in late November 1951 to the Arab states that it would not favor their joining any alliance with the West, Egypt was reportedly trying in early 1952 to promote the idea that the Arab Collective Security Pact should be considered a regional security agreement and developed with the assistance of the West.[19] For some time, rumors persisted that negotiations were to be conducted between the Arab League and Turkey on some sort of extension of NATO—and Turkey was even reported about to join the Arab League.

The results of the discussions and negotiations were negligible, although the British did eventually grant *de facto* recognition of the Arab League Collective Security Pact in connection with the 1954 Anglo-Egyptian agreement on the British bases in the Suez Canal Zone. But the two sides were poles apart. The West was intent on obtaining a political and military commitment from the Arab League states in terms of "collective self-defense" against the Soviet Union, as viewed from standpoint of Article 51 of the UN Charter.[20] The West refused to accept the League's Joint Defense Treaty as a substitute

[18] *Facts on File*, 1951, p. 371. See also p. 363 of the same volume for additional details of an Egyptian proposal for a Middle East defense organization sponsored by the Arab states. See *al-Ahram* [Cairo], January 2, 1952, on Nuri's proposal.

[19] *Middle Eastern Affairs*, IV (1952), 115.

[20] As one Western observer commented regarding the Western plan, "the aim was more political than military" (Spain, *op.cit.*, p. 252).

for its own military proposals, particularly since the Arab League plans would have established an autonomous agency beyond Western control—even if within the framework of the collective security mechanism of the UN. The Arab counter plans, in which the Arab League Security Pact figured as a starting point for a regional defense organization, appealed to Article 52 of the Charter.[21] In the balance, Great Britain and the United States shifted their emphasis to the "Northern Tier" approach and eventually fathered the Baghdad Pact. In its turn, the Arab League Council took the official stand that the Arab Collective Security Pact was adequate for Arab policy and that no member of the Arab League should become a party to an agreement [with a Western power] that was likely to affect the sovereignty and independence of Arab League member states.[22]

The adherence of Iraq to the Northern Tier scheme and the subsequent formation of the Baghdad Pact represented a limited victory for the West in the tug-of-war with the Arabs, but it almost wrecked the Arab League. An unsuccessful attempt was made to expel Iraq, for example, and Egypt threatened to withdraw. Iraq's position, in the face of Arab criticism of the step, was that the tie with the West served to strengthen the Arab League. In fact, Iraq never abrogated the 1950 Arab Collective Security Pact but, rather, continued to offer military assistance to the Arab League in support of its regional security policies. The 1955 treaty between Iraq and Turkey refers to the Arab Collective Security Pact in the preamble. The treaty was left open to any Arab League member concerned with the security of the area.[23] In actuality, however, the Collective Security Pact

[21] Nuri's plan, for example, was geared to Article 52 (see *al-Ahram* [Cairo], January 2, 1952).

[22] Resolution of the 21st session of the League Council, April 6, 1954, reported in *Middle Eastern Affairs*, v (1954), 275.

[23] Text of treaty in *Middle East Journal*, IX (1955), 177-78. A

became a dead issue as Egypt attempted to establish her own security community by a series of treaties with Syria and Saudi Arabia (1955), and, eventually, with Jordan and Yemen (in 1956).

THE REVIVAL OF ARAB COLLECTIVE SECURITY

Projects for strengthening Arab regional defense capabilities proliferated after the Suez incident of 1956. In particular, pressures increased after mid-1958 for a joint Arab policy toward Israel with special reference to Israeli plans to divert Jordan River waters to the parched Negev and alleged Israeli attempts to develop nuclear weapons. Ironically, however, the most significant Arab experience in the collective security field was to be the Arab League's intervention in Kuwait, where a joint Arab force in the fall of 1961 warded off an Iraqi annexation threat. Meanwhile, armed clashes between Arab League members and barely disguised attempts at internal subversion broke a long-standing tradition that Arab relations in the area never degenerated to the point of armed conflict and made a genuine collective security arrangement vitally necessary.

The military coup d'etat in Iraq and the succcessful Arab League mediation of the Lebanese crisis, both in mid-1958, paved the way for the revival of the League's Collective Security Pact.[24] Iraq's withdrawal from the Baghdad Pact in 1959 removed the principal obstacle to

---

report in *an-Nasr* [Damascus], January 25, 1955, stated that the Turkish Government had tendered an official invitation to each Arab League state to join the Iraqi-Turkish treaty on January 22, 1955. The personal account of the American Ambassador to Iraq on the formation of the Baghdad Pact is in Waldemar Gallman, *Iraq Under General Nuri* (Baltimore: Johns Hopkins Press, 1964), Chaps. IV and V.

[24] See Majid Khadduri, *Modern Libya* (Baltimore: Johns Hopkins Press, 1963), pp. 295-96, for an insight into the League's handling of the crisis in Lebanon, June 1958.

the Arab collective security approach. Iraq resumed its role in the Arab League Council in September 1960 in a gesture of Arab solidarity. In late April 1961, the military chiefs of staff of Iraq, Jordan, Lebanon, Saudi Arabia, the UAR, and Yemen—signatories of the Collective Security Pact—and observers from Libya, Morocco, and the Sudan met in Cairo to discuss joint Arab defense policies. The meeting of the Arab chiefs of staff led to the June 1961 session of the Joint Defense Council (the first in several years) to discuss Arab policy toward Israel. The details of the meeting are less important than the fact that it was held and that, on June 13, 1961, Morocco adhered to the security pact. The final communiqué issued by Lieutenant General 'Ali 'Ali Amer, the League's Assistant Secretary General for Military Affairs (and UAR Chief of Staff), expressed optimism for the future of Arab collective security. Barely three months later, the Collective Security Pact was invoked for the first time in its ten-year history to permit the Arab League to intervene in the dispute between Iraq and Kuwait.

Kuwait had long planned to join the Arab League as an independent state, a move encouraged by other Arab League members who hoped to benefit from the sheikhdom's enormous oil revenues.[25] Secretary General Hassouna had conferred with Sheikh Sabah in Kuwait in April 1961, and Kuwait formally applied for membership in the Arab League on June 22 after terminating its special treaty relationship with the British. Thus, the Arab world was staggered a few days later when Iraq's erratic General Kassem laid claim to Kuwait as a lost province of Iraq. Subsequent action by the Arab League suggests that the League's collective defense system was not as weak as most people had believed.

Secretary General Hassouna and Assistant Secretary

[25] Kuwaiti spokesmen announced a plan to join the Arab League in September 1958. *Washington Post*, September 25, 1958.

General Said Nawfal flew to Baghdad on July 1 to confer with Kassem and his Foreign Minister, Hashim Jawad, and meet with the heads of Arab diplomatic missions in the Iraqi capital. On July 4, Hassouna arrived in Kuwait for discussions with responsible officials there. Before he returned to Cairo, Hassouna also traveled to Riyadh for talks with King Saud, who had already provided military and other support to Kuwait. Meanwhile, Kuwait had requested the British to implement their defense treaty with the sheikhdom in the face of an expected attack from Iraq. The British, in turn, requested a special meeting of the UN Security Council on Kuwait's behalf. The meeting convened on July 2, but after several sessions the Security Council was unable to act because of Egyptian and Soviet efforts to force the withdrawal of British troops. A British draft resolution calling for the Security Council to guarantee Kuwait's independence was defeated by a Soviet veto on July 7, and the Security Council tacitly turned the affair back to the Arab League.[26]

An extraordinary meeting of the League Council convened in Cairo on July 4 to discuss Kuwait's application for membership. After some delaying tactics by the Iraqi delegate, the meeting adjourned until July 12 to await the results of Hassouna's talks with officials in Iraq, Kuwait, and Saudi Arabia. When the League Council reconvened, Secretary Hassouna proposed either that Kassem withdraw his claim to Kuwait and publicly acknowledge its independence or that the Arab League form a joint Arab force to replace the British troops in Kuwait. After some debate, the Council voted on July 20 to admit Kuwait to membership in the Arab League and to provide "effective help for the preservation of Kuwait's independence, upon that country's request."[27] Kuwait

[26] A detailed survey of the situation is available in Benjamin Schwadran's two-part article "The Kuwait Incident," *Middle Eastern Affairs*, XIII (January and February 1962), 2-13, 43-53.

[27] Quoted by Schwadran, *op.cit.*, p. 49.

agreed to adhere to the Joint Defense Treaty and undertook to request the evacuation of the British forces, moves in preparation for the entry of the proposed Arab task force.

On August 12, 1961, a formal agreement concluded between the Arab League and the government of Kuwait provided the legal and operational framework for the joint Arab force.[28] Secretary General Hassouna was assisted in the negotiations on the agreement and in arrangements for the reception of the Arab League command by Assistant Secretary General Said Nawfal and by Lieutenant General Ahmad Halim Imam, chairman of the League's Permanent Military Commission. On September 10, the first elements of the 3,300-man Arab League force began to arrive in Kuwait. The force, drawn from Saudi Arabia, the UAR, the Sudan, Jordan, and Tunisia, was placed under a Saudi commander, Major General Abdullah al-Isa.[29] British troops began their withdrawal upon the arrival of the Arab forces and were out of Kuwait at the end of 30 days. Except for the withdrawal of the UAR contingent in December 1961, the Arab League force remained in Kuwait until it was officially dissolved in February 1963. By this time the crisis had long since passed.

The revival in 1961 of the Collective Security Pact, and the solid success of the Kuwait solution under its terms, encouraged additional interest in the problems of regional defense. The adherence of Morocco and Kuwait widened

[28] Text of the agreement is available in UN Security Council document S/5007, November 30, 1961 (mimeo. in English).

[29] Saudi Arabia and the UAR each provided 1,200 troops; Sudan provided 400, Jordan, 300, and Tunisia, 200, *Middle East Journal*, xv (1961), 435. Schwadran, *op.cit.*, p. 51, states that about 2,000 more troops were eventually levied from the UAR and Sudan. A new Saudi commander took over in July 1962: Major General Abdullah al-Mutlaq.

the scope of action under the pact. One Arab military leader reviewed the security pact and recommended the following improvements:

"(1) the Joint Defense Council should be composed of permanent representatives and meet at least weekly; the original composition of the Defense Council (i.e., defense ministers and foreign ministers) would be retained for purposes of annual or semi-annual policy meetings;

"(2) a permanent Military Affairs Department under a 'Deputy Secretary General' should be established within the League Secretariat to support the Defense Council;

"(3) permanent representatives from each Arab member state should augment the Chiefs of Staff advisory group; they would review plans prepared by the Permanent Military Committee;

"(4) the Permanent Military Commission, comprising officers from all armed forces of the Arab member states, should be organized as a joint planning staff and should eventually become the headquarters of a 'Unified Arab Command.' "[30]

At least some of these ideas were incorporated into the League's plans, developed during the fall and winter of 1963, for joint Arab action to counteract Israel's plan to divert the Jordan. The January 1964 Cairo summit meeting of the heads of Arab League member states approved the establishment of a joint Arab command under General 'Ali 'Ali Amer, an annual defense budget of about $42 million—principally to strengthen the armed forces of Syria, Lebanon, and Jordan—and a permanent joint planning staff of about one hundred military experts under the general supervision of General Imam, chairman of the Permanent Military Commission. As a gesture of Arab solidarity, the remaining non-adherents—Algeria,

[30] Hassan Mustapha, "Arab Military Cooperation," *Middle East Forum*, xxxvii (1961), 23.

Tunisia, Libya, and the Sudan—joined the Collective Security Pact during the second "Arab summit meeting," held at Alexandria in September 1964.

From the Westerner's point of view, it is a regrettable if indisputable fact that during most of its history the Arab League has been obsessively convinced that the only real threat to peace in the Arab region comes from Israel—or Israel's supporters outside the region. In actuality, of course, the Arab area has been rocked by disputes unrelated either to Israel or to Western "intervention" that the Arab League has been unable to solve. Since 1958, these disputes have become increasingly violent. And since 1962, the peace of the Arab region has been shattered by bloody wrangling over Yemen (involving Saudi Arabia, Jordan, and the UAR, in addition to two rival Yemeni governments), border disputes between Syria and Lebanon, and a major border incident between Algeria and Morocco.

The new look in Arab collective security may well put some teeth in the 1950 security pact. But it is essential that the League maintain its status as a regional organization in any future elaboration of security plans. The formation of a joint Arab command as a permanent feature of the Arab League will hardly be applauded if its sole purpose is to prepare for an invasion of Israel.[31] On the other hand, a lightly armed and specially trained joint command under the control of the Arab League could effectively carry out the task of maintaining peace

[31] The decision to form a joint Arab command in January 1964 was based on the expressed need for coordinated Arab defense policy vis-à-vis the military *threat* from Israel. The semantic relevancy of "defensive" *vs.* "offensive" military planning is obscure at best, however, and difficult to evaluate. It is worth noting that in the debate between the two major power blocs each accuses the other of "aggressive" military preparations. Most Westerners are just as convinced that NATO, for example, is a defensive agency as most Soviet bloc residents are convinced that it exists only for the ultimate attack on the Socialist camp.

and security within the region or of providing special forces for UN security actions in peripheral areas. Several Arab League states provided military forces for UN operations in the Congo, for example, and an Arab League peacekeeping force was proposed by Archbishop Makarios during the Cyprus crisis in early 1964.

PEACEFUL SETTLEMENT OF DISPUTES

While military security measures are intrinsically more spectacular and controversial, the greatest need of a regional agency remains that of effective mechanisms for peaceful settlement of disputes, whether between members or between a member and a third party. In general terms, the Arab League has not had effective, institutionalized mechanisms for the peaceful settlement of disputes. Meanwhile recent inter-Arab disputes have shown a disconcerting tendency to erupt into armed conflict. In practice, of course, internal (regional) disputes have been handled by the traditional methods of mediation, conciliation, and/or arbitration—often by the Secretary General or one of his representatives. But the efforts have not always been successful.

Article 5 of the Pact of the League of Arab States lays down the principle of voluntary arbitration by the League Council and mandatory mediation by the League Council of all disputes which threaten to lead to war. Decisions on arbitration and mediation are by majority vote, not including the votes of the disputants. The extreme sensitivity of the Arab states to the matter of state sovereignty, however, limits the effect of the proposed arbitration procedure. Article 5 excepts from the purview of the League Council any dispute which concerns "a state's independence, sovereignty, or territorial integrity." The only other reference to mechanisms for peaceful settlement of disputes is the suggestion of a future "Arab Tribunal of Arbitration" in Article 19.

The 1950 Arab Collective Security Pact failed to add any detailed procedure for peaceful settlement of disputes, though Article 1 reaffirmed the intention of contracting parties "to settle their international disputes by peaceful means, whether such disputes concern relations among themselves or with other Powers." The subsequent "Convention on the Privileges and Immunities of the League of Arab States," drawn up and signed in 1953, provides for the submission of disputes arising out of the interpretation or application of the convention to the "Arab Court of Justice."[32] But no Arab Court of Justice had been established by the end of 1964.

The lack of formal machinery for the settlement of disputes, along with the sweeping restrictions on the jurisdiction of the League Council, undoubtedly contribute to the apparent inability of the Arab states to agree among themselves while the Arab League remains impotent. In effect, all political disputes between member states are excluded from the cognizance of the Arab League. Though minor legal disputes are subject to Arab League mediation, no juridical body has been established to hear the complaints.[33] As a result, the League has at varying times used the good offices of the Secretary General or his assistants, has established *ad hoc* investigating commissions, or has resorted to informal means of conciliation in an attempt to circumvent legal and practical restrictions on its jurisdiction and authority.[34]

In at least one case, that of Lebanon in 1958, the Council found itself unable to act, with the result that

[32] Text in Arab League's *Treaty Series*, pp. 46-52. See Article 33, particularly.

[33] In 1950, Jordan argued that the League Council was not competent to judge the question of Jordan's annexation of Palestine. See, for example, Ezzeldin Foda, *The Projected Arab Court of Justice* (The Hague: Martinius Nijhoff, 1957), p. 43.

[34] In May 1949, for example, Syria and Lebanon agreed to submit an extradition dispute to Saudi Arabia and Egypt for arbitration. *International Organization*, III (1949), 349.

a regional dispute was referred to the UN Security Council for action. In the case of Lebanon, the League was able to reach a decision before the United Nations could take action, however. The situation in Yemen following the military coup d'etat there in September 1962 was beyond the capabilities of the Arab League and required action by the United Nations. The border dispute between Algeria and Morocco in October 1963 was also excepted from Arab League action because Morocco refused to accept a League mediation commission.

The League has been hardly more successful in mediating problems between its members and non-member countries. Attempts at mediation have been numerous in the Arabian peninsula and have included the Buraimi Oasis question between Saudi Arabia and the United Kingdom, and the continuing dispute between Yemen and British authorities in Aden. An agreement on the Yemeni-Aden border was mediated by the Secretary General in 1954, but the dispute erupted again after the 1962 coup in Yemen. Outside of the membership of the League, action has been taken to mediate relations between the British and the Sultan of Oman and between the French and its former North African dependencies without success. In July 1961, the Secretary General was involved in discussions aimed at settling the grievances between France and Tunisia that led to the armed clash at Bizerte.

Some sort of improved procedure for the peaceful settlement of intra-regional disputes is clearly indicated to permit the League to take official and effective action to forestall the frequently acid and increasingly violent attacks on one member state by another. Procedure is obviously not the entire answer and, in the first place, no "political" dispute can be handled by the League until the Pact has been amended to permit it. Once Article 5 has been revised and a few cases handled, however, improved confidence should result in improved relations. Simultaneously, the establishment of an Arab Court of Justice, proposals for which have been under study since 1950, could provide a basis for settlement of legal disputes and would help keep such issues from becoming inflamed.[35] In the future, the closer cooperation between Arab League members envisaged in the plans for an Arab Common Market, among other schemes, will make the establishment of such an Arab Court—within the system of regional courts suggested by the Statute of the International Court of Justice—an absolute necessity.[36]

[35] For a detailed discussion of the impediments to peaceful settlement under the Pact of the League and the proposed Arab Court, see Foda, *op.cit.*

[36] The Arab Press in early 1964 reported a proposal for an amendment to the Charter to make arbitration of disputes mandatory. Final plans for a nine-member Arab court were also reported in June 1964; cases referred to the court would require the consent of both parties.

CHAPTER 11 INTERACTION WITH OTHER INTERNATIONAL AGENCIES

ONE of the fundamental problems faced by the Arab League since its formation is the proper scope and nature of its relation to the United Nations. The Dumbarton Oaks Proposals, which had been studied by the founders of the Arab League, for the first time in the history of international organization had given some status to "regional arrangements." Proponents of regionalism had envisaged a close, harmonious relationship between the new universal organization and the proposed regional organizations, particularly in the field of functional activities. And Article 3 of the Pact of the League of Arab States had anticipated cooperation with future international bodies "in order to guarantee security and peace and regulate economic and social relations." Under the circumstances, the Arab League countries at the time of the UNCIO proceedings in San Francisco in 1945 sought some tangible form of "recognition" for the League of Arab States as a "regional arrangement" satisfying the provisions of Chapter VIII of the UN Charter approved there.

The Arab delegations gave the UNCIO Secretariat a copy of the Pact of the League of Arab States, which was subsequently circulated as an official document for the information of all conferees. They worked closely with the Latin American delegations in an effort to secure *de jure* "recognition" of both the Union of American Republics and the Arab League as regional arrangements by having them named in the text of the Charter. Although the primary orientation of the Arab League states was to regional functional integration, the discussions at UNCIO tended to emphasize the role of regional agencies in the maintenance of international peace and security. Under the circumstances, neither the Arab states nor the Latin American states were able to obtain "recognition" of their respective regional organizations in the Charter. More significantly, perhaps, the Charter contained no guide to the criteria for "recognition" in the future. Moreover, it specified no policies or procedures according to which to integrate the activities of the regional arrangements with those of the universal organization. The unofficial understanding was left, however, that "recognition" by the United Nations would be contingent upon the establishment of effective regional collective security mechanisms.

The effect of UNCIO on would-be regional organizations, therefore, was to encourage a reorientation toward regional security problems and away from functional programs. About a year after the formation of the Arab League, Lord Altringcham declared that the Arab League expected too much in aspiring to UN recognition as a regional organization. Only after the League had demonstrated, along with other regional organizations charged with world security, its capability to assume responsibility for the Middle East—in case of necessity—would the League be justified in its request for recognition.[1] The ease with which the Organization of American States obtained subsequent *de facto* acceptance as a regional organization within the meaning of Chapter VIII, immediately after the establishment of the 1947 Rio Treaty, served to emphasize the validity of the unwritten rule.

[1] Cited in Salim Cattan, "La Lega Araba nel suo primo quinquennio," *Oriente Moderno*, xxx (1950), 107.

It was no coincidence that the first serious movement toward an institutionalized regional collective security agency by the Arab League took place soon after the United Nations invited the Organization of American States to send an observer to the UN General Assembly.

In April 1950, the League Council recommended that member states request the UN Secretary General to include in the agenda of the next General Assembly the subject of the status of the Arab League as a regional organization.[2] In July 1950, a month after the signature of the Joint Defense Treaty, often called the Collective Security Pact, the Syrian delegate to the United Nations requested the UN Secretary General to place on the agenda of the General Assembly the matter of a "permanent invitation to the Arab League to attend sessions of the General Assembly." The matter was discussed by the Sixth (Legal) Committee at the fall session of the General Assembly, a draft resolution calling for the invitation was approved, and the matter was referred to the General Assembly for decision. The Arabs argued that formal recognition was not required by the Charter, but that it merely states that the activities of regional organizations should be consistent with the Charter. Furthermore, the Arab spokesman emphasized, the Pact of the Arab League provided for collaboration with the United Nations.[3]

[2] League Council Resolution 290, April 1, 1950, in Khalil, *op.cit.* Document No. 57, p. 147.

[3] Discussion summarized in *Yearbook of the United Nations, 1950* (New York: United Nations, 1951), pp. 870-73. See also *Repertory of United Nations' Organs*, Vol. II (Art. 23-54), pp. 432-47, for UN attitude toward regional organizations. In 1948, Kamāl al-Ghālī had advanced the argument that the League's regional status was determined by its adherence to UN principles and purposes, citing the decision of ECOSOC to establish a "Middle East Economic Commission" in 1947 in which the Arab League was mentioned as a "regional organization" (al-Ghālī, *op.cit.*, p. 163, citing the *United Nations Bulletin*, Nov. 4, 1947, p. 603).

On November 1, 1950, League Secretary General 'Azzam renewed previous assurances to the General Assembly that the Arab League would continue to cooperate closely with the United Nations. He informed the General Assembly of the League's cooperation with FAO, WHO, and the Economic and Social Council and declared that the Arab League looked forward to closer collaboration with the United Nations and its Specialized Agencies—especially in the social, economic, and cultural fields. Meanwhile, he extended a standing invitation to the UN Secretary General to visit the Arab world.[4] The General Assembly approved the recommendation of the Sixth Committee on the same day and requested the Secretary General to invite the Arab League's Secretary General to attend the Sixth United Nations General Assembly.

The invitation to the Arab League Secretary General, accepted by action of the League Council on October 13, 1951, has subsequently been reextended for each session of the UN General Assembly.[5] While the resolution of the Sixth Committee was understood by all concerned as "an act of courtesy" not to be construed as a decision on the status of the Arab League as a regional organization within the meaning of Chapter VIII of the Charter, the League has since regarded the step as an important one toward *de facto* "recognition" by the United Nations.[6] Negotiations continued between the Arab League Secretary General and the UN Secretary General in an effort to develop a basis for *de jure* "recognition," particularly

[4] Khalil, *op.cit.*, Document No. 34, pp. 81-82.

[5] The League Council took formal notice of the invitation and approved it for acceptance by the Secretary General (Resolution 403, October 13, 1951, in *Egypt and the UN*, p. 134). The Secretary General had already attended sessions of the General Assembly in an unofficial capacity in 1947. *International Organization*, I (1947), 539.

[6] Mohammed Fathalla el-Khatib, *The Status of the League of Arab States in the International Community* (New York: Arab Information Center, 1958), p. 6.

during the period from 1958 to 1960. Independent negotiations have also been carried on with several of the Specialized Agencies with the result that ILO, UNESCO, WHO, and FAO have concluded agreements with the Arab League acknowledging its status as a regional organization. The Secretary General of the Arab League has reported additional negotiations for the exchange of observers to meetings of the UN Economic Commission for Africa (UNECA).

The closest approach to a formal agreement between the United Nations and the Arab League was made in December 1960. At that time, the Secretary General of the United Nations forwarded to his Arab League counterpart a memorandum intended to serve as a guide to future cooperation between the secretariats of the two organizations. The memorandum set forth recommended procedures on such matters as mutual consultation, joint action in the economic and social fields, exchanges of information and documentation, and representation and liaison.[7] The memorandum recommended that the two organizations subsequently appoint liaison officers as a step toward systematic coordination of activities of mutual interest.

The letter transmitting the agreement of August 1961 between the Arab League and Kuwait, relating to the League's security force, refers to paragraphs 7 and 8 of the UN memorandum as "embodying the principles agreed upon between the Secretary General of the United Nations and the Secretary General of the Arab League regarding the means of communication between the League of Arab States and the United Nations."[8] In effect, the transmittal of the agreement to the UN Secretary

[7] Letter to author from Legal Counsel, United Nations, January 1962. The memorandum to the Arab League has not been made public.

[8] Document S/5007, November 30, 1961, UN Security Council, in English.

General (for referral to the Security Council and eventual deposit in the UN archives) also carried out the provision of Article 54 of the UN Charter that the Security Council be kept informed of peacekeeping moves. According to UN policy, however, the memorandum of the UN Secretary General is not an agreement between the two organizations and no *de jure* "recognition" is involved. There is no question, however, but that the memorandum does contribute to the *de facto* "recognition" of the Arab League by the United Nations.

The question of *de jure* "recognition" of the Arab League may be academic in the long run. No provision for any type of recognition was made in the United Nations Charter. But the basic problem is that the United Nations is an organization of independent sovereign states and, as such, cannot extend membership to an organization such as the Arab League. And *de jure* recognition of the Arab League, in effect, would mean membership in some form. Indeed, the suggestion was made during World War II that the members of the United Nations should be subordinate regional organizations instead of independent states, but the United Nations Charter did not sanction such a situation. Even if membership could be accorded the League, there then would arise the question of representation for member states of the League. Would they continue to be regarded as members of both organizations? Or would the representatives of the member states of the Arab League be required to withdraw in favor of one representative for the League as a collectivity? It would seem that the solution is rather one of closer coordination between the universal agency and the several regional organizations than of restructuring the United Nations.

THE ARAB LEAGUE AND THE UN: POLICIES AND PROCEDURES

Although the question of "recognition" remains open, the

Arab League has developed considerable leverage in the activities of the United Nations. It is impossible to narrate the history of Arab League actions vis-à-vis the United Nations within the scope of this study, however, and the principal purpose of this portion of the discussion is to illustrate the procedures and techniques used by the League in effecting this leverage.

The essence of the Arab League approach to the United Nations is the development of the "united front," manifested in all possible activities and in all organs of the United Nations. Very early in the history of the League, in December 1946, the Political Department of the League Secretariat was designated the principal agency of the organization to deal with matters concerning the United Nations. The Political Department, of course, is subject to the League Council in matters of policy in accordance with Article 3 of the Pact of the League of Arab States. Other departments of the League Secretariat have assumed responsibility for coordinating aspects of the League's programs with the United Nations: particularly the Department of Cultural Affairs, the Department of Social Affairs, the Economic Department, and the Palestine Department. In general terms, however, the Political Department retains the primary responsibility for coordinating UN affairs.

The impetus for the united front presented by the Arab League states in the United Nations derives from official resolutions of the League Council. In its September sessions, the League Council reviews the agenda of the UN General Assembly and considers other business associated with the United Nations—brought before it in terms of memoranda or draft resolutions prepared by the Political Department of the Secretariat. Once a decision has been made, the permanent representatives of the member states to the United Nations are informed and appropriate action is taken to implement the resolution in the proper organ of the world organization. In addition to coordinating the activities of the permanent representatives, the resolution may direct each member state to make representations to appropriate diplomatic missions in the Arab capitals in an effort to gain support for a League-Council course of action. Arab diplomatic missions abroad attempt to line up support in the foreign ministries of the world. And the permanent representatives themselves engage in the inevitable lobbying and caucusing in the corridors and lounges at the UN— concentrating particularly on the Afro-Asian and Latin American delegations.

League Council resolutions related to the United Nations and its activities vary from broad policy guidance to specific instructions to the Secretary General and/or the permanent delegations. The following categories of questions are typical of those that become subject to League Council resolutions:

1. decisions on existing General Assembly agenda items, usually those of indirect interest to the Arab League (Indonesian independence, peacekeeping operations in the Congo, etc.);

2. proposals to add items to the General Assembly agenda, usually those of direct interest to the Arab League (the Arab refugees, independence for the Arab dependencies in French North Africa, the status of Oman, etc.);

3. nominations for membership or office in United Nations organs, committees, and commissions;

4. Arab representation in the staff of the UN Secretariat; and

5. matters concerning the organization of the United Nations (more power for the General Assembly, Charter amendments, enlargement of the Security Council and ECOSOC, etc.).

Arab League policies on subjects brought up at emergency sessions of the General Assembly or the Security Council are apt to be formulated without filtering them through the League Council. Coordination is effected, for example, by the League Secretariat through the Arab member states' delegations in Cairo or by direct contact with the various Arab foreign offices. A recent innovation has been the convening of an extraordinary session of the League Council in New York during the General Assembly sessions. Several such League Council sessions at the foreign ministers' level have been held since 1961.

The Arab League's "permanent observer" at the United Nations is normally the senior representative of the Arab League, although the Secretary General is usually present for at least part of each General Assembly session. The permanent observer has no vote in any organ of the United Nations, but he is responsible for seeing that League Council policies are implemented. This is done by means of weekly or more frequent meetings of the Arab representatives and observers at the United Nations (at least during the annual General Assembly sessions) at which decisions on current problems are made. Considerable latitude is afforded the representatives in New York when the League Council decision has been made at the level of policy guidance. The role of the permanent observer is, therefore, extremely important. He is, in effect, the Arab League's "parliamentary whip."

The effectiveness of these procedures in the General Assembly is well-documented. During the first twelve sessions of the United Nations General Assembly, members of the Arab League at the UN had a record of 90.2 per cent in terms of internal cohesion on recorded General Assembly roll-call votes.[9] Table 10 shows the voting pat-

---

[9] "Internal cohesion" is the measure of agreement within the Arab voting bloc and includes votes in which all members voted alike plus votes in which members abstained rather than vote

terns in the General Assembly for the Arab members of the United Nations as a group on various types of questions.

TABLE 10

VOTING PATTERNS IN THE GENERAL ASSEMBLY[a]
FOR ARAB STATES

Type of Issue	Identical Votes (%)	Solidarity Votes (%)	Internal Cohesion (% of all votes)
Collective Measures	61	37	98
Peaceful Settlement	58	39	97
Self-Determination	74	22	96
Functional Cooperation	64	21	85
Human Rights	51	41	92
Development of International Law	48	34	82
Administrative and Procedural	57	23	80

[a] Adapted from Hovet, *Bloc Politics in the United Nations,* Chart 14, p. 135.

In his study of voting behavior in the General Assembly, Thomas Hovet evaluated voting behavior for each Arab country in terms of the percentage deviation from the position of the majority of the Arab bloc during the first thirteen Assembly sessions. His data, shown in Table 11 illustrates the influence of the internal rift within the Arab League following Iraq's adherence to the Baghdad Pact in 1955. It is significant, however, that internal differences among Arab League states had little effect on voting in the General Assembly during most of the period studied. When the League was at its low-

against the majority of the other Arab members. See Thomas Hovet, *Bloc Politics in the United Nations* (Cambridge, Mass.: Harvard University Press, 1960), p. 62. A less detailed, but confirmatory study, is available in Arend Lijphart, "The Analysis of Bloc Voting in the General Assembly: A Critique and a Proposal," *American Political Science Review,* LVII (December 1963), 902-17.

TABLE 11

DEVIATION BY COUNTRY FROM VOTE OF
ARAB MAJORITY AT GENERAL ASSEMBLY SESSIONS
(per cent)[a]

Country	UNGA Sessions I-IX (1946-54)	UNGA Sessions X-XIII (1955-58)
Lebanon	2.32	7.80
Saudi Arabia	1.45	0.71
Egypt	1.16	0.00
Yemen	0.96	0.71
Iraq	0.86	10.60
Syria	0.86	0.71
Jordan[b]	—	3.70
Libya[b]	—	2.78
Sudan[b]	—	0.00

[a] Source: Hovet, *Bloc Politics in the United Nations*, p. 61.
[b] Not members of United Nations until after 1954.

point, 1955-58, Iraq, Jordan, and Lebanon voted with, or, more properly stated, did not vote *against* the rest of the Arab League states on the overwhelming majority of issues. Even in 1962, when Nasser was threatening to withdraw from the Arab League, the UAR delegation to the General Assembly continued to exchange views with other Arab delegations on issues to be debated at the session although it refused to be drawn into any formal Arab League meeting.[10]

Margaret Ball, author of an earlier study on bloc voting in the United Nations, Hovet, and others working in the field seem to be unaware of the fact that the so-called Arab bloc in the General Assembly is in fact carrying out policy decisions of the Arab League Council. Both Hovet and Ball refer to the meetings of the Arab League members as a "caucus," a term which technically inter-

[10] See *Middle East Journal*, xvii (Winter-Spring 1963), 104 for report from *al-Ahram* [Cairo].

preted would impute greater authority and independence of action to delegates from Arab countries than is actually the case.[11] Both observers of the Arab bloc in the General Assembly have noted, however, that the dissenting members usually abstain rather than vote against the other Arab members. Margaret Ball notes also that the Arab bloc, in general, is dedicated to increasing the power of the General Assembly. She illustrates this by reference to the lack of Arab support (with only Iraq voting pro) of UN action in Korea, followed by unanimous Arab support for the "Uniting for Peace" resolution.[12] Hovet, furthermore, observes that the Arab bloc is the oldest bloc in the United Nations and that it dates from UNCIO in San Francisco.

All these observations are correct and are, in fact, readily traced to Arab League policies, a factor which both authors appear to ignore. Hovet concluded, for example, that external influences hold the Arab group together, particularly opposition to Israel and to the "so-called colonial powers." He noted that the unity of the Arab bloc tended to decrease after the formation of the Baghdad Pact but offered no explanation. Elsewhere Hovet characterizes the "Arab Caucusing Group" as an organized unit within the Asian-African group, thereby implying its temporary nature.

While the behavior of the Arab bloc in the General Assembly may appear to be erratic, the fact that the Arab League Council is pulling the wires from backstage helps to explain apparent inconsistencies. It was the League Council that decided to bring the Moroccan question to the General Assembly as early as 1951, to introduce the Tunisian question to the Security Council in 1952, and to

[11] See Margaret Ball, "Bloc Voting in the General Assembly," *International Organization*, v (February 1951), 26, and Hovet, *op.cit.*, section on "Arab Caucusing Group," pp. 58f.

[12] Ball, *op.cit.*, pp. 23, 25, 26.

initiate numerous other moves—some failures and some successes—related to regional political problems: e.g., alleged Israeli aggression, the question of Algeria, the question of British relations with Oman. In October 1953, when the Arab states at the United Nations petitioned the Security Council in behalf of Jordan—not then a UN member—to discuss the "aggression by armed forces of Israel upon Jordan at Qubaya, Shuqba, and Budrus," the Arab League Political Committee was discussing the same question in Amman. On October 23rd, Charles Malik, of Lebanon, speaking for the Arab states, temporarily withdrew the request. On the same day, the League's Political Committee instructed the Assistant Secretary General, then Ahmed Shukairy, to go to New York to confer with Arab delegates at the United Nations in order to convey the decisions of the committee and to insure common action.[13]

One of the techniques used in both the General Assembly and the Security Council is for one Arab delegate to act as temporary spokesman for the rest of the Arab states on major issues. Thus, in October 1953, the Lebanese delegate opened the General Assembly debate on the Tunisian question. The Saudi Arabian delegate brought the "grave situation in Algeria" to the attention of the Security Council in January 1955; in 1957, the Syrian delegate raised the same issue before the General Assembly's eleventh session, and the Tunisian delegate presented the Algerian case before the twelfth session. During the thirteenth General Assembly, the principal spokesman was again the Tunisian representative.

These few examples illustrate the flexibility with which the Arab League can implement its decisions regarding the United Nations. It is interesting that the North Afri-

[13] See *Middle Eastern Affairs*, IV (1953), 390 for Malik's action (Lebanon was a member of the Security Council in 1953), and *Oriente Moderno* XXXIII (1953), 459 for a report on the League's Political Committee.

can cases were handled by French-speaking Arabs, among them representatives of states which had only recently become independent of France themselves. It is perhaps at least as significant that the Tunisian representative acted as spokesman for the Arab League states in December 1958, following a diplomatic break with Cairo over Tunisia's allegations that Egypt controlled the League.

A corollary to the Arab League's decisions on procedure at the General Assembly is, of course, that it can decide not to have an issue raised. Thus, in several recent years, the League Council has voted not to bring the Palestine issue before the General Assembly. Similarly, the League Council has assumed the role of regional authority and interposed itself between the United Nations and a League member on at least one occasion. In the aftermath of the abortive Arab complaint of Israeli military action on the Jordanian border in October 1953, for example, the Israeli government called upon the United Nations to arrange a meeting with Jordan which would involve direct, bilateral talks on the issue. The Jordanian government informed the Arab League of the UN's invitation to the proposed meeting and requested that the Political Committee be convened.[14] The Political Committee examined the problem in December 1953 and recommended that the request be rejected on the grounds that existing armistice machinery was adequate and that acceptance of Israel's demands for bilateral discussions would amount to recognition of Israel. This recommendation of the Political Committee was approved by the League Council at a meeting in Cairo in January 1954, and Jordan subsequently informed the UN Secretary General that it would not accept the bid to meet with Israel.

[14] *Middle East Journal*, VIII (Spring 1954), 199. Jordan was not then a UN member; this was a sensitive issue because Jordan, as an Arab League member, had pledged herself not to enter into separate negotiations with the Israelis.

In furtherance of Arab League objectives, the Arab delegates at the United Nations have frequently worked closely with the delegates of the Organization of American States and with the loosely organized Afro-Asian bloc at the United Nations, in both cases as a result of League Council decisions. This is a complex situation, which cannot be examined in detail here. In effect, however, the Arab League member states' delegations at the United Nations, acting under broad policy guidance by the League Council, attempt to secure the support of the Latin American and Afro-Asian blocs for their own resolutions and measures on a *quid pro quo* basis.

In the case of the Afro-Asian bloc, regular meetings are held during General Assembly sessions in which the Arab states' delegations participate as a sub-bloc. Cooperation between the Arab League and the Asian members of the United Nations began with the Arab League's support of independence for Indonesia in 1946 and has been extended outside the United Nations, largely as a result of the influence of the Bandung Conference of 1955. One of the first meetings of the leaders of the then Arab-Asian bloc outside UN conference halls was held in Cairo, however, at the instance of the Arab League in December 1952. The meeting, which included India, Ethiopia, Iran, Afghanistan, Indonesia, and Pakistan in addition to the Arab League members, formulated policies in support of independence for French North Africa which were later carried out in the United Nations. In 1954, League Council Resolution 605 took formal notice of the close ties between the Arab states and other states of the Afro-Asian bloc in the United Nations and recommended that diplomatic ties between the Arab states and other states of the Afro-Asian bloc in the United Nations be strengthened, that periodic meetings be convened, and that political, cultural, and economic cooperation be increased. The same provisions were to apply to Arab League relations with the Latin American states.[15]

The interest of the Arab League does not exhaust itself in the political organs of the Security Council and General Assembly, though it is in these two organs that the activities of the Arab states have been particularly well publicized. The Arab League Council periodically reviews the personnel requirements of governing boards of such UN organs as the Economic and Social Council (ECOSOC), the various ECOSOC agencies, the Trusteeship Council, and the International Court of Justice and nominates qualified Arab candidates to fill vacant seats. The same procedure is, of course, also followed with the Security Council—in which one seat is normally filled by a Middle Eastern country—and the General Assembly and its committees. Once a nomination, either of a member country or of a particular individual, is agreed upon by the League Council, the Arab states' delegations at the United Nations are expected to support the official decision.[16] The selections by the League Council do not always meet with general approval, however, as was illustrated by the election of Charles Malik to the presidency of the General Assembly in 1958. The Council had endorsed Mohammed Mahgoub, the Sudanese Foreign Minister, for the position, but by a *majority* decision (Lebanon objecting). Malik ran for the post with the support of Lebanon and defeated Mahgoub, 45 to 31 votes on September 16, 1958.

Table 12 suggests the extent to which the Arab League states at the United Nations have maintained their influence in the Economic and Social Council and in the

[15] Text of League Council Resolution 605, January 21, 1954, in *Egypt and the UN*, p. 139. Note that the 1962 Afro-Asian Economic Conference also took place in Cairo at the Arab League headquarters building.

[16] For an example of this, see Resolution 589, September 7, 1953, in *ibid.*, p. 136.

Security Council. Two distinguished General Assembly presidents have also been elected from among the Arab League states—Charles Malik (Lebanon) and Mongi Slim (Tunisia). These postings tell only part of the story, of course. The Arab League states seek election to the advisory committees and working commissions of the General Assembly and the Economic and Social Council and frequently succeed. The emphasis is on certain areas of interest to many of the smaller UN members including those pertaining to territories that have not attained self-government, to questions of administration and organization of the Secretariat, and to technical assistance and economic development. The preselection of nominees for important assignments is, of course, a procedure followed by other blocs in the United Nations. The difference lies in the fact that in the case of the Arab states, the decisions are made at the Arab League headquarters in Cairo and not in the lounges of UN headquarters in New York.

National representation on the staff of the United Nations Secretariat has also been a matter of interest to the League Council. Article 101/3 of the UN Charter, regarding the appointment of staff members to the Secretariat, states that "due regard shall be paid to the importance of recruiting the staff on as wide a geographical base as possible." That this is an ideal not always to be realized in practice is generally understood, if only because well-qualified personnel are not equally available from all countries. It was perhaps for this reason that the Arab League Council in 1950 drafted a policy which stated that, though every Arab state has an equal right to representation on the UN Secretariat, those states which do not choose to exercise their right may relinquish it in favor of another Arab state.[17] Any UN Secretariat position not claimed by an Arab state, moreover, was to

[17] Resolution 286, 1 April 1950, in *ibid.*, p. 131.

TABLE 12

UN MEMBERSHIP DATA FOR ARAB LEAGUE STATES

ntry	Date of membership in UN	Membership in ECOSOC	Membership in Trusteeship Council	Service on Security Council
eria	October 8, 1962	1964-66	—	—
	October 30, 1945[a]	1964-66	1947-52	1957-58
lan	December 14, 1955	1961-63	—	—
vait	May 14, 1963	—	—	—
anon	October 15, 1945[a]	1946-49	—	1953-54
ya	December 14, 1955	—	—	—
occo	November 12, 1956	—	—	1963-64
di Arabia	October 18, 1945[a]	—	—	—
an	November 12, 1956	1958-60	—	—
ia	October 19, 1945[a]	—	1953-58	1947-48
isia	November 12, 1956	—	—	1959-60
R (Egypt)	October 22, 1945[a]	1952-57	1959-61	1949-50 1961-62
nen	September 30, 1947	—	—	—

Original member; date refers to ratification of UN Charter.

be referred to the League Secretary General for reapportioning.

That such a policy could be unilaterally supervised by the Arab League is doubtful, but subsequent League Council decisions confirmed the policy in 1951 and 1952, recommending that the question of proportional representation be taken up with the Fifth (Administrative) Committee of the General Assembly and the Personnel Department of the UN Secretariat.[18] In 1955, the League's Political Committee reviewed the situation at the UN Secretariat and found the Arab share of posts to be inadequate. The Committee recommended that every effort be made to secure posts in Secretariat offices "compatible with Arab commitments to the United Nations."

[18] Resolution 383, October 10, 1951, and 428, September 14, 1952, in *ibid.*, pp. 133 and 135, respectively.

A special effort was to be made to place an Arab in one of the Assistant Secretary General posts.[19]

There is no way for anyone outside the Secretariat to determine the extent to which Arab League policies and pressures have influenced the composition of that portion of the staff subject to geographical distribution. The problem of geographical distribution, in any event, is a large one of no little consequence to many members of the United Nations. The Secretariat has tacitly subordinated the question of geographical representation to that of efficiency of the operation, despite pressures from some sources for representation on the basis of population or some other empirical factor. Nevertheless, the number of Arabs on the UN Secretariat staff has increased over the years, and recent reports by the Secretary General show the staffing patterns to be well within the "ranges" established for most Arab member states of the United Nations.[20]

Between 1960 and 1963, the number of Secretariat officials from Arab League states increased from 39 to 66. About one-third of the Arab staff members were Egyptians in 1963, compared to about one-half in 1960 and before. Other Arab League states relatively over-represented—possibly on the basis of the relative abundance of technically proficient candidates—were Syria, the Sudan, Lebanon, and Jordan. Conversely, Algeria, Kuwait, and Yemen were not represented in 1963. In June 1963, an Arab achieved the rank of Assistant Secretary General for the first time when the director of the UAR's National Planning Institute was appointed UN Commissioner for Industrial Development.

A noteworthy exception to the carefully coordinated

[19] Resolution 1018, October 1, 1955, in Khalil, *op.cit.*, p. 150.

[20] As of August 31, 1963, 1,389 Secretariat positions were subject to geographical distribution. See "Geographical Distribution of the UN Staff of the UN Secretariat," A/C.5/987, October 11, 1963.

policy of close affiliation with all phases of UN activity is found in the fact that the Arab League does not regularly forward to the UN Secretariat copies of treaties and agreements negotiated between its members. Nor, so far as can be determined, have Arab League members submitted copies of these treaties to the United Nations under the provisions of Article 102 of the UN Charter. The United Nations *Treaty Series* contains only the original Pact of the League of Arab States of 1945, a copy of which was submitted to UNCIO, and a convention concluded between the Arab League and the International Labor Organization, submitted by the ILO. While no obligation exists to submit such documents to the United Nations, it would appear to be mutually advantageous to both the Arab League and the United Nations to have Arab League treaties and agreements on file at UN headquarters.

In addition there has been no regular procedure for transmitting to the United Nations such documents as the League's annual reports or the resolutions of the League Council. Although each case is treated differently, such Arab League documents as are received may merely be circulated to interested officials within the UN Secretariat and then filed. In a few other instances, usually at the request of the Arab League, League communications have been circulated as UN documents. The draft agreement of December 1960 between the two organizations presumably provides for the establishment of regular channels of communication between the two secretariats.

THE UNITED NATIONS AND THE ARAB LEAGUE

While the Arab League has developed closely coordinated procedures to accomplish its objectives within the framework of the United Nations, the reverse has not been true. United Nations contacts with the Arab League have been on an *ad hoc* basis and are only beginning to be regularized as a result of the memorandum drafted in 1960 by the UN Secretary General. Contacts between the two Secretary Generals have been fairly frequent— particularly between the late Dag Hammarskjold and Dr. Hassouna—but officially "unofficial." The Arab League Secretariat frequently contacts the United Nations Secretariat and occasionally dispatches to it copies of certain League Council resolutions and other messages, practices initiated in its earliest days. Only in September 1951, however, did the League Secretariat receive its first official message from the United Nations. The message was a routine acknowledgment of the receipt of a League Council resolution on the Anglo-Egyptian controversy.[21] It is worth noting, however, that this first official communication followed the General Assembly's invitation to the League Secretary General.

Four UN agencies, an information center, and the UN Emergency Force (UNEF) have offices in Cairo where, with the notable exception of UNRWA, they have generally operated with little or no reference to the activities of the Arab League.[22] This is not particularly surprising, considering the fact that the work of the United Nations is with the governments of its member states. On the other hand, discussions regarding future coordination of activities of mutual interest—particularly in the economic field—have been in progress between senior officials of the Arab League and of the United Nations almost since UNCIO.

[21] *Oriente Moderno,* xxxi (1951), 126.
[22] UN agencies with offices in Cairo are the UN Technical Assistance Board (UNTAB), the United Nations Children's Fund (UNICEF), the United Nations Relief and Works Agency for Palestine Refugees (UNRWA), and the United Nations High Commissioner for Refugees (UNHCR). For a critical article on UN activities in Egypt, see Walter R. Sharp, "The United Nations System in Egypt," *International Organization,* x (1956), 235-60. Sharp stressed the lack of coordination between the several UN agencies.

UN agencies and *ad hoc* commissions have taken notice of the Arab League from time to time, particularly during the period immediately before, during, and after the Arab-Israeli War of 1948. As a result of a League Council decision, the Arab states presented a joint declaration to the UN Special Commission on Palestine (UNSCOP), at Beirut in July 1947.[23] During the brief visit of UNSCOP to the Middle East, the group invited the Arab League to send a liaison officer to Geneva for the final sessions of the committee. During the war in 1948, Count Folke Bernadotte found it expedient to include the Arab League in his discussions and held frequent conferences with the League Secretary General and other League officials. Subsequent to the Arab-Israeli War, the Arab League Secretariat was in direct contact with the UN on the problem of refugee relief.[24]

Since the Arab-Israeli War, the League has continued its interest in UN activities resulting from the fighting. As an outgrowth of the League's involvement in the campaigns of 1948, for example, the Secretary General in 1964 stepped in to coordinate the activities of the Arab delegations to the Mixed Armistice Commissions that assist the United Nations in supervising the truce between Israel and the adjoining Arab states. The first meeting of the Arab MAC delegations was held in Jerusalem in February 1964 under the chairmanship of Dr. Said Nawfal, Assistant Secretary General, and was attended by the chief of the Palestine Department of the Arab League Secretariat. Subsequent meetings were scheduled at six-month intervals.

The Arab League has generally cooperated with the United Nations Relief and Works Agency for Palestine Refugees (UNRWA) since it started functioning in May 1950. League Council Resolution 325, June 12, 1950, es-

[23] See *Middle East Journal*, i (October 1947), 444.
[24] *Middle East Journal*, iii (January 1949), 78.

tablished a policy of cooperation (and coordination) between the League and UNRWA, always reserving the rights of the refugees to receive compensation for lost or sequestered property and to return to "Palestine."[25] In 1952, the League Council adopted the policy that Arab League member states harboring Palestine refugees should cooperate with UNRWA in projects to ameliorate the condition of the refugees and to permit them to qualify for employment.[26] The resolution provided that the Palestine Department in the League Secretariat should coordinate the joint Arab-UNRWA programs. UNRWA reports show that between 1950 and 1963, the Arab League "host" governments (Jordan, Lebanon, Syria, and the UAR) had contributed almost $50 million in direct assistance to the refugees, principally for education, social welfare, housing, and medical assistance, and continue to contribute about $5.5 million a year. These expenditures are in addition to pledges to the general UNRWA operation—at a rate of about one million dollars a year and totaling another $9.5 million at the end of 1962—from the Arab League member states.

Official contacts between the United Nations and the Arab League have also extended to the difficult problem of resettlement of the Arab refugees. John Blandford, the first director of UNRWA, addressed a subcommittee of the Arab League Political Committee in October 1951 to outline proposals for the settlement of the refugees.[27] The proposals of the UN Secretary General for a settlement of the refugee problem were conveyed to the League Secretariat in 1959 for study and comment. The Arab League rejected Mr. Hammarskjold's proposals, and it is worth noting that the report to the UN Secretary General was signed by all Arab League members at a

[25] See *Egypt and the UN*, pp. 168-69.
[26] Resolution 462, September 23, 1952, in Khalil, *op.cit.*, pp. 170-71.
[27] *Middle Eastern Affairs*, II (1951), 373.

time when Iraq and Tunisia were boycotting the League Council. A similar united front approach resulted in the League's rejection of the Joseph Johnson plan for resolution of the refugee problem in October 1962. The precondition of all Arab League discussions of the Arab refugee problem has remained the same: explicit recognition of the right of the Arab refugees to return to "Palestine"— with compensation for damages and losses of property— whether or not they choose to exercise the right. This right, Arab leaders point out, is recognized by paragraph 11 of General Assembly resolution 194, adopted in 1948 and frequently reaffirmed by the General Assembly, despite the fact that it remains unimplemented.

The close cooperation with the United Nations in the matter of regional functional integration, anticipated by the architects of the Arab League and the proponents of regionalism alike, has never materialized. United Nations offices and agencies in the Middle East and North Africa, of course, have undertaken development programs in the various member states of the Arab League. But direct contact between the United Nations and the Arab League as a means of coordinating regional programs has been the exception.

The policy of the UN Technical Assistance Board (UNTAB), one agency that could coordinate development programs of regional scope, for example, has discriminated in favor of the individual country approach. The trend in the technical assistance programs supervised by the United Nations has been toward the regional approach since 1955, however, and there is some evidence of increased coordination between the operating agencies of the United Nations and the Arab League Secretariat. A movement is afoot to decentralize the activities of UNTAB (along with the Special Fund) and to place them under the general supervision of the Secretariats of the regional economic commissions. Because there is no "Economic Commission for the Middle East," an effort is being made to expand the economic and social programs of the UN office in Beirut, including the possible creation of a technical assistance coordination unit there.[28]

The reasons for the lack of closer coordination between the Arab League and United Nations offices like UNTAB are difficult to ascertain. Several factors have operated to preclude close regional cooperation in the past, including the tendency for development agencies to plan in terms of country programs, the lack of sufficient specialists in the Arab League states to coordinate regional programs, and the highly particularistic attitude of the member states of the League itself. Some qualified observers would add the jealously guarded autonomy of the UN Specialized Agencies as a factor, since they would be required to participate in any extensive regional program under UNTAB supervision. But the fact remains that the Middle East lags far behind most of the other less-developed areas of the world in terms of regional development projects coordinated by the United Nations. In 1958, for example, these regional projects, in terms of dollar expenditures, were distributed as follows:[29]

	Per cent
Latin America	33.5
Asia and the Far East	22.8
Middle East	11.2
Europe	8.5
Africa	5.2
Inter-regional	18.8

[28] *Report of the Economic and Social Council: 4 August 1962— 2 August 1963*, UN Doc. A/5503 (New York: United Nations, 1963), pp. 32-33.

[29] Walter R. Sharp, *Field Administration in the United Nations System* (London: Stevens and Sons, Ltd., 1961), p. 339. Included are projects financed from all sources. Inter-regional projects are those, like the Desert Locust Program, that extend into several of the regions specified above.

Well-established regional economic commissions were already operating in Latin America and the Far East in 1958, and a vigorous development program has since been initiated by the Economic Commission for Africa. In Latin America—with one-third of the regional programs in 1958—the regional economic commission cooperates closely with the subsidiary organs and affiliated agencies of the Organization of American States. The absence of a similar "Economic Commission for the Middle East" is undoubtedly a factor in limiting cooperative regional economic and social programs by the Arab League and the United Nations. And the history of the abortive moves to establish a Middle East economic commission provides an instructive example of the negative influence exerted by the Arab-Israeli conflict.

Since a primary concern of the Arab League has been that of economic development, Arab planners placed considerable emphasis on the early establishment of a regional economic agency under the sponsorship of the United Nations, similar to the economic commissions formed under the auspices of ECOSOC for other regions. At the fifth session of ECOSOC (February-March 1947), Charles Malik (Lebanon) proposed the establishment of an Economic Commission for the Middle East. A year later, the sixth session of ECOSOC constituted an *ad hoc* committee to study the problem. The Arab League Council, watching these developments, approved the idea of economic coordination in Resolution 206, February 22, 1948. Unfortunately, the outbreak of hostilities in Palestine and the subsequent refusal of the Arab League states to deal with Israel combined to sabotage the idea of any effective Economic Commission for the Middle East under the sponsorship of the United Nations.

An unsuccessful attempt to revive the plan, without Israel and only marginally supported by the United Nations and the Arab League, was made by the Lebanese in 1954-55.[30] A conference of the Arab League states, Turkey, Ethiopia, Iran, and Pakistan convened in Beirut in May 1955. The meeting decided to establish a permanent body to study the question of regional economic cooperation. Nothing concrete came of the effort, and Arab thinking has turned to the concept of an Arab Common Market as a solution to the economic problems of the region.

The establishment of the Economic Commission for Africa in 1958 has had some influence on economic development in at least some of the Arab League states: the Sudan, Egypt, Libya, Tunisia, Morocco, and Algeria. Rather than working toward regional integration, however, the ultimate effect of the ECA could well be to split the Arab League as the Arab states in Africa turn more and more southward. Symptoms of this effect have already appeared as the moves toward African political and economic integration motivate the Arab states in the northern regions of the continent to line up with newly independent states south of the Sahara in the Organization for African Unity.

In the long run, it would seem that considerably more scope exists for close cooperation between the United Nations and the Arab League in the matter of regional functional integration. It is to be hoped that the new approach to cooperation between the two organizations embodied in the memorandum of December 1960 between the two Secretaries General will have a salutary effect on future regional activities of mutual concern. The close coordination already existing between the United Nations and the Organization of American States indicates that the United Nations is not unwilling to work with regional organizations. Paradoxically, however, UN actions with respect to the Arab League have seldom

[30] *Oriente Moderno*, xxxiv (1964), 551, and xxxv (1955), 258.

promoted cooperation between the two organizations. And so long as the question of Arab-Israeli relations remains unsettled, it appears that any major change in the relations between the two organizations will be effected only with difficulty.

The Arab League and the Specialized Agencies

Unlike the situation with the United Nations itself, the Arab League has had close and continuing relations with several of the UN Specialized Agencies since its early days (see Table 13). Not only are member states encouraged to join the agencies, but formal agreements for regional coordination of programs of mutual interest have been signed between the Arab League and UNESCO, ILO, FAO, and WHO. In general terms, these agreements are similar to those between the Specialized Agencies and the Organization of American States, the Council of Europe, and other inter-governmental bodies.[31] The agreements provide for exchange of information and documents, consultation on matters of mutual interest, cooperation in planning and implementing regional programs, exchanges of observers, delegations, and experts, and—under certain conditions—joint activities. Moreover, agreements normally provide for direct communication between the Arab League Secretary General and the director general (or equivalent) of the Specialized Agency. In practice, regional offices maintained in Egypt by WHO

[31] The Arab League agreement with UNESCO was approved by the UNESCO Executive Board in June 1957; text is in Khalil, *op.cit.*, pp. 92-94. The ILO-Arab League convention was signed May 28, 1958; text is in UN *Treaty Series*, Vol. 302. An agreement with WHO, signed in June 1961, replaced an early exchange of memoranda between the League and the Mediterranean Regional Director of April 1954. See also *International Organization*, viii (1954), 271, for note on cooperation between the Arab League and the WHO Regional Office for the Eastern Mediterranean prior to 1954. The Agreement with FAO was signed in June 1960.

and FAO assist with active programs, while the League's contact with UNESCO is through the Paris headquarters and, with ILO, through the regional office in Istanbul.

In all instances, informal cooperation between the Arab League and the Specialized Agencies has preceded the formal agreements. Thus the development of coordination between the League and the Specialized Agencies has been evolutionary—in the case of UNESCO, since 1946—and the agreements merely help to formalize already existing relations. Nevertheless, considerable liaison will be required before some of the autonomous Specialized Agencies change their mode of operations from that of working with individual countries to that of working through an established regional organization.

This situation is particularly true of UNESCO. This agency has worked in the Middle East for many years, sometimes using a regional approach. However, the Arab League adopted a policy in May 1951 that, in effect, sabotaged any broad "regional" approach by UNESCO and other UN Specialized Agencies: no Arab state was to participate in any regional conference which included Israel.[32] As a direct result of this policy, a 1953 regional UNESCO conference was canceled.

Despite Israeli efforts to ward it off, UNESCO concluded an agreement with the Arab League which aims at regional cooperation. The agreement protected UNESCO's existing bilateral programs, however, and working-level collaboration on the regional level between UNESCO and the Arab League has developed slowly. The Arab League maintains a permanent representative in

[32] See Resolution 356, May 19, 1951, in *Egypt and the UN*, pp. 169-171. The policy is based on the Arab legal position that Israel does not exist as a state. The same policy led to the refusal of Arab League states to participate in a proposed FAO regional training center (see Resolution 385, October 10, 1951, *ibid.*, pp. 172-73). In 1952, the policy was extended to non-governmental organizations by Resolution 463 (see Khalil, *op.cit.*).

TABLE 13

AB LEAGUE COUNTRY MEMBERSHIP IN UN SPECIALIZED AGENCIES, 1963

untry	*IAEA*	*ILO*	*FAO*	*UNESCO*	*WHO*	*FUND*	*BANK*	*IFC*	*IDA*	*ICAO*	*UPU*	*ITU*	*WMO*	*IMCO*
q	G	m	m	m	G	m	m	m	m	m	m	m	m	o
dan	o	m	m	m	G	m	m	m	m	m	m	m	m	o
wait	o	m	m	m	m	m	m	m	m	o	m	m	m	m
banon	m	G	G	m	m	m	m	m	m	G	G	m	m	o
ya	o	m	m	m	m	m	m	m	o	m	G	m	m	o
rocco	m	G	G	G	m	m	G	G	G	m	m	G	m	m
di Arabia	m	o	m	m	m	m	m	m	m	m	m	m	m	o
dan	m	m	m	m	m	m	m	m	m	m	m	m	G	o
ria	o	m	m	m	m	m	m	m	m	m	m	m	m	m
nisia	m	G	m	m	G	m	G	G	G	G	m	G	m	o
R	m	G	G	m	m	G	m	m	m	G	m	G	G	m
men	o	o	m	m	m	o	o	o	o	o	m	m	o	o

Source: *Yearbook of the United Nations, 1962*
Symbols: m—member; o—non-member; G—member and represented on the cutive or governing body

Paris at UNESCO headquarters, and consultations between the Arab League Secretariat and the UNESCO Director General's office are frequent. Under the circumstances, despite a tendency for UNESCO to continue to work directly with member states, those Middle East regional programs which have been developed by UNESCO are virtually "Arab regional programs" and apparently satisfy at least some Arab League requirements.

In addition to its Arab States' Fundamental Education Center near Cairo (virtually limited to Arab League members), UNESCO coordinates the UNRWA educational programs among Arab refugees. Many of the

UNESCO "experts" serving in the Arab states are themselves Arabs, another factor which enhances its programs in the area. Several UNESCO programs for the Arab area are operated from the center at Beirut, which is almost entirely an Arab regional facility. Since 1960, the Beirut center has actively promoted regional educational development, with special emphasis on improving teaching techniques and developing professional cadres in the education ministries in the Arab states.

In 1962, UNESCO sponsored an all-Arab roundtable meeting on "The Cinema and Arab Culture" which promised to lead to a regional program of film development. The establishment of an Arab regional center for bibliography and documentation at Cairo grew from a UNESCO seminar in October 1962. At Algiers in March 1964, a conference of UNESCO national commissions from Arab League states agreed to establish a regional literacy campaign, asked UNESCO to assist the Arab states with the development of sciences and technology, and called for long-range improvement of Arab educational systems. The conference was attended by observers from UNESCO and the Arab League Secretariat. As a result of this meeting, a regional conference on literacy in the Arab states was later proposed for September 1964 in Cairo.

Arab League relations with the Food and Agriculture Organization (FAO) have been established on a practical foundation. Not only do the League and FAO exchange technical reports and observers, but the two organizations collaborate on sponsoring (and paying for) technical meetings. The League also has an advisory status with respect to FAO social welfare activities.[33] The FAO has used an Arab League desert-locust expert, on a loan basis, to direct the anti-locust program in Saudi Arabia, thus providing a refreshing change of direction in the

[33] Interview with FAO Regional Economic Advisor, Cairo, December 1960.

flow of technological know-how. In another working-level arrangement, the League has provided FAO the facilities of its Social Service Center in Yemen for use in connection with agricultural extension work.

In contrast to the UNESCO agreement with the Arab League, furthermore, the FAO-Arab League agreement specifies broad joint objectives to be reached in the future, including improvements in nutrition, conservation of plant and animal resources, increasing agricultural credit facilities, and improved marketing and distribution networks for agricultural products. Contracts and joint activities between the League and FAO are coordinated in Cairo by the regional office of FAO. During 1962, for example, FAO sponsored a training seminar on agricultural planning at Cairo, convened in Amman a committee on agricultural statistics for the region, held a seminar in Beirut on food consumption in the Arab states (a joint endeavor with WHO and UNICEF), and conducted a watershed management course.

Cooperation between the Arab League and the International Labor Office (ILO) is also carried out at a working level, in addition to exchanges of representatives, data, plans, and documents.[34] The annual labor seminars conducted by the Arab League since 1949, originally completely UN—ILO affairs, have been conducted entirely by Arab League personnel and with Arab League funds since 1952; ILO, however, continues to provide technical support. The ILO has provided half the funds for the ambitious League project of translating into Arabic all ILO international conventions, and also provides technical assistance for the Arab social welfare seminars, with particular reference to labor problems. Conversely, the Arab League in 1964 agreed to contribute to the support of an international vocational training center in Turin,

[34] Interview with Assistant Director, ILO branch office, Cairo, December 1960.

Italy. In the interests of encouraging labor education and organization in the Arab states, the ILO has recognized the International Confederation of Arab Trade Unions as a regional labor organization. Most of this activity is supervised by the ILO field office in Istanbul, but communications between the League Secretariat and the Geneva offices of ILO pass through the branch office in Cairo.

The World Health Organization (WHO) has maintained a regional office in Alexandria, Egypt, since about 1950 and has conducted annual health conferences for the Eastern Mediterranean area since 1951. The agreement between WHO and the Arab League, signed in 1961, formalized cooperative programs that had been in progress since 1954. Calling for cooperation "in all matters that arise in the field of health," the agreement provides for exchanges of non-voting representatives at conferences on health held by either organization and technical cooperation on problems of mutual interest.[35]

In addition, regional programs of interest to the Arab League are also carried out by several other UN agencies with which the League has no formal agreements. The World Bank was influential in drawing up the charter for the Arab Development Bank, for example. In 1962 the World Meteorological Organization (WMO), which is organized on the basis of six regional associations, completed a comprehensive study of climatology in the Near East. In recent years the International Civil Aviation Organization (ICAO) has conducted several regional seminars in the Arab states on such subjects as air traffic control, aeronautical communications, and weather forecasting, and plans to inaugurate in Beirut in 1965 a civil aviation flight safety center—a joint venture of the ICAO, the UN Special Fund, and the Lebanese Government— as a training center for students from the Near East and

[35] *Arab News and Views,* July 1, 1961.

Africa. A regional isotope training center was established in Cairo in 1962 as a joint venture of the International Atomic Energy Agency and participating Arab states, with some funds from the UN technical assistance program.

Arab League interest in the activities and programs of the UN Specialized Agencies extends beyond the agreements already concluded with ILO, FAO, WHO, and UNESCO. The Arab League Secretary General long ago recommended that the Arab League member states adopt a common policy on representation to all the Specialized Agencies. He also recommended the establishment of joint Arab offices at the headquarters of these agencies and urged the League Council to study ways and means to make use of these offices. A basic League policy for some time has been prior consultation among Arab states represented at the Specialized Agencies.[36] The League Council regularly considers nominations for executive posts in the governing bodies of most of the Specialized Agencies, encourages its members to join the agencies so as to represent the Arab viewpoint, and monitors their programs. Special conferences of Arab "experts" are sometimes convened by the Arab League to shape a unified "Arab policy" in advance of important conferences of the Specialized Agencies. The techniques, in short, resemble those applied to UN organs and were described earlier in this chapter.

In the field of functional integration, the Arab League has been relatively successful in its relations with the Specialized Agencies. This was the hope and expectation of the founders of the Arab League, but much remains to be done to integrate the diverse programs already initiated in order to avoid duplication of effort and make the best use of available economic and human resources. Although the problem of future coordination is at least part-

[36] Hassouna, *op.cit.*, p. 176.

ly political in nature because of the refusal of the Arab League to work with Israel, it appears that a great deal of regional cooperation can be promoted even under existing conditions. More significantly, perhaps, neither the United Nations nor most of its Specialized Agencies are fully accustomed (or willing) to operate in terms of regional programs, especially if local control and supervision were to be delegated to another organization such as the Arab League. On the other hand, the broad interests of WHO, FAO, and ILO, based on experience and programs that predate the United Nations, have enabled them to apply regional concepts successfully, in concert with the Arab League.

One approach to the problem of future regional economic and social programs, already suggested above, will almost certainly be the establishment of Arab League "specialized agencies." These agencies would function autonomously in the League's area of operations but in close coordination with the Specialized Agencies and the regional technical assistance coordinating center of the UN. Such a scheme, if properly implemented, could reduce the administrative and operating burdens of the Specialized Agencies and, at the same time, avoid duplication of effort. A proposal for an Arab League "UNESCO" has already been floated by the League's Cultural Committee, and a proposal for an "Arab Health Organization" developed from an Arab League medical congress in 1961. The future of such proposals, however, depends to a great extent on the willingness of the Specialized Agencies and the appropriate UN bureaus to change their present operating procedures. The World Health Organization, for example, has already had an unsatisfactory experience with the Pan-American Health Organization during which the WHO headquarters in Geneva virtually lost control of PAHO's operations, reportedly to the detriment of its own worldwide programs.[37]

[37] See Sharp, *op.cit.*, pp. 315-16.

PART IV CONCLUSIONS

CHAPTER 12 SOME REFLECTIONS ON REGIONAL ORGANIZATION

THE ARAB LEAGUE IN PERSPECTIVE

THE League of Arab States is the second oldest continuously existing inter-governmental organization of its kind, only the Organization of American States (a continuation of the Union of American Republics) has a longer history. This fact is in itself remarkable. When it was formed in the period of chaos during World War II by politicians more experienced in intrigue than in the debate, mediation, and compromise of international relations, the League's membership included four states that had barely achieved their independence (Egypt, Iraq, Syria, and Lebanon) and three others that had hardly advanced beyond the Middle Ages (Transjordan, Saudi Arabia, and Yemen). The organization seemed to meet few if any of the objective preconditions for longevity. A prediction that during the next twenty years the Arab League would survive two catastrophic military actions, a series of bitter internecine feuds, and almost continual political and social revolution would have seemed little short of incredible to its founders. Not only has the League survived, but between 1945 and 1962 its membership almost doubled. And each new member (Sudan, Libya, Morocco, Tunisia, Kuwait, and Algeria) represented a newly independent state that, in some measure at least, owed its very existence to the Arab League.

At this point in the discussion, after allowing the facts to speak largely for themselves, it seems appropriate to stand aside and make an effort to put the subject of the Arab League as a regional organization into perspective. There can be little doubt that the Arab League is a regional organization, both in terms of the model developed in Chapter 1 and in terms of Kaplan's dynamics, which are summarized in the introduction to Part II. In accordance with these standards, the strengths and weaknesses of the Arab League have been analyzed and discussed. What remains, perhaps, is to develop some critical framework within which to evaluate the operational theory and techniques of regionalism itself. First, it is worth while reviewing some of the main points discussed earlier.

The internal instability of the Arab League, the basis of much adverse comment during the last two decades, is in fact an inherent characteristic of regional organization. In its structure, the Arab League is a loose but permanently constituted confederation of independent states, sanctioned by treaty, to which each member state has transferred only a limited amount of its sovereignty in the interests of realizing stated common goals and objectives. More than an alliance but less than a sovereign federation, the Arab League, like any regional organization, is subject to internal stresses and strains moderated only by the degree to which its member states assign realistic priorities to objectives that can be obtained only (or best) through the organization.

It is a truism that the nationalistic pressures that led to the establishment of a half-dozen new sovereign Arab states in the two decades after 1941—and to political revolutions in most of the others—have increased and not decreased regional tension. On the other hand, the Arab League has been the agency through which the Arab states have consciously confirmed their own national sovereignties and secured their region from external control, if not always from external interference. The liberation movements in North Africa illustrate this function most strikingly. But Syria, Lebanon, Iraq, Egypt, Jordan, and Sudan have been assisted by and through the Arab League to shed the remaining vestiges of a former

European hegemony. And the tragedy of Palestine is the more acute because the Arab League is the self-appointed surrogate for Arab Palestine and all Palestinians. That the movement toward national independence has been concurrently a movement away from extra-regional control is a factor often ignored or overlooked by the outsider. This factor, however, helps to illuminate many of the regional crises of the 1950's.

The power struggle between Iraq and Egypt, which survived the change from "reactionary" monarchies to "liberated" republics, has been another more or less constant factor in accounting for the instability of the Arab League. Nevertheless, the fact is that both major Arab powers have agreed most of the time on the basic objectives of the Arab League and have cooperated inside the organs of the League even when engaged in campaigns of mutual recrimination and vilification outside them. Indeed, no Arab League member state has gone so far as to attempt to destroy the organization in order to obtain its own goals. This circumstance, in the final analysis, is much more significant than the fact that the League's objectives are sometimes circumscribed by predictable political tensions.

The development of the Arab League, in terms both of its structure and its functions, has been in line with the principal fields of action of regional organizations: (1) common efforts in the field of functional integration, (2) regional security, and the peaceful settlement of disputes, and (3) a close working relationship with the United Nations. The burden of the argument so far has been that the Arab League as a regional organization is interested in regional security matters primarily from the point of view of threats originating from within the region. This view, of course, further emphasizes the need for close relations with the United Nations, which organization ostensibly disposes of the means to deal with threats to the peace originating outside the region.

Within the framework of these broad fields of action, the League has made significant progress with its regional economic, social, and cultural programs. Throughout most of its history, the Arab League has actively fostered regional integration and provided newly emerging Arab states with an increasingly effective institutional framework within which they can synthesize national and regional goals and objectives. The League's constitutional organs, its specialized agencies, and its affiliated "associational interest groups" provide a diversified regional apparatus which reaches out to influence most aspects of contemporary Arab life.

Although progress in the vital field of regional economic integration has been slower than expected, this is largely because economic activity has a high political content. But progress has been genuine in all these functional areas. By 1964, hardly a week went by without an important meeting of some Arab regional professional society, or a special seminar sponsored by the Arab League, or a session of one of the permanent committees of the Arab League, or a meeting of one of the League organs. Thousands of Arabs have benefited by working together on regional problems during the last twenty years, and millions have had their lives influenced by the activities of the Arab League in such fields as education, science, economics, medicine and public health, and cultural affairs.

The Arab League has also developed very effective operating mechanisms to influence its relations with the United Nations in the functional areas, although neither the United Nations nor its specialized agencies has been as prone to work with the League on problems of mutual concern as the founders of the Arab League had expected. Nevertheless, the Arab League has long functioned effectively as the coordinating agency for the achievement of regional goals through the agency of the United Nations. Comprising one of the oldest and probably one of the most effective voting blocs in the United Nations, since 1945 the Arab League states have persistently influenced the course of world affairs to no little extent. The League has always sought to strengthen the role of the smaller powers in the United Nations, both by enlarging the Security Council on a regional basis and by seeking more power for the General Assembly, where Great Power politics and conflicts are less influential as determinants of organizational policies, programs, and activities. It has, therefore, encouraged the development of the Afro-Asian bloc within the United Nations and helped focus the awesome capabilities of the Great Powers on constructive programs of international economic, social, and cultural development.

In the field of international security, the exclusive concern of the UN Charter for regional security mechanisms as an extension of the functions of the Security Council has tended to influence the role of the Arab League vis-à-vis the United Nations. However, the Arab League has concentrated on the problem of internal threats—including threats from Israel, since the Arab states officially regard that country as "occupied Arab territory" —despite Cold-War pressures on the League to orient its security mechanisms to external threats. It is indeed an irony that the West's preoccupation with regional security pacts formed under Article 51 of the UN Charter has only reinforced inherent tendencies to regional exclusiveness in the Arab World and limited the ability of the Western powers to influence events in the region.

The Arab League states have effectively policed their own region during most of the League's history. Despite bitter propaganda exchanges between rival Arab states, there have been surprisingly few breaches of the peace by Arab League members. And despite somewhat inadequate machinery, most of the breaches of the peace that have occurred have been settled satisfactorily. The Lebanese crisis of 1958 was eventually settled within the Arab League family, although it threatened to become an issue for the United Nations. In 1961, the League's handling of the Kuwait incident was efficient and expeditious. Most other internal threats to the peace of the region have been settled amicably before they became inflamed, usually by means of arbitration and mediation, and often by the direct intervention of the League's Secretary General.

The principal failures are exceptions to the rule. The split within the League membership on the issue of the 1962 Yemeni revolution required the establishment of a UN observation mission in Yemen. But even in this situation, Arab League actions—in the form of personal diplomacy by the Secretary General and the Chairman of the League Council—exerted a restraining influence and prevented the dispute from spreading. Later, the border incident between Algeria and Morocco in November 1963 was mediated by the Organization of African Unity when the Moroccans refused to accept an Arab League arbitration proposal.

Neither failure, however, undermines the utility of the League's claim to take the first action in the case of regional disturbances. The UN Charter, after all, not only established the system for using regional organizations as enforcement agencies, but it exists to support the regional organization in its attempts to maintain peace within its area of responsibility. Much more significant is the fact that the application of the 1950 Arab Collective Security Pact to the Kuwait crisis proved its adequacy to the regional situation. On the other hand, the procedures for the peaceful settlement of disputes within the region embraced by the Arab League have not always been effective, since virtually all disputes are excepted from the cognizance of the organization in deference to the exaggerated concepts of national independence and sovereignty held by its member states. Recent moves to strengthen the Pact on this point may improve the peacekeeping potentials of the Arab League.

Despite limitations in the operational context, the Arab League has developed effective, permanent agencies that have contributed much to the continued existence of the organization in the face of dissension within the membership. Perhaps the most significant agency is the League Secretariat, which plays a critical role in the administration and execution of policies established by the League Council and other Arab League organs. The Secretariat, considerably strengthened during the tenure of the present Secretary General, Abdel Khalek Hassouna, provides evidence that the diverse interests of member states can be redirected toward constructive ends within the scope of the goals and objectives of the organization. In an important sense, the contribution of the Secretariat has also been to heighten the consensus on procedure that seems to be so difficult to achieve in the Arab world—compared to the consensus on goals, on which most Arabs readily agree.

Each of the operating agencies under the control of the Secretary General, including the Arab Narcotics Bureau, the Institute of Advanced Arab Studies, and the Social Service Centers, makes a concrete contribution to procedures calculated to assist with the achievement of regional goals. The recent establishment of affiliated agencies, such as the Arab Telecommunications Union, the Arab Postal Union, and the Arab Development Bank suggests the development of decentralized specialized agencies, within the Arab League's range of interests but outside its immediate control. Such moves should be encouraged because the limited staff of the Secretariat is already overworked. Furthermore, the proliferation of these agencies not only acts to catalyze regional integration but serves to define the independent character of the Arab League which has been gradually emerging over a period of twenty years.

The expanding roles of the Secretariat and other more or less permanent organs have also served to circumvent to some extent the limitations on policy formulation imposed by the unanimity rule in the League Council. Thus, the staff departments of the Secretariat not only supervise the execution of policies decided by the League Council, but also tend to initiate policy in the course of background studies and analyses of regional problems. The permanent committees, the Economic Council, and the Joint Defense Council, as well as an increasing number of "consultative bodies" (operating in an undefined region between the Secretariat and the League Council and not subject to the unanimity rule) also contribute to the decision-making process by formulating or acting on "recommendations" that are often ratified by the League Council without discussion. In September 1964, for example, the League Council meeting was to be preceded by meetings of the Economic Council, the "Follow-up Committee" (the personal representatives of the Arab chiefs of state who met in January 1964), the Arab chiefs of staff, the Joint Defense Council, and the permanent committee of Arab foreign ministers.

The rather complex decision-making procedures of the League, therefore, tend to insure thorough study and discussion of regional problems—particularly those in the context of functional integration—which in turn result in the "recommendation" of policies that can be approved by the League Council. This procedure works best when problems with significant political content are not involved. Emergency situations involving the limitation of member sovereignties are, of course, not so amenable to resolution by this process.

REGIONALISM, NATIONALISM, AND THE COLD WAR

This study was not designed to be a simple history of the Arab League or, for that matter, an analysis of the economic, political, and social development of the Arab Middle East. But it is inevitable that the detailed discussion of a regional organization should raise questions which can only be answered by reference to events occurring within the region but not necessarily associated with the Arab League. Moreover, the tendency of most observers is to ask, in effect, how the Arab League could be considered effective when in fact the region has moved from one crisis to another for the past twenty years. The glib answer to that question is another question: "What has the United Nations been doing for the past twenty years while the world has moved from crisis to crisis?" For, within limits, the functions, operations, and activities of regional organizations and the United Nations are analogous.

What is indicated, however, is a reexamination of regionalist theory in the light of the experience of the Arab League—and other regional organizations—since the end of World War II. Most critics of the Arab League (or other similar organizations) tend to be captives of widely accepted but unexamined theories of regional organization. Hopefully, the few comments that follow will encourage a thorough-going examination and critique of regionalist theory, but this is unfortunately outside the scope of this study. Most of the points raised here have been discussed elsewhere in one form or another. They are based primarily on the fundamental conflict between the functional approach to regionalism and the security approach. This conflict subsumes the opposing concepts of regional exclusiveness (leading to neutralism) and that of Great Power hegemony over the several regions of the world (leading to regional security communities). And, finally, the divisive issue of nationalism is also raised.

In its early stages at least, regionalist theory was developed by Europeans in a European context and oriented to European problems. That is, regionalism was applied to an already existing system of relatively mature nation states. Ideally, in the European context, it seemed possible to separate *functional* problems from *political* issues and to resolve them on a regional scale on a non-political basis. Under the circumstances, however, it would have been more realistic to postulate that, because of their maturity, the Western European states could afford to delegate some of their sovereignty to a functionally oriented regional organization without destroying the political equilibrium of the region. Europe's subsequent experience with the European Economic Community seems to confirm this latter view.

The difficulties of applying regionalist theory to the newly emerging areas of the world were apparently not recognized by the "regionalists" or were perhaps simply ignored in the chaotic optimism of the World War II period. By 1945 and the time of the San Francisco Conference, the leaders of the "sponsoring powers" saw things quite differently from their regionalist Arab and Asian—or even Latin American—colleagues. The sponsoring powers clearly expected to exercise a long-term political tutelage over the rapidly increasing number of former mandates, ex-colonies, and dependencies that were already being described in the minutes of the conference as the "regional powers." They were also committed to the idea of eventual warfare *between* regions. Thus the United Nations Charter made "regional arrangements" subordinate to the Security Council, where the wartime victors were permanently installed. Economic, social, and cultural integration was clearly subordinated to the primary problem of the maintenance of world peace and security.

The "regional powers" (meaning the non-European states) at UNCIO clearly favored a form of regional arrangement that would exclude the Great Powers (meaning the United States and the European powers sponsoring the United Nations). Some among them anticipated the emergence of new nation states following the total collapse of the remaining extra-European empires, although they foresaw few of the problems such a development would generate. Rather, they expected to be the beneficiaries of a guarantee of postwar peace by the United Nations, meaning defense against European interference. And, at the same time, they expected to receive from the former colonial powers the necessary material and non-material aid (preferably through the United Nations) that would make functionalism a reality. Unlike the sponsoring powers, they expected to be able to maintain peace in their own regions without Great Power intervention. Regionalists of this persuasion tended to be both functionalists and neutralists.

Although no one had really anticipated the Cold War in 1945, its onset in 1947-48 convinced the United States and, presumably, Great Britain that their view of regionalism was the correct one. They therefore began to work toward the establishment of regional security communities in which the predominant Western power would commit itself to the defense of the region from external attack—i.e., from the USSR and the Soviet-controlled region of Eastern Europe. Since they were unable to insure their own freedom of action within the United Nations, and specifically within the Security Council, the Western powers acted outside the United Nations and frustrated the whole rationale of regional organization as seen by the "regionalists." This movement by the West to insure the security of world regions inevitably collided with the opposing trend in the newly emerging areas toward regional exclusiveness and emphasis on functional development and thereby abetted the vaguely defined struggle against "imperialism."

Coming back to the observation that the history of the contemporary Arab world seems to be a continuation of crises, it can be argued that the major incidents since 1945 have been precipitated by agencies and forces outside the region and beyond the control of the Arab League. The "Palestine problem" is the most important example of the chronic inclination of the Great Powers to attempt to control the course of events in the region. The Tripartite Agreement of 1950 (by which the United States, France, and Great Britain attempted to forestall a regional arms race and guaranteed the integrity of Israel, by armed force if necessary) and the abortive attempt to establish a "Middle East Defense Organization" in the early 1950's confirmed the reluctance of the Western powers to permit the Arab states the necessary luxury of exercising their individual and collective sovereignties to control their regional destiny.

The eventual formation of the Baghdad Pact in 1954-55 probably hindered rather than helped the defense of the region. It almost destroyed the Arab League by enticing Arab member states away from its objectives of regional integration in favor of a worldwide Western-sponsored struggle against international Communism. Ironically, Iraq, the only Arab state that joined the West in the Baghdad Pact, later came closest to succumbing to the dubious appeals of Communism.

Also during the 1950's, the U.S. policy of employing or withholding foreign aid to reward its friends and punish its enemies led to further fragmentation of the Arab region, although the United States earlier had encouraged the formation of the Arab League for the purpose of promoting regional economic, social, and cultural integration. Specifically, the withdrawal in 1956 of the American offer to collaborate in the Egyptian project for a high dam at Aswan, not only led to the Suez crisis and the punitive expeditions staged by Israel, France, and Great Britain, but also opened the door for the unrestrained development of Soviet bloc influence in the area and thereby destroyed the utility of the Baghdad Pact. The Eisenhower Doctrine of 1957 was, in retrospect, a ludicrous postscript to the events of 1956.

Lest the theme that the West has been the villain of the Arab Middle East be overplayed, it is necessary to observe that many of the crises in the region were originated or intensified by agents and forces internal to the region but operating outside the context of the Arab League. Thus, as the Cold War between the United States and the Soviet Union is essentially outside the United Nations (as have been most of the incidents associated with it, from the Berlin blockade to the Cuban missile crisis of 1962), so the power struggle between Iraq and Egypt has been largely outside the Arab League.

Moreover, many of the tensions within the region are the result of the almost continuous social and political revolutions that have confirmed national independence and sovereignty in a dozen Arab states since 1945. The opposed forces of nationalism and regionalism, enunciated as variants of Arab nationalism and Arab unity, further complicate the situation. Long-standing issues involved in internal crises since 1945 include: Fertile Crescent unity and the Greater Syria schemes; the dynastic rivalries between the Hashemites of Jordan and Iraq and the House of Sa'ud; the question of control of the Nile Valley; antipathy between Christian and Muslim

Arabs and between Sunni Muslims and Shia Muslims; and the whole question of the role of North Africa in the Arab nationalist movement.

Nevertheless, the continued involvement of the West in the regional affairs of the Arab Middle East from 1945 to 1960 did not strengthen the region but, rather, at various times exacerbated regional tensions and increased regional instability, frustrated regional goals, opened the area to the Cold War, and diverted attention from regional functional integration to non-productive security measures by ignoring the Arab League almost entirely. Thus, although nationalism has served to undermine regional goals, extra-regional international tensions generated by Great Power policies have not only conflicted with regional programs but have led directly or indirectly to regional crises. And even when regional crises have not resulted, the possibility of constructive relations between the Great Powers and the regional agency has been all but obviated because of the continued reliance on bilateral diplomacy by the Powers and the failure to utilize the United Nations effectively in dealing with regional organizations.[1]

It is no exaggeration to say that the regional security pacts fostered by the United States in the 1950's have failed to accomplish their objectives. Even NATO, which has been effective largely because of the massive U.S. physical resources committed to it, seems in danger of disintegrating. Revision of the "Atlantic Community" concept is being advocated by some Europeans to eliminate U.S. participation in the regional affairs of Europe. Under the circumstances, an interesting sidelight on the current U.S. approach to regionalism is the fact

[1] The United States, for example, refused to permit the Point Four program to be tied to the UN technical assistance program in order to preclude possible foreign control. Wilmington, "The Middle East Supply Center," *op.cit.*, p. 156.

that, in an apparent effort to save the regional security pacts, the United States is encouraging them to broaden their programs to emphasize *functional* activities. This is particularly true of the Central Treaty Organization (CENTO), the successor to the ill-starred Baghdad Pact, in which a sizeable regional technical assistance program has already had considerably more impact than its military activities.[2]

The United States in 1964 appeared to have moved closer to the regionalist point of view and its emphasis on the functional approach to peace, especially as it affects regional security. Furthermore, the United States has modified the somewhat rigid stand on neutralism it held in the late 1950's. This is not to say that the regionalists have all the best arguments, for it is evident that functional problems can seldom be divorced from the political context of the region. But it is apparent that the firm political support of the Western powers for any regional organization, preferably through the medium of the United Nations, could do much to obviate some of the regional political tensions and the obstructionist national policies of the regional powers that now divert attention from constructive regional activities.

The reasons for these shifts in emphasis are probably based on the exigencies of practical relations between the United States and the regional powers. Nevertheless, it is of some interest to note that the United States has been pressured in the direction of functionalism by the Organization of American States since the Panama Conference of 1956, eventually resulting in the establishment in

[2] Iran, Pakistan, and Turkey agreed on a ten-point regional development program outside CENTO at a meeting in Istanbul, July 20-21, 1964. Included were a regional airline, a shipping firm, a joint Chamber of Commerce, uniform postage rates, highway construction programs, a regional trade zone, joint economic projects, and a broadened technical assistance program.

1961 of the Inter-American Development Bank and the Alliance for Progress. Until that time, security from extra-regional attack was the foundation of the OAS, and the relationship between the OAS and the United Nations was seen primarily in the light of regional collective security, at least by the United States.[3]

Like the other security communities sponsored by the United States, the hemispheric defense system of the OAS has not been a huge success. Since the establishment of the Castro regime in Cuba, the United States to its daily embarrassment has confronted many of the problems faced by the Arab League in dealing with Israel. The similarities are striking: Cuba represents a bridge-head in the region established at the expense of an indigenous population and maintained by an international movement alien to the region. Several hundred thousand refugees have congregated in nearby regional countries, where they plot and agitate for an invasion of the homeland to drive out the usurpers, often to the embarrassment of the host countries. Tensions increase as both sides seem to arm for a showdown, and the issue inspires unrivaled oratory on both sides. Attempts at joint military action fail, but an economic boycott is finally established—which extra-regional countries promptly ignore. The leading power in the region boosts its military assistance programs in order to prepare other regional states to fight if necessary, under the terms of a regional collective security pact. Meanwhile, everyone agrees that this would never have happened if the country had been economically and socially healthy and all resolve that the region needs intensified action to shore up its economic and social shortcomings. In the wake of the economic and social revolution, an incipient political

[3] See Manuel Canyes, *The Organization of American States and the United Nations* (Washington: Pan American Union, 1963), pp. 44-46.

revolution threatens to rock the region to its traditionalist underpinnings.

So striking are the similarities, in fact, that the Cuban situation described above would be regarded by most Arabs as almost an exact parallel of the Arab experience with Israel, except, of course, the "alien movement" to them is the "international Zionist movement," not Communism. While the United States may not be influenced to favor the Arab League's functional programs on this account, it may be comforting to the Arabs to know that Americans are experiencing somewhat the same kind of frustration they have felt regarding the establishment of Israel since 1948.

Furthermore, some of the contemporary problems faced by regional theory are illustrated by the U.S. experience with Cuba in the context of the OAS, and with the defense of Europe and the Middle East in the contexts of NATO and CENTO. In the first place, regionalism in its classic sense has been applied to underdeveloped areas where politicalization of issues has often frustrated would-be functional solutions to regional problems. But even in the European Community, the locus of power is said to be shifting from the functionally oriented supra-national commission to the politically motivated inter-governmental Council of Ministers.[4] And while the political content of regional functional problems is recognized by such regional agencies as the Arab League and the European Community, the danger of overemphasizing the political approach and applying it to "security" to the exclusion of other problems is increasingly borne home on the United States and its partners in the OAS and in the several regional security communities where increased attention is devoted to functional problems.

[4] Gordon, "Economic Regionalism Reconsidered," *op.cit.*, p. 243.

Whenever a problem causes a contemporary organization to misfunction, its manipulators immediately call for structural and procedural changes to put it right again. In the case of regionalism, at least, it seems that the first problem is the need to reexamine and revise basic theoretical formulations in the light of fifteen or twenty years of field experience. For example, will a shift from a unanimous vote to a majority vote strengthen a regional organization when its real problems are the reluctance of its members to carry out any decision that impinges on their sovereignty? Conversely, can a regional security community really function as it is supposed to when the basic economic and social problems of its members are all but ignored?

Secondly, the actual or potential exclusivity of a region could endanger world peace and security if it were carried to its logical extreme. Ironically, this potential is increasingly apparent in proportion to the success of the European Economic Community. The EEC's policies with regard to the importation of the raw materials exported by most of the underdeveloped regions of the world are being questioned by other regional agencies.[5] The Arab League states have called the EEC system a new form of "imperialism," referring to its extension to the "associated states" and to its indirect control over the economies (and domestic politics) of the other underdeveloped states who compete for European markets for their raw materials and semiprocessed goods. This EEC exclusiveness and the possibility of retaliating to these policies is perhaps one of the reasons that the Arab states are again raising the issue of regional controls over "Arab oil."

The possibility of inter-regional conflict is not entirely

[5] See *The Effects of the European Economic Community on the Latin American Economies* (Washington: Pan American Union, 1963), Chap. i, for some policy implications foreseen by the OAS.

remote: could the abortive Suez War have foreshadowed it? The principal outcome of regional exclusivity to date has been neutralism, however. Arab neutralist tendencies are deeply embedded in the dynamics of the region, although they have recently been reaffirmed by Gamal Abdel Nasser. The trend of events in some Latin American states suggests that neutralist or non-alignment tendencies in the OAS area may present a problem to the United States in the future. Some Arab observers even saw a French move toward non-alignment in early 1964 when de Gaulle recognized Communist China.

Finally, the problem of the relationship to be established between the United Nations and bona fide regional organizations in any but the security context remains to be solved. Functionalism has been taken over by the Great Powers as a basis for national policy, thus cutting out the United Nations to a large extent. (In the case of the Soviet Union, the UN is cut out entirely since the USSR does not contribute to its technical assistance program.) Bilateralism prevails in the diplomatic sphere, and there are no developed means for contact between the Western powers that could meaningfully support regional functional integration and the regional agency.

U.S. support of the Inter-American Development Bank, its sponsorship of a limited regional technical assistance program within CENTO, and its contributions to UNTAB suggest that the problems are not insurmountable, however. It is worth pointing out again that the regionalists of the World War II era expected the major powers to contribute directly to the functional development of the newly emerging regions of the world, so long as they did not attempt to dictate terms incompatible with valid regional objectives. The Columbo Plan presumably illustrates the potential for direct cooperation between a major European power and a developing region. There would seem to be no conflict of aims if the Western powers were to work through the UN on some problems and directly with regional agencies on others, assuming mutual consultation. But the United Nations should probably remain the primary agency for channeling and coordinating functional aid to the developing regions.

FUTURE PROBLEM AREAS

Four major areas of emphasis for the future of the Arab League seem to emerge from the analysis and discussion already presented. First, and by far the most important, is the relationship of the Arab League to the Arab unity movement. Second, assuming that the League will continue to operate in the indefinite future, a concerted effort must be made to realize the potential for close working relationships with the United Nations. Third, the need exists for improved procedures and mechanisms to insure regional security and the peaceful settlement of disputes between Arab League members. And, finally, a realistic approach to the problems of regional functional integration is essential.

The Question of Arab Unity

One of the major deficiencies of the Arab League has been its reluctance to accept its role as a regional organization. The inclination has been to regard the League as a step along the path to Arab unity despite the decision, made in 1945 and frequently reaffirmed, that political unification was not a feasible objective of the Arab League and that the League should function as a regional organization. Nevertheless, the pull toward some form of Arab unity has remained a vital factor in the League's programs and policies.

The failure of the Arab League to prosecute the Arab-Israeli War of 1948 successfully led to a series of proposals to "strengthen" the organization, usually by means of a federal or supra-national structure, with the emphasis on reform of the voting procedure in the League Council to permit a binding majority vote. The major proponents of such reforms have been the Iraqis and the Syrians, whose ideas have adhered closely to the original proposals of Nuri as-Sai'id: an Arab federal state with central control over defense, economic development, and social and cultural affairs.

A proposal advanced to the League Council by Nazim al-Kudsi, Prime Minister of Syria, in 1951, for example, postulated immediate Arab union. According to al-Kudsi, the Arab League "has frustrated the hopes of the Arabs, has been prodigious in declarations and discussions [but] barren of results and actions; everyone knows that the dominant spirit [of the Arab League] is not attune to the reality of the moment, to the pace of the times, to the gravity of events, that it does not follow a constructive path in the fields of defense, economics, and cultural and social affairs."[6] The plan was formally submitted to the League Council on January 23, 1951, for study and comment. Needless to say, it was shelved. One Arab observer later complained that "instead of working toward a greater consolidation of Arab ties, the League has immobilized the relations between the Arab states at the stage where it found them."[7]

Another major scheme for a federal union was proposed in January 1954 by Iraq's Prime Minister Fadhil al-Jamali. This plan envisaged unification of Arab ministries of foreign affairs, education, war, and finance and economics. The plan was to be implemented with the unification of any two Arab states. Within a few days

[6] Quoted in *Oriente Moderno* xxxi (1951), 2, from *al-Ahram* [Cairo], January 26, 1951 (my translation). See also *Middle Eastern Affairs*, ii (March 1951), 100-104, and *Middle East Journal*, v (Spring 1951), 201.
[7] Nejla Izzeddin, *The Arab World: Past, Present, and Future* (Chicago: Henry Regnery Co., 1953), p. 324.

after Jamali had offered his plan to the League Council, the Political Committee issued a statement thanking the Iraqi Prime Minister for his plan and proposing that it be studied by the members of the Committee. This was tantamount to a refusal; the plan was never heard of again. A few months later, however, a conference of the Parliament of Arab Graduates, meeting in Jerusalem, drew up a constitution for a "federal Arab state," the prologue of which stated: "Whereas the League of Arab States has fulfilled its purpose as the first step to the common ground of Arab Unity. . . ."[8]

This sort of agitation from outside the League has continued. And the idea has gained ground within Arab League circles that the Arab League is somehow delinquent if it does not at least give lip service to the concept of Arab unity. Spokesmen from within the League itself have objected that no provision exists for popular representation and that the organization provides only for the "coordination" of Arab policies.[9] Secretary General Hassouna himself since 1958 has suggested amendments to the Pact which would provide for binding majority votes in the League Council, a consultative assembly elected by the parliaments of member states (so as to have representation of the people), and a regularly constituted Council of Foreign Ministers.

Behind these moves is the compulsive urge for contemporary Arab leaders to repudiate the founders of the Arab League as "imperialist stooges" who attempted to sabotage the Arab unity movement. As a recent Arab League publication put it: "The Arab League is not an

[8] Foda, *op.cit.*, p. 66, n1.

[9] See Fayez Sayegh, *Arab Unity: The Hope and the Fulfillment* (New York: Devin-Adair, 1958), written while Sayegh was a member of the Arab States delegation in New York, p. 122.

end in the Arab aspirations for unity . . . it is simply a regional organization including every Arab state from Morocco . . . to Iraq. [But] unlike . . . other regional organizations, the Arab League views itself as a stepping stone toward complete unity. . . . It is a step in the direction of complete political, economic, social, and cultural unity for the Arabs."[10] But the history of the past twenty years suggests that, regardless of the validity of the impulse toward Arab unity, the prospects for realization of "complete political, economic, social, and cultural unity" in the full sense of the term are as remote as Wendell Willkie's "One World."

The frenetic search for a political rationale for the entire Arab area has only revealed the impossibility of political unity and, paradoxically, impeded the progress of the Arab League in the economic, social, and cultural fields. The assumption by Egypt of the leadership of the Arab national movement during World War II and the independence of the North African states changed the ground rules of the old Arab unity movement. The perpetuation of differing levels of economic development and varying shades of political behavior—largely the heritage of the Ottoman and the 19th century "imperialist" periods—only add to the existing problems. That the Arab League has been rescued by its members more than once from the brink of disaster reveals a widespread perception in the Arab world that the League contributes to common goals what particularistic Arab states, jealous of their newly won independence and sovereignty, have been unable or unwilling to do. In a real sense, then, coexistence is a more appropriate regional slogan than Arab unity. It is an indisputable fact that much more can be accomplished toward the realization of legitimate regional goals by means of the Arab League acting as a

[10] *The Arab World* [New York], VII (March 1961), 3-6.

regional organization than as a federal or unitary state, even if it were possible to envisage such a state.

The future of the Arab League is not a matter that can be decided outside the Arab world. Nevertheless, it should be urged that the extensive analysis of the Arab League presented above indicates not that the League suffers from structural weaknesses—indeed, the flexibility of the Pact works to its advantage—but from the inability of member states to work consistently together on programs of mutual interest. As a former Assistant Secretary General put it in 1953, almost everything the League attempts is contrary to the practices, usages, or traditions of some member. The permanent organs of the Arab League have been able to make some progress, despite the particularism of member states, when some common area of agreement exists. In the critical areas of economic integration and regional security, however, little real headway has been made. One student of regional organization has even argued that the preconditions for "integration" (i.e., upgrading common objectives) are lacking among Arab states; the only possible solution is "forcible integration—conquest."[11] However, the success of the 1964 Arab summit conferences suggests that Arab leaders can work together constructively if they wish.

Thus it appears that the Arab League, as a loose confederation, offers about the best hope for inter-governmental action that can be expected in the near future. Forcible integration, everyone now recognizes, offers no hope at all for the future. This does not rule out the possibility of subregional amalgamations—a "polycentrist" solution—as in the Fertile Crescent or in the North African Maghreb. Nor is the basic ethnic identity undermined. But the urge for complete Arab unity is demonstrably exaggerated, unless the term is understood in its

[11] Hass, "International Integration," *op.cit.*, p. 381.

allegorical context.[12] There should be no cause for dismay, however, if the true potential of the Arab League for regional coordination were to be realized.

As a regional organization, the Arab League can be strengthened by an increased delegation of authority from member states to the central organization without amending the Pact to provide for binding majority decisions. Increased confidence in the role of the Arab League as a truly regional organization is, of course, mandatory. The future role of Egypt, for example, must be that of a regional leader, not that of a despotic commander. Possible prods toward greater confidence—some of them already under way—include the decentralization of Arab League activities to avoid overemphasis on the Cairo headquarters; the appointment of permanent representatives to the League Council; improved recruitment and personnel policies to provide a career service attractive to the best talent available from all member states; the development of public records; the establishment of specialized agencies capable of extending the existing scope of economic, social, and cultural cooperation; and the establishment of permanent Arab League offices in each of the Arab capitals for liaison, coordination, and public relations.

Future Relations with the United Nations

The Arab League offers many advantages for genuine regional integration, chief of which is its ability to draw on the vast resources of the United Nations and/or to influence United Nations policies in its favor. It is apparent that the essential precondition to effective opera-

[12] In a 1964 interview, President Nasser said, significantly, that the real meaning of Arab unity is unity of action in the face of danger; Arabs must work together. Constitutional unity, he said, is different and will be difficult to achieve, if it is possible at all. *London Observer*, July 5, 1964.

tion of the Arab League as a regional organization is the ability of its member states to work more closely together toward realizable regional objectives. Conversely, however, the United Nations must be persuaded of the necessity to minimize its emphasis on regional security and increase its concern for regional development in the functional areas.

The Hammarskjold note of December 1960 seems to offer encouragement for future relations between the Arab League and the United Nations. More pertinent, perhaps, is the fact that increased responsibility within the membership of the regional organization will tend to encourage increased support by the universal body. In this respect, it will be important for the Arab League to justify the respect and confidence of the West as well as of the Afro-Asian and Latin American powers. The Arab States cannot afford to overlook the fact that Western encouragement was a major factor in the establishment of the League in 1944-1945. Moreover, the 1950 invitation to the Arab League to send an observer to the sessions of the General Assembly was secured as a result of Western support.[13] While the West withdrew its support of the League during the period of the Baghdad Pact, it now appears to be more sympathetic to the idea of supporting the League once again as a major force in regional integration.

The political objectives of the Arab States—independence and freedom from Western political control—have been satisfied for the most part and the West has more

[13] The Arab League Secretary General conferred with the U.S. Ambassador in Cairo in September 1950 on the matter of an Arab League request for an invitation to UN General Assembly sessions, and secured the promise of U.S. support. Later the British Government conveyed its support in a letter to the Arab League Secretary General. The French demurred because of the League's position on North Africa, *Oriente Moderno*, xxx (1950), 133, from *al-Ahram* [Cairo], September 13, 1950.

or less acknowledged the failure of its Cold-War policies in the Arab Middle East. The critical issue of Arab-Israeli relations remains, of course, but this can only be settled with the support of the West. Channeling future Western support of the Arab League through the agency of the United Nations seems to hold considerable promise for the future, therefore, particularly as the Arab states demonstrate their willingness to cooperate among themselves within the context of the existing regional organization.

Regional Security Prospects

The question of future relations with the West, in or out of the United Nations, will also be determined by the Arab League's capacity for effective regional security and the peaceful settlement of disputes. At the risk of oversimplifying the problem, it appears that the orientation of the Arab League as a regional organization toward the problems of regional security has been correct in principle. The problem facing the Arab League is less one of defense from attacks originating outside the area than defense against threats from within the area. The problem of defense against external threats is essentially one for the United Nations, as has already been demonstrated by the United Nations action during the Suez Crisis of 1956.

A major concern, of course, is the exaggerated animosity between Israel and the Arab League, a circumstance which suggests to some observers that any external support to an Arab League regional security mechanism would only embroil the region in another war. So far, this has not been the case despite massive Soviet military aid to Egypt, Syria, and Iraq since 1955. In the final analysis, however, the equitable settlement of the Arab-Israeli question is essential to the establishment of effective regional security mechanisms. If this obstacle can be overcome, then it may be possible for the Western powers to provide technical assistance and equipment in support of an Arab League regional security agency—preferably through the United Nations under Article 47 of the Charter—in sufficient quantity to give the region a base for self-defense against external attack as well as an adequate measure of defense against possible threats to regional peace from within the region.

Under the circumstances, however, the problem of improved procedures for peaceful settlement of disputes between Arab League members is probably more significant than the problem of regional security. No effective procedures for peaceful settlement of disputes were included within the terms of the Pact of the League of Arab States, largely as a concession to the exaggerated concern for national independence and sovereignty exhibited by member states of the League. A number of suggestions have been made to remedy this situation, including compulsory arbitration of disputes between members and the establishment of an Arab Court of Justice, but the key to the problem is again less that of procedure than of increased confidence on the part of member states in the regional organization. An amendment to the Pact would be required, particularly of Article 5, which limits the jurisdiction of the League Council only to that type of dispute between members "which does not concern a state's independence, sovereignty, or territorial integrity," and Council decisions apply only "if the parties to the dispute have recourse to the Council for the settlement of this difference." In effect, this provision rules out all substantive disputes.[14] The development of a regional "Arab Court of Justice," well under way in 1964, should

[14] A draft amendment to the Pact to make arbitration of disputes compulsory was discussed by the League Council in early 1964, according to *al-Jaridah* [Beirut], March 24, 1964.

also contribute to the capacity of the Arab League to keep peace among its members.

Improved Programs for Regional Functional Integration

The final requirement of the Arab League is reorientation toward realistic and realizable programs in the field of regional functional integration, particularly as concerns economic and social development. Functionalism presumes the existence of more or less sophisticated social and economic institutions that are almost totally lacking in the Arab world where the tradition has been one of personalized, autocratic rule. The tug of war between the traditionalists and the reform-minded modernists—inevitably involving the question of what final political form shall prevail in the area—tends to preclude the establishment of these institutions within the nascent national state. Problems of economic and social reform, for example, are seen primarily in their political context by insecure political leaders or governments. One of the most significant contributions of the Arab League, therefore, has been its encouragement of non-governmental regional associational interest groups—medical societies, labor unions, scientific associations, a regional chamber of commerce, and other professional groups—which help to span this institutional gap.

The future functional programs and activities undertaken by the League must recognize inherent limitations on available resources and must be compatible with both the needs and desires of the region. There is no room for spectacular solutions or self-deception—seemingly fatal characteristics of Arab planners. The human and material resources of the region are inadequate, and external support is critically needed. On the other hand, more efficient utilization of existing Arab League resources and agencies, together with encouragement of new operating agencies, is necessary.

Some form of multilateral regional development planning such as, for example, a joint project between UN-TAB, the Arab League Secretariat, and the UN Specialized Agencies applied to country programs in the Arab League area could well be coordinated with the appropriate department of the League Secretariat (and the appropriate League specialized agency) to avoid duplication of effort, to insure the best utilization of available material and human resources, and to provide the basis for a coordinated program approach to the development of the region. To facilitate such coordination, the professional capacities of Arab League staff members are steadily increasing, and constructive working relationships between the UN Specialized Agencies and the Arab League can be anticipated for the future.

Within the purview of the League itself, the movement toward some form of Arab Common Market suggests that the particularistic policies of member states may be giving way to genuine concern for regional objectives. To be effective, such a move must be constructive and carried out on a higher level than the context of the "threat" posed by the existence of the European Common Market. A starting point might be the newly established Council of Economic Union, now freed of the limitations imposed by the 1950 Collective Security Pact and open to all Arab League states.

Following any concrete program of regional economic integration, an Arab Common Market might well be within reach as a logical further step. It should not be a means of disguising a forced move toward Arab unity but, rather, a voluntary associational enterprise based on the recognition that regional economic integration is an essential prerequisite to national economic development. The Arab Common Market is merely a means to an end, and not an end in itself as a substitute for some sort of Arab federation.

Finally, the proposed "Arab Educational, Scientific, and Cultural Organization" (ARESCO) can perform a genuine service by implementing some of the long-planned programs to unify and standardize educational curricula, teacher training, school administration, higher education, scientific terminology, and even—the regional *ne plus ultra*—the Arabic language. It can serve to encourage scientific research at the same time that it works closely with the devotees of the arts and letters. But it would be useless to promulgate the drastic structural change in the League's machinery envisaged by the establishment of ARESCO (the League Secretariat's Cultural Department would all but disappear, for example) without providing the new agency with the necessary prestige and authority to carry out its programs.

It is of no little significance that the four problem areas discussed above depend for their solutions upon the increased capacities of the Arab states to work together toward long-range objectives of mutual benefit to the members of the Arab League. As emphasized throughout this study, the apparent ease of functional integration is a myth. Every major step toward regional economic integration, for example, involves fundamental political decisions. It is not sufficient that the Arab League states react to threats from outside the region. The real problems facing the Arab League in the mid-1960's and after are those originating from within the region.

The problems confronted by individual Arab states are not unknown in other parts of the world, however, where regional programming has taken effect in one form or another. In his analysis of the stages of economic growth, Rostow describes the general situation in terms that may be applied to the Arab League as well as to its member states:

"A reactive nationalism was likely to be an initial unifying element, making for a purposeful effort to supplant the traditional society, binding up disparate elements into an *ad hoc* coalition. Once the new coalition had attained power against the older traditional groups, or the colonial power, or both, it faced a choice between three lines of policy; or, more accurately, of striking a balance between them. Specifically the new leaders faced this question: should nationalism be turned to assert dignity and power on the world scene; should an effort be made to consolidate the power of the central government over the residual traditional forces in the regions; or should economic and social modernization be the primary objective?"[15]

The balance has not yet been attained between these three choices in any collective sense by the Arab League states, principally because the immediate need of individual Arab states has been to consolidate national power. This need has largely been met, and the Arab liberation movement—as it is now called—is virtually complete. To a large extent, the Arab League has been the instrument through which the Arab nationalist movement has successfully asserted its dignity and power on the world scene. The urgent need now is for regional action to realize the full potential of the power over their own destinies acquired by the Arab states since 1945. The existing machinery of the Arab League is capable of directing this new national power into constructive channels for economic and social modernization in the Arab world if it is properly employed.

[15] W. W. Rostow, *The Stages of Economic Growth* (Cambridge: Cambridge University Press, 1960), p. 113.

APPENDICES

APPENDIX A: THE ALEXANDRIA PROTOCOL[1]

THE chiefs and members of the Syrian, Trans-Jordanian, Iraqi, Lebanese and Egyptian delegations at the Preliminary Committee of the General Arab Conference,

Anxious to strengthen and consolidate the ties which bind all Arab countries and to direct them toward the welfare of the Arab world, to improve its conditions, insure its future, and realize its hopes and aspirations,

And in response to Arab public opinion in all Arab countries,

Have met at Alexandria from Shawwal 8, 1363 (September 25, 1944), in the form of a Preliminary Committee of the General Arab Conference, and have agreed as follows:

1. LEAGUE OF ARAB STATES

A League will be formed of the independent Arab States which consent to join the League. It will have a council which will be known as the "Council of the League of Arab States," in which all participating states will be represented on an equal footing.

The object of the League will be to control the execution of the agreements which the above states will conclude; to hold periodic meetings which will strengthen the relations between those states; to coordinate their political plans so as to insure their cooperation, and protect their independence and sovereignty against every aggression by suitable means; and to supervise in a general way the affairs and interests of the Arab countries.

The decisions of the Council will be binding on those who have accepted them except in cases where a disagree-

[1] Source: *The Arab World* [Arab Information Center, New York] v (April 1959), 15-16.

ment arises between two member states of the League in which the two parties shall refer their dispute to the Council for solution. In this case the decision of the Council of the League will be binding.

In no case will resort to force to settle a dispute between any two member states of the League be allowed. But every state shall be free to conclude with any other member state of the League, or other powers, special agreements which do not contradict the text or spirit of the present dispositions.

In no case will the adoption of a foreign policy which may be prejudicial to the policy of the League or an individual member state be allowed.

The Council will intervene in every dispute which may lead to war between a member state of the League and any other member state or power, so as to reconcile them.

A subcommittee will be formed of the members of the Preliminary Committee to prepare a draft of the statutes of the Council of the League and to examine the political questions which may be the object of agreement among Arab States.

2. COOPERATION IN ECONOMIC, CULTURAL, SOCIAL AND OTHER MATTERS

A. The Arab States represented on the Preliminary Committee shall closely cooperate in the following matters:

(1) Economic and financial matters, i.e., commercial exchange, customs, currency, agriculture, and industry.
(2) Communications, i.e., railways, roads, aviation, navigation, posts and telegraphs.
(3) Cultural matters.
(4) Questions of nationality, passports, visas, execution of judgments, extradition of criminals, etc.
(5) Social questions.
(6) Questions of public health.

B. A subcommittee of experts for each of the above subjects will be formed in which the states which have participated in the Preliminary Committee will be represented. This subcommittee will prepare draft regulations for cooperation in the above matters, describing the extent and means of that collaboration.

C. A committee for coordination and editing will be formed whose object will be to control the work of the other subcommittees, to coordinate that part of the work which is accomplished, and to prepare drafts of agreements which will be submitted to the various governments.

D. When all the subcommittees have accomplished their work the Preliminary Committee will meet to examine the work of the subcommittee as a preliminary step toward the holding of a General Arab Conference.

3. Consolidation of These Ties in the Future

While expressing its satisfaction at such a happy step, the Committee hopes that Arab States will be able in the future to consolidate that step by other steps, especially if postwar events should result in institutions which bind various Powers more closely together.

4. A Special Resolution Concerning Lebanon

The Arab States represented on the Preliminary Committee emphasize their respect of the independence and sovereignty of Lebanon in its present frontiers, which the governments of the above States have already recognized in consequence of Lebanon's adoption of an independent policy, which the Government of that country announced in its program of October 7, 1943, unanimously approved by the Lebanese Chamber of Deputies.

5. A Special Resolution Concerning Palestine

A. The Committee is of the opinion that Palestine constitutes an important part of the Arab World and that the rights of the Arabs in Palestine cannot be touched without prejudice to peace and stability in the Arab World.

The Committee also is of the opinion that the pledges binding the British Government and providing for the cessation of Jewish immigration, the preservation of Arab lands, and the achievement of independence for Palestine are permanent Arab rights whose prompt implementation would constitute a step toward the desired goal and toward the stabilization of peace and security.

The Committee declares its support of the cause of the Arabs of Palestine and its willingness to work for the achievement of their legitimate aim and the safeguarding of their just rights.

The Committee also declares that it is second to none in regretting the woes which have been inflicted upon the Jews of Europe by European dictatorial states. But the question of these Jews should not be confused with Zionism, for there can be no greater injustice and aggression than solving the problem of the Jews of Europe by another injustice, i.e., by inflicting injustice on the Arabs of Palestine of various religions and denominations.

B. The special proposal concerning the participation of the Arab Governments and peoples in the "Arab National Fund" to safeguard the lands of the Arabs of Palestine shall be referred to the committee of financial and economic affairs to examine it from all its angles and to submit the results of that examination to the Preliminary Committee in its next meeting.

In faith of which this protocol has been signed at Faruq I University at Alexandria on Saturday, Shawwal 20, 1363 (October 7, 1944).

APPENDIX B: PACT OF THE LEAGUE OF ARAB STATES[1]

HIS EXCELLENCY THE PRESIDENT OF THE SYRIAN REPUBLIC;
HIS ROYAL HIGHNESS THE AMIR OF TRANS-JORDAN;
HIS MAJESTY THE KING OF IRAQ;
HIS MAJESTY THE KING OF SAUDI ARABIA;
HIS EXCELLENCY THE PRESIDENT OF THE LEBANESE REPUBLIC;
HIS MAJESTY THE KING OF EGYPT;
HIS MAJESTY THE KING OF THE YEMEN;

Desirous of strengthening the close relations and numerous ties which link the Arab States;

And anxious to support and stabilize these ties upon a basis of respect for the independence and sovereignty of these states, and to direct their efforts toward the common good of all the Arab countries, the improvement of their status, the security of their future, the realization of their aspirations and hopes;

And responding to the wishes of Arab public opinion in all Arab lands;

Having agreed to conclude a Pact to that end and having appointed as their representatives the persons whose names are listed hereinafter, have agreed upon the following provisions:

Article 1. The League of Arab States is composed of the independent Arab States which have signed this Pact.

Any independent Arab State has the right to become a member of the League. If it desires to do so, it shall submit a request which will be deposited with the Permanent Secretariat General and submitted to the Council at the first meeting held after submission of the request.

Article 2. The League has as its purpose the strengthen-

[1] Signed March 22, 1945. Source: *The Arab World*, v (April 1959), 16-18.

319

ing of the relations between the member states; the coordination of their policies in order to achieve cooperation between them and to safeguard their independence and sovereignty; and a general concern with the affairs and interests of the Arab countries. It has also as its purpose the close cooperation of the member states, with due regard to the organization and circumstances of each state, on the following matters:

A. Economic and financial affairs, including commercial relations, customs, currency, and questions of agriculture and industry.

B. Communications; this includes railroads, roads, aviation, navigation, telegraphs, and posts.

C. Cultural affairs.

D. Nationality, passports, visas, execution of judgments, and extradition of criminals.

E. Social affairs.

F. Health problems.

Article 3. The League shall possess a Council composed of the representatives of the member states of the League; each state shall have a single vote, irrespective of the number of its representatives.

It shall be the task of the Council to achieve the realization of the objectives of the League and to supervise the execution of agreements which the member states have concluded on the questions enumerated in the preceding article, or on any other questions.

It likewise shall be the Council's task to decide upon the means by which the League is to cooperate with the international bodies to be created in the future in order to guarantee security and peace and regulate economic and social relations.

Article 4. For each of the questions listed in Article 2 there shall be set up a special committee in which the member states of the League shall be represented. These committees shall be charged with the task of laying down the principles and extent of cooperation. Such principles shall be formulated as draft agreements, to be presented to the Council for examination preparatory to their submission to the aforesaid states.

Representatives of the other Arab countries may take part in the work of the aforesaid committees. The Council shall determine the conditions under which these representatives may be permitted to participate and the rules governing such representation.

Article 5. Any resort to force in order to resolve disputes arising between two or more member states of the League is prohibited. If there should arise among them a difference which does not concern a state's independence, sovereignty, or territorial integrity, and if the parties to the dispute have recourse to the Council for the settlement of this difference, the decision of the Council shall then be enforceable and obligatory.

In such a case, the states between whom the difference has arisen shall not participate in the deliberations and decisions of the Council.

The Council shall mediate in all differences which threaten to lead to war between two member states, or a member state and a third state, with a view to bringing about their reconciliation.

Decisions of arbitration and mediation shall be taken by majority vote.

Article 6. In case of aggression or threat of aggression by one state against a member state, the state which has been attacked or threatened with aggression may demand the immediate convocation of the Council.

The Council shall by unanimous decision determine the measures necessary to repulse the aggression. If the aggressor is a member state, his vote shall not be counted in determining unanimity.

If, as a result of the attack, the government of the state attacked finds itself unable to communicate with the Council, that state's representative in the Council shall have the right to request the convocation of the Council for the purpose indicated in the foregoing paragraph. In the event that this representative is unable to communicate with the Council, any member state of the League shall have the right to request the convocation of the Council.

Article 7. Unanimous decisions of the Council shall be binding upon all member states of the League; majority decisions shall be binding only upon those states which have accepted them.

In either case the decisions of the Council shall be enforced in each member state according to its respective basic laws.

Article 8. Each member state shall respect the systems of government established in the other member states and regard them as exclusive concerns of those states. Each shall pledge to abstain from any action calculated to change established systems of government.

Article 9. States of the League which desire to establish closer cooperation and stronger bonds than are provided by this Pact may conclude agreements to that end.

Treaties and agreements already concluded or to be concluded in the future between a member state and another state shall not be binding or restrictive upon other members.

Article 10. The permanent seat of the League of Arab States is established in Cairo. The Council may, however, assemble at any other place it may designate.

Article 11. The Council of the League shall convene in ordinary session twice a year, in March and in October. It shall convene in extraordinary session upon the request of two member states of the League whenever the need arises.

Article 12. The League shall have a permanent Secretariat-General which shall consist of a Secretary-General, Assistant Secretaries, and an appropriate number of officials.

The Council of the League shall appoint the Secretary-General by a majority of two-thirds of the states of the League. The Secretary-General, with the approval of the Council shall appoint the Assistant Secretaries and the principal officials of the League.

The Council of the League shall establish an administrative regulation for the functions of the Secretariat-General and matters relating to the Staff.

The Secretary-General shall have the rank of Ambassador and the Assistant Secretaries that of Ministers Plenipotentiary.

Article 13. The Secretary-General shall prepare the draft of the budget of the League and shall submit it to the Council for approval before the beginning of each fiscal year.

Article 14. The members of the Council of the League as well as the members of the committees and the officials who are to be designated in the administrative regulation shall enjoy diplomatic privileges and immunity when engaged in the exercise of their functions.

The building occupied by the organs of the League shall be inviolable.

Article 15. The first meeting of the Council shall be convened at the invitation of the head of the Egyptian Government. Thereafter it shall be convened at the invitation of the Secretary-General.

The representatives of the member states of the League shall alternately assume the presidency of the Council at each of its ordinary sessions.

Article 16. Except in cases specifically indicated in this Pact, a majority vote of the Council shall be sufficient to make enforceable decisions on the following matters:

A. Matters relating to personnel.

B. Adoption of the budget of the League.

C. Establishment of the administrative regulation for Council, the committee, and the Secretariat-General.

D. Decisions to adjourn the sessions.

Article 17. Each member state of the League shall deposit with the Secretariat-General one copy of every treaty or agreement concluded in the future between itself and another member state of the League or a third state.

Article 18. If a member state contemplates withdrawal from the League, it shall inform the Council of its intention one year before such withdrawal is to go into effect.

The Council of the League may consider any state which fails to fulfill its obligations under this Pact as having become separated from the League, this to go into effect upon a unanimous decision of the states, not counting the state concerned.

Article 19. This Pact may be amended with the consent of two-thirds of the states belonging to the League, especially in order to make firmer and stronger the ties between the member states, to create an Arab Tribunal of Arbitration, and to regulate the relations of the League with any international bodies to be created in the future to guarantee security and peace.

Final action on an amendment cannot be taken prior to the session following the session in which the motion was initiated.

If a state does not accept such an amendment it may withdraw at such time as the amendment goes into effect, without being bound by the provisions of the preceding article.

Article 20. This Pact and its Annexes shall be ratified according to the basic laws in force among the High Contracting Parties.

The instruments of ratification shall be deposited with

the Secretariat-General of the Council and the Pact shall become operative as regards each ratifying state fifteen days after the Secretary-General has received the instruments of ratification from four states.

This Pact has been drawn up in Cairo in the Arabic language on this 8th day of Rabi' II, thirteen hundred and sixty-four (March 22, 1945), in one copy which shall be deposited in the safekeeping of the Secretariat-General.

An identical copy shall be delivered to each state of the League.

[Here follow the signatures]

(1) *Annex Regarding Palestine*

Since the termination of the last great war the rule of the Ottoman Empire over the Arab countries, among them Palestine, which had become detached from that Empire, has come to an end. She has come to be autonomous, not subordinate to any other state.

The Treaty of Lausanne proclaimed that her future was to be settled by the parties concerned.

However, even though she was as yet unable to control her own affairs, the Covenant of the League (of Nations) in 1919 made provision for a regime based upon recognition of her independence.

Her international existence and independence in the legal sense cannot, therefore, be questioned, any more than could the independence of the other Arab countries.

Although the outward manifestations of this independence have remained obscured for reasons beyond her control, this should not be allowed to interfere with her participation in the work of the Council of the League.

The states signatory to the Pact of the Arab League are therefore of the opinion that, considering the special circumstances of Palestine and until that country can effectively exercise its independence, the Council of the

League should take charge of the selection of an Arab representative from Palestine to take part in its work.

(2) *Annex Regarding Cooperation with Countries Which Are Not Members of the Council of the League*

Whereas the member states of the League will have to deal in the Council as well as in the committees with matters which will benefit and affect the Arab world at large;

And whereas the Council has to take into account the aspirations of the Arab countries which are not members of the Council and has to work toward their realization;

Now, therefore, it particularly behooves the states signatory to the Pact of the Arab League to enjoin the Council of the League, when considering the admission of those countries to participation in the committees referred to in the Pact, that it should spare no effort to learn their needs and understand their aspirations and hopes; and that it should work thenceforth for their best interests and the safeguarding of their future with all the political means at its disposal.

(3) *Annex Regarding the Appointment of a Secretary-General of the League*

The states signatory to this Pact have agreed to appoint His Excellency Abdul-Rahman 'Azzam Bey, to be Secretary-General of the League of Arab States.

This appointment is made for two years. The Council of the League shall hereafter determine the new regulations for the Secretary-General.

APPENDIX C: JOINT DEFENSE AND ECONOMIC COOPERATION TREATY BETWEEN THE STATES OF THE ARAB LEAGUE[1]

The Governments of:

> THE HASHIMITE KINGDOM OF JORDAN
> THE SYRIAN REPUBLIC
> THE KINGDOM OF IRAQ
> THE KINGDOM OF SAUDI ARABIA
> THE LEBANESE REPUBLIC
> THE KINGDOM OF EGYPT
> THE MOTAWAKILITE KINGDOM OF YEMEN

In view of the desire of the above-mentioned Governments to consolidate relations between the States of the Arab League; to maintain their independence and their mutual heritage; in accordance with the desire of their peoples, to cooperate for the realization of mutual defense and the maintenance of security and peace according to the principles of both the Arab League Pact and the United Nations Charter, together with the aims of the said Pacts; and to consolidate stability and security and provide means of welfare and development in the countries.

The following government delegates of . . . , having been duly accredited and fully authorized by their respective governments, approve the following:

Article 1. The Contracting States, in an effort to maintain and stabilize peace and security, hereby confirm their desire to settle their international disputes by peaceful

[1] Signed by Egypt, Lebanon, Syria, Saudi Arabia and Yemen on June 17, 1950; by Iraq on February 2, 1951; and by Jordan on February 16, 1952. Source: *The Arab World,* v (April 1959), 18-19.

means, whether such disputes concern relations among themselves or with other Powers.

Article 2. The Contracting States consider any [act of] armed aggression made against any one or more of them or their armed forces, to be directed against them all. Therefore, in accordance with the right of self-defense, individually and collectively, they undertake to go without delay to the aid of the State or States against which such an act of aggression is made, and immediately to take, individually and collectively, all steps available, including the use of armed force, to repel the aggression and restore security and peace. In conformity with Article 6 of the Arab League Pact and Article 51 of the United Nations Charter, the Arab League Council and U. N. Security Council shall be notified of such act of aggression and the means and procedure taken to check it.

Article 3. At the invitation of any one of the signatories of this Treaty the Contracting States shall hold consultations whenever there are reasonable grounds for the belief that the territorial integrity, independence, or security of any one of the parties is threatened. In the event of the threat of war or the existence of an international emergency, the Contracting States shall immediately proceed to unify their plans and defensive measures, as the situation may demand.

Article 4. The Contracting States, desiring to implement fully the above obligations and effectively carry them out, shall cooperate in consolidating and coordinating their armed forces, and shall participate according to their resources and needs in preparing individual and collective means of defense to repulse the said armed aggression.

Article 5. A Permanent Military Commission composed of representatives of the General Staffs of the armies of the Contracting States shall be formed to draw up plans of joint defense and their implementation. The duties of the Permanent Military Commission which are set forth in an Annex attached to this Treaty, include the drafting of necessary reports on the method of cooperation and participation mentioned in Article 4. The Permanent Military Commission shall submit to the Joint Defense Council, provided hereunder in Article 6, reports dealing with questions within its province.

Article 6. A Joint Defense Council under the supervision of the Arab League Council shall be formed to deal with all matters concerning the implementation of the provisions of Articles 2, 3, 4, and 5 of this Treaty. It shall be assisted in the performance of its task by the Permanent Military Commission referred to in Article 5. The Joint Defense Council shall consist of the Foreign Ministers and the Defense Ministers of the Contracting States or their representatives. Decisions taken by a two-thirds majority shall be binding on all the Contracting States.

Article 7. The Contracting States, in order to fulfill the aims of this Treaty, and to bring security and prosperity in the Arab countries, and in an effort to raise the standard of living in them, undertake to cooperate in the development of their economies and the exploitation of their natural resources; to facilitate the exchange of their respective agricultural and industrial products; and generally to organize and coordinate their economic activities and to conclude the necessary inter-Arab agreements to realize such aims.

Article 8. An Economic Council consisting of the Ministers in charge of economic affairs, or their representatives if necessary, shall be formed by the Contracting States to submit recommendations for the realization of all such aims as are set forth in the performance of its duties, seek the cooperation of the Committee for Financial and Economic Affairs referred to in Article 4 of the Arab League Pact.

Article 9. The Annex to this Treaty shall be considered an integral and indivisible part of it.

Article 10. The Contracting States undertake to conclude no international agreements which may be contradictory to the provisions of this Treaty, nor to act, in their international relations, in a way which may be contrary to the aims of this Treaty.

Article 11. No provision of this Treaty shall in any way affect, or is intended to affect, any of the rights or obligations developing upon the Contracting States from the United Nations Charter or the responsibilities borne by the United Nations Security Council for the maintenance of international peace and security.

Article 12. After a lapse of 10 years from the date of the ratification of this Treaty, any one of the Contracting States may withdraw from it, providing 12 months' notice is previously given to the Secretariat-General of the Arab League. The Secretariat-General of the League shall inform the other Contracting States of such notice.

Article 13. This Treaty shall be ratified by each Contracting State according to the constitutional procedure of its own government. The Treaty shall come into force for the ratifying States 15 days after the receipt by the Secretariat-General of the instruments of ratification from at least four States. This Treaty is drafted in Arabic in Cairo on April 13, 1950. One signed copy shall be deposited with the Secretariat-General of the Arab League; equally authentic copies shall be transmitted to each of the Contracting States.

MILITARY ANNEX

1. The Permanent Military Commission provided for in Article 5 of the Joint Defense and Economic Cooperation Treaty between the States of the Arab League, shall undertake the following:

(a) in cooperation with the Joint Defense Council,

to prepare plans to deal with all anticipated dangers or armed aggression that may be launched against one or more of the Contracting States or their armed forces, such plans to be based on the principles determined by the Joint Defense Council;

(b) to submit proposals for the organization of the forces of the Contracting States, stipulating the minimum force for each in accordance with military exigencies and the potentialities of each State;

(c) to submit proposals for increasing the effectiveness of the forces of the Contracting States in so far as their equipment, organization, and training are concerned; so that they may keep pace with modern military methods and development; and for the unification and coordination of all such forces;

(d) to submit proposals for the exploitation of natural, agricultural, industrial, and other resources of all Contracting States in favor of the inter-Arab military effort and joint defense;

(e) to organize the exchange of training missions between the Contracting States for the preparation of plans, participation in military exercises and maneuvers and the study of their results, recommendations for the improvement of methods to ensure close cooperation in the field, and for the general improvement of the forces of all the Contracting States;

(f) to prepare the necessary data on the resources and military potentialities of each of the Contracting States and the part to be played by the forces of each in the joint military effort;

(g) to discuss the facilities and various contributions which each of the Contracting States, in conformity with the provisions of this Treaty, might be asked to provide, during a state of war, on behalf of the armies of such other Contracting States as might be operating on its territory.

2. The Permanent Military Commission may form temporary or permanent subcommittees from among its own members to deal with any of the matters falling within its jurisdiction. It may also seek the advice of any experts whose views on certain questions are deemed necessary.

3. The Permanent Military Commission shall submit detailed reports on the results of its activities and studies to the Joint Defense Council provided for in Article 6 of this Treaty, as well as an annual report giving full particulars of its work and studies during the year.

4. The Permanent Military Commission shall establish its headquarters in Cairo but may hold meetings in any other place the Commission may specify. The Commission shall elect its Chairman for two years; he may be reelected. Candidates for the Chairmanship shall hold at least the rank of a high commanding officer. Each member of the Commission must have as his original nationality that of the Contracting State he represents.

5. In the event of war, the supreme command of the joint forces shall be entrusted to the Contracting State possessing the largest military force taking actual part in field operations, unless, by unanimous agreement, the Commander-in-Chief shall be assisted in directing military operations by a Joint Staff.

SUPPLEMENTARY PROTOCOL TO THE TREATY OF JOINT DEFENSE AND ECONOMIC COOPERATION BETWEEN THE ARAB STATES AND TO THE MILITARY ANNEX[2]

A consultative military organization shall be composed of the Chiefs of Staff of the Contracting States to supervise the Permanent Military Commission provided by

[2] Signed on February 2, 1951 at the 13th session of the League Council. Text from *League of Arab States Treaty Series* (no date, no place of publication), p. 18, with change of "Common" to "Joint" in *Joint Defense*; "Collaboration" to "Cooperation" in *Economic Cooperation*.

Article 5 of the Treaty and to direct it in all the functions specified in Article 1 of the Military Annex.

The reports and proposals of the Permanent Military Commission shall be submitted to the Consultative Military Organization before submitting them to the Joint Defense Council provided for by Article 6 of the Treaty.

The Consultative Military Organization shall submit its reports and proposals regarding its functions to the Joint Defense Council that it may examine them and take the necessary decisions.

The present Protocol shall have the same force as the Treaty and its Appendix [Military Annex] as regards the provisions of Articles 5 and 6 of the Treaty and Article 3 of the Military Appendix [Annex].

APPENDIX D[1]: INTERNAL REGULATIONS OF THE COUNCIL OF THE LEAGUE OF ARAB STATES, OCTOBER 13, 1951

Article 1. The Member States of the League shall elect their representatives who compose the Council and who shall be furnished with credentials covering their delegation to the Council as well as with documents covering their powers, whenever necessary. Their names shall be communicated to the Secretary-General.

Article 2. The delegates shall retain their representative character in the Council unless the Secretariat-General is notified of any changes which Member States wish to make in their delegations, and every new delegate shall be furnished with his credentials and powers.

Article 3. The credentials and the documents covering the powers (of the delegates) shall be delivered to the Secretary-General, who shall submit to the Council the results of his examination thereof to be entered in the minutes of the meeting.

Article 4. The Secretary-General shall fix the date for the commencement of each of the ordinary sessions for March and October.

Each session shall continue until all the questions on the agenda have been discussed, unless the Council decides to end the session before this (has been done).

Article 5. The Council shall meet in extraordinary session within a period not exceeding one month from the date of receipt by the Secretary-General of the official request from the meeting.

Article 6. In the cases of aggression referred to in Article 6 of the Pact, the meeting shall take place at the earliest

[1] English translation courtesy of Muhammad Khalil, *The Arab States and the Arab League: A Documentary Record*, Vol. II (Beirut: Khayat's, 1962).

possible time within three days from the date of the receipt by the Secretary-General of the official request (for the meeting).

Article 7. The Secretary-General—or any one acting for him in case of his absence—shall send notices for convening the ordinary sessions one month at least before the date fixed for the opening of the sessions.

As for the extraordinary sessions, the notice shall be sent by telegram five days before the date fixed for the meeting.

Article 8. The Secretary-General shall prepare the draft agenda of the Council and communicate it to the Member States together with the notice of the meeting.

The Member States may suggest within a period not exceeding 15 days from the date of their notification of the draft agenda the entering of new questions thereon, and the Secretary-General shall draw up an additional list of these questions and communicate it to the Member States ten days before the meeting of the Council.

The agenda of every ordinary session shall contain a report covering the activities of the Secretariat-General between the two sessions and the measures taken for the implementation of the Council's resolutions.

There shall be annexed to the agenda detailed memoranda on the subjects submitted (for discussion) along with any available reports, whether submitted by the committees or by others.

Article 9. The Council shall approve the agenda at the beginning of each session, and may add, by a decision approved by the majority, other questions not included thereon.

Article 10. There shall not be included on the agenda of extraordinary session any questions other than those for the discussion of which the extraordinary session has been convened.

The Council may by a majority of votes decide to discuss other questions.

Article 11. The meeting of the Council shall be considered legal if attended by representatives of the majority of the Member States. As for resolutions, these can only be valid if approved by a majority of the votes of the Member States of the League or by a two-thirds majority or by the unanimous votes of the (Member) States in accordance with the provisions of the Pact in each case.

Article 12. The meetings of the Council shall be secret except in those cases when the Council decides by a majority of votes to make them public.

Article 13. The meeting of the Council of the League shall be attended by the Secretary-General or by any one delegated by him from among his Assistants to act for him.

Article 14. The presidency of the Council shall be entrusted by rotation at the opening of every ordinary session to each of the Member States according to the alphabetical order of their names.

The President shall continue in the exercise of his functions as President until the presidency is entrusted to his successor at the opening of the following session.

Article 15. The President opens, prorogues and adjourns the meetings; he directs the activities of the Council; sees to it that the provisions of the Pact and of the Internal Regulations are applied; announces the closing of the discussion; submits a proposal for a vote; takes the steps for the formation of the committees as decided by the Council; notifies the Council of all messages within its competence, and supervises the implementation of its decisions.

Article 16. Should the President be for any reason unable to carry out his functions as President, these should be assumed in his stead by any one of the representatives of his country according to the order in which they are accredited. When his country has no other representative the temporary presidency should be entrusted to the head of the delegation of the State which has the right to the presidency for the following session.

Article 17. The Council may entrust to any of its members the study of a given question and the role of *rapporteur* on that question to the Council.

The reports submitted on such questions shall be distributed to the members at least one day before the meeting during which these questions will be discussed. The report shall be read during the meeting or, at the discretion of the Council, the mere distribution of the report in the manner described above may be considered sufficient. The *rapporteur* may, however, give to the Council any such explanations as he may deem necessary.

Article 18. The Council shall form at the beginning of every ordinary session the following committees:

1) The Committee for Political Affairs
2) The Committee for Economic Affairs
3) The Committee for Social and Cultural Affairs
4) The Committee for Administrative and Financial Affairs
5) The Committee for Legal Affairs

It may also form other committees if necessary.

Every delegation shall elect at the beginning of every session from among its members its representatives to each of these committees, and may seek the assistance of experts and specialists.

The Council shall refer the questions on the agenda to the committees, each according to its competence, for study and the submission of a report thereon containing their recommendations.

The Council may permit the committees to travel to the Member States of the League should it find this necessary to ensure an exhaustive study of the questions referred to these committees.

The Council may also discuss the questions entered on the agenda before referring them to the competent committees should this be decided upon by a majority of votes.

Article 19. All matters referred to the Council by the committees shall be accompanied by reports, and the committee concerned shall appoint a *rapporteur* who will attend the meeting of the Council in order to furnish whatever explanations he may be required to submit. The *rapporteur* shall participate in the discussions but shall not participate in the voting, unless he is a member of the Council.

Article 20. The Secretary-General may draw the attention of the Council or the Member States to any question which may be prejudicial to the existing relations between Member States or between Member States and other States.

Article 21. The Secretary-General shall undertake the organization of the Secretariat of the Council and of the Secretariat of the committees formed by the Council.

The Secretary-General may be assisted or superseded during the Council's meetings by one or more delegates chosen by him.

The Secretary-General or his delegates may, at any time, with the approval of the President, submit to the Council verbal reports or statements on any question under discussion by the Council.

Article 22. The Secretary-General shall supervise the drawing up of records or minutes of all the deliberations which take place and of all the resolutions adopted during the ordinary and extraordinary meetings of the Council.

Article 23. The Secretariat-General shall receive, print and notify all the documents, reports and resolutions; shall register, print and notify the records and minutes of the meetings; shall file the documents of the Council in the archives of the League; shall translate any of these as may be necessary; shall publish the accounts of the meetings; and shall, in general, undertake all the functions which the Council of the League may entrust to it.

Article 24. The Secretariat-General shall undertake the preparation of these records and minutes, the printing and distribution thereof among the members of the Council with the least possible delay. Whoever wishes to correct his statements shall notify the Secretariat-General to this effect within the following forty-eight hours.

After the lapse of the period prescribed for the correction of the statements, the Council shall adopt the records and minutes which shall be signed by the President and the Secretary-General.

Article 25. The Council may decide not to draw up minutes of its meetings, in which case it will be sufficient to make only a record of the text of the resolution adopted by the Council. This record, as in the case of the minutes, shall be distributed among the members. It shall then be approved by the Council and signed by the President and the Secretary-General.

Article 26. The debates in the Council shall take place according to the following procedure:

1) The President shall submit the question in a general manner, and shall call upon the Secretary-General to give any explanations he may deem necessary, if required.

2) The record shall be given to the *rapporteur* and then to those who follow him according to the order in which they have asked to speak.

3) The President shall submit to the Council the proposal for closing the discussion, and, if (it is) approved by the majority of the Council, announce the decision to this effect.

4) Draft resolutions, amendments and proposals intended to be submitted to a vote shall be made in

writing, and the vote shall be taken by roll-call, and the President shall announce the results of the voting.

Article 27. These Internal Regulations shall not be amended unless a proposal to this effect is submitted and approved by the Council by a majority of votes.

APPENDIX E[1]: INTERNAL REGULATIONS OF THE COMMITTEES OF THE LEAGUE OF ARAB STATES, OCTOBER 13, 1951

Article 1. The functions of the Committees referred to in Article 2 of The Pact of the League shall be regulated in the following manner:

Article 2. Each Member State of the League shall be represented in each Committee by one or more delegates. It shall have (only) one vote.

One and the same person may be charged with the representation of his State in more than one Committee.

The States shall notify the Secretary-General of the names of their delegates, and shall also specify the Committee or Committees in which (these delegates) represent them.

Article 3. The delegates shall retain their representative character, each in the Committee to which he is appointed, unless replaced by their States.

Article 4. The Secretariat-General shall assist the Committees in the performance of their work, in order to enable them to acquaint themselves with the subjects under discussion.

Article 5. The Council shall appoint for each of the Committees referred to in the Pact, a chairman for a period of two years, subject to renewal.

Should (the chairman) be absent, the Committee shall elect another to take his place during his absence. The Secretariat-General shall delegate one from among its employees to represent it in the Committees.

Article 6. The Secretary-General shall delegate one of the employees of the Secretariat-General, specialized in the

---

[1] English translation courtesy of Muhammad Khalil, *The Arab States and the Arab League: A Documentary Record*, Vol. II (Beirut: Khayat's, 1962).

matters entrusted to each Committee, to act as Secretary thereto.

Article 7. The Committees shall convene at the headquarters of the League. They may, with the approval of the Secretary-General, decide to meet in another of the League's countries, should the requirements of the work so demand.

Article 8. Each Committee shall be convened by the Secretary-General. In fixing the dates of the meetings, (the Secretariat-General) shall pay due regard to the time needed for the reception of the summons and for the arrival of the members traveling from the farthest country to the headquarters of the League.

Article 9. The quorum in each Committee shall be constituted by the attendance of the representatives of the majority of the States Members of the League.

The resolutions shall be passed by a majority of those present.

The meeting of the Committees shall be secret.

Article 10. Two or more Committees may meet (jointly) for considering a given subject. The meeting shall be presided over by the senior chairman of the assembled committees. The quorum shall be constituted if the majority of delegates in each Committee attend the meeting.

The resolution shall be passed by a majority of those present.

Article 11. Minutes shall be made of the meetings of the Committees, in which a summary of their deliberations and the full text of the resolutions passed by them shall be recorded.

Article 12. The work of the Committees in matters assigned to them by the fact shall be of a preparatory nature, and shall be drawn up in a form of draft agreements to be submitted to the Council of the League. (The Committees) may also submit to the Council any recommendations or suggestions that may arise in the course of their discussions.

Article 13. The principal Committees may form, from among their members, sub-committees, each to be designated for one of the technical questions which the principal Committee is studying.

Article 14. Each Committee may recommend the calling of meetings of experts representing the States Members of the League and the other Arab countries, if necessary, in order to be guided by their views on matters coming within the jurisdiction of the Committee.

The Secretary-General shall be responsible for contacting the League States for the implementation of this recommendation.

Article 15. These regulations shall come into force as from the date on which they are approved by the Council, namely, October 13, 1951.

APPENDIX F[1]: INTERNAL REGULATIONS OF THE SECRETARIAT-GENERAL OF THE LEAGUE, MAY 10, 1953

Article 1. The Secretary-General shall, in the name of the League, implement the resolutions of the Council and shall take the financial measures within the limits of the budget approved by the Council. He shall also, in his capacity as Secretary-General of the League, attend the meetings of the Council of the League and of the Committees, and shall perform such other duties as may be entrusted to him by these bodies.

He shall be exclusively responsible to the Council of the League for all acts of the Secretariat-General and for the implementation of office regulations in the Departments and Divisions of the Secretariat-General which carry out their functions under the supervision and approval of the Secretary-General.

Article 2. The appointment of the Secretary-General shall be for five years, subject to renewal.

Article 3. The Secretary-General shall be assisted in the supervision of the duties of the Secretariat-General by Assistant Secretaries. Each one of the Member States shall have the right to nominate, from among its own nationals, an Assistant Secretary, whose appointment shall be made with the approval of the Council. Each of (these Assistant Secretaries) shall be in charge of at least one of the Departments of the Secretariat-General.

Article 4. Should there happen anything necessitating the absence of the Secretary-General, he shall delegate one of his available Assistants to replace him.

---

[1] English translation courtesy of Muhammad Khalil, *The Arab States and the Arab League: A Documentary Record*, Vol. II (Beirut: Khayat's, 1962).

Article 5. The Secretariat-General shall be constituted of the following Departments:

1) *Conference Secretariat*: This shall carry out (all) correspondence concerning public affairs not coming under the competence of the other Departments; the performance of the functions of the Council's Secretariat during its sessions, and (also) protocol affairs.

There shall be attached to it the Archives Registry which shall be charged with all matters relating to the receipt and dispatch of mail; the filing and classification of the League's papers and official documents; the registration of out-going and incoming correspondence; the supervision of the final disposition of matters referred to the various Departments, and the (sending of) reminders thereon on the dates prescribed by instructions. The Registry shall also keep in good order the circulation and progress of files.

The library, too, shall be attached to the Conference Secretariat.

2) *Finance and Administrative Department*: This shall carry out all the financial affairs of the League, including the preparation and control of its budget, the bookkeeping of the accounts of the League and of the employees, the Provident Fund, supplies, and all matters relating to the employees financially and administratively.

The Director of the Department shall act as Secretary to the body supervising the management of the Provident Fund.

3) *Political Department*: This shall carry out the study of the political affairs relating to the Arab countries, follow up those international affairs of (special) interest to the Arab League, and prepare the studies and reports connected with the above.

4) *Economic and Communication Affairs Department*: This shall prepare, in general, the studies required by

the work of the Economic and Communications Committees.

It shall prepare the statements and statistics concerning the economic situation in the Member States.

It shall prepare the studies relating to the progress and implementation of the commercial agreements concluded among the Member States.

It shall furnish the appropriate Departments in the Governments of the Member States with economic statements and statistics, and may make suggestions on all (matters) relating to the economic conditions, or economic stability (of the Palestine refugees) in the countries of the Member States.

It shall compile studies published in international, economic and commercial magazines, pertaining to the economies of the countries of the Member States.

5) *Social and Health Affairs Department*: This shall carry out studies relating to migration, labour and labour movements, child protection, health matters and questions of co-operation among the Arab countries concerning these matters.

6) *Legal Department*: This shall carry out the study of legal matters in general and shall prepare studies relating to nationality, passports, visas, execution of judgements, extradition of criminals, and the study and preparation of the various draft laws, leading to the achievement of co-operation among the Member States.

It shall discuss international legal matters likely to arise out of a given international situation.

It shall act as an advisory department concerning all affairs of the Secretariat-General.

It shall have the right to appear before the courts in suits brought by or against the League.

It shall undertake the drafting and drawing up of

agreements prepared by the League, as well as the registration of agreements deposited by the Member States, in accordance with the provisions of Article 17 of the Pact.

7) *Information and Publication Department*: Its duty shall be the making of propaganda for the Arab countries, furnishing the newspapers with communiqués and other (documents), and (also) controlling whatever is published therein, as well as furnishing the League with all matters relating to propaganda and publication.

8) *Cultural Affairs Department*: This shall carry out the preliminary study of cultural and educational matters.

Article 6. Each Department shall have officials according to the need and necessity of the work, as provided for in the budget.

APPENDIX G: CHRONOLOGY OF ARAB LEAGUE COUNCIL SESSIONS, 1945-1963[1]

Session: 1
Date: June, 1945
Place: Cairo
Chairman: Egypt

Summary of Activities
Discussion of dispute between Syria and Lebanon and France. Any international meeting to resolve dispute should include Arab League (Resol. 1). Council supported Syria and Lebanon against France (Resol. 2). Communiqué demanded withdrawal of French troops from Syria and Lebanon, June 8.

Session: 2
Date: October, 1945
Place: Cairo
Chairman: Syria

Summary of Activities
Boycott of Jewish goods established and plans made to establish committee to enforce boycott (Resol. 16). Council approved up to three representatives from Palestine (Resol. 17).

Session: 3
Date: March, 1946
Place: Cairo
Chairman: Syria

[1] Since Arab League Council proceedings are secret and only selected actions are publicized, this summary is by no means complete. Sources of information are the chronology sections of *International Organization, Middle Eastern Affairs, Middle East Journal, Oriente Moderno*, etc. Resolutions enumerated are summarized in the Appendix of *Egypt and the United Nations.*

Summary of Activities

Council supported Egypt's demand for withdrawal of British troops from Suez; decision to be communicated to British by Secretary General (Resol. 25). Plans for common Arab citizenship, Arab financial institution for agricultural development discussed. A decision was made to initiate liaison activities with UNESCO (Resol. 38). Council declared support of independence for Indonesia (Resol. 45). Council approved draft note to Peace Council with Italy urging unity and independence for Libya (Resol. 41).

Session: 4
Date: June, 1946
Place: Bludan, Syria
Chairman: Jordan

Summary of Activities

Council decided Arab League should be included in any future discussion on Libya (Resol. 59). Secretary General charged with following progress of Libyan commission of inquiry (Resol. 62); all Arab governments urged to help secure freedom of Arab peoples still outside the Arab League (Resol. 63). Boycott program extended to all Arab League countries (Resol. 70). Plan to establish "Higher Arab Executive" to unify efforts in Palestine approved (Resol. 82).

Session: 5
Date: October, 1946
Place: Cairo
Chairman: Iraq

Summary of Activities

Council recommended League members recognize Indonesia (Resol. 83). Secretary General directed to request British to halt Italian immigration in Libya; League governments requested to make diplomatic representations (Resol. 143). Secretary General directed to request status of reforms proposed for Spanish Morocco by Spanish Government (Resol. 138). Secretary General directed to send note to British request action to stop Jewish terrorism in Palestine (Resol. 140). Council affirmed that Palestine was a vital part of the Arab motherland (Resol. 142). Member Governments urged to have representatives in the U.S. inform U.S. Government that interference in Palestine was resented by the Arabs. Boycott of Jewish goods extended to land transfers. Note on North Africa prepared for dispatch to French. Political Department of Secretariat made responsible for UN affairs. Council approved draft aviation agreement, draft of model treaty between Arab states and foreign powers.

Session: 6
Date: March, 1947
Place: Cairo
Chairman: Saudi Arabia

Summary of Activities
Session attended by a Spanish delegation. Council confirmed support of Egypt in dispute with British (Resol. 148). Secretary General directed to attempt to have League included in any future inquiry or referendum in Libya (Resol. 157). Member states urged to coordinate efforts of UN delegations on the coming debate over Palestine (Resol. 167). Plan for Arab citizenship, referred to member governments, included abolition of passports. Question of relations between Syria and Jordan debated.

Session: 7-ɪ
Date: October, 1947
Place: Aley, Lebanon
Chairman: Lebanon

Summary of Activities

£E 15,000 appropriated for liaison with UN (Resol. 185). League Cultural Comm. to advise Arab delegations to UNESCO Conference, Beirut (Resol. 198). Council approved proposed economic cooperation with UN (Resol. 206). Support for Egypt and independence for Libya confirmed by Council; Council declared its support for independence of Morocco (Resol. 211). Funds allocated to fight famine in Tripoli and Tunis (Resol. 213). Material and moral support pledged Arabs in Palestine; necessity for military precautions on Arab borders asserted (Resol. 181). Boycott Committee report approved, procedures tightened. Draft of Arab Army agreement approved.

Session: 7-II
Date: December, 1947
Place: Cairo
Chairman: Lebanon

Summary of Activities

No public announcement of decisions. Council reportedly debated policy on military intervention in Palestine, decided against formal intervention unless U.S. and British intervened militarily.

Session: 8
Date: February, 1946
Place: Cairo
Chairman: Saudi Arabia

Summary of Activities

Yemen absent; Palestine represented. Council approved plan for political, military, and economic measures to be taken in face of Palestine crisis, including withholding petroleum concessions and possible sanctions against countries aiding the Zionists. Mission to Yemen investigated murder of Imam Yahya. All-Arab news agency plan approved. A Syrian plan for an Arab collective security pact was discussed. Council reaffirmed support for an independent Libya. Unification of trade marks, commercial documents recommended.

Session: 9
Date: October, 1948
Place: Cairo
Chairman: Yemen

Summary of Activities
Council protested to UN against el-Doweima massacre (Resol. 218). Partition plan for Palestine rejected. Cable to UN Security Council urging Council order Dutch to halt military operations in Indonesia.

Session: 10
Date: March, 1949
Place: Cairo
Chairman: Jordan

Summary of Activities
Council affirmed policy of return of Arab refugees to Palestine, safeguard of Arab property (Resol. 231). League members at UN given freedom to determine proper course with regard to Ethiopia's claim to Eritrea (Resol. 232). Council decided to send letter to Nehru pledging Arab cooperation with Asian bloc in their common interests (Resol. 241). Secretary General authorized to assist the formation of a Libyan delegation to the UN (Resol. 240).

Session: 11
Date: October, 1949
Place: Cairo
Chairman: Syria

Summary of Activities
Agreement in principle on a collective security organization. Decision made to reduce power of Secretariat by

requiring consultation before policy decisions announced by Secretary General. A permanent Palestine Committee was formed (Resol. 256). Proposed plan for unity of Syria and Iraq regarded as an internal affair, not subject to Council action. Policy of non-recognition of Israel approved. Arab delegates at UN urged to support independence for Libya.

Session: 12
Date: April, 1950
Place: Cairo
Chairman: Iraq

Summary of Activities
Council affirmed status of League as a regional organization; UN members to request inclusion of matter in UN General Assembly agenda (Resol. 290). Egypt nominated to ICAO Council; Egypt nominated to ECOSOC. Boycott of Israel extended, member states prohibited from unilateral peace with Israel. Policy toward Palestine approved: liberation, not conquest. Co-operation with UN-RWA approved (Resol. 325). Direct negotiations between Yemen and UK encouraged on dispute; League members to encourage conciliation (Resol. 291). Draft security pact initialed. Temporary boycott of Council by Jordan, over Jordan's acquisition of Eastern Palestine.

Session: 12-Extra
Date: May, 1950
Place: Cairo
Chairman: Iraq

Summary of Activities
Special session discussed steps to be taken against Jordan for her unilateral action in Palestine. Expulsion supported by Egypt. Saudi Arabia, Lebanon, Syria. Compromise regarded Jordan as "trustee" of East Palestine, sponsored by Iraq.

Session: 12-Extra
Date: June, 1950
Place: Alexandria
Chairman: Iraq

Summary of Activities
Jordan absent. Council approved plan to consider Jordan as "trustee." Collective security pact signed, June 17, except Jordan and Iraq.

Session: 13-I
Date: October, 1950
Place: Cairo
Chairman: Saudi Arabia

Summary of Activities
Council adjourned to await return of Arab delegations from UN General Assembly.

Session: 13-II
Date: February, 1951
Place: Cairo
Chairman: Saudi Arabia

Summary of Activities
Council affirmed support for world peace, pledged support of principles of UN (Resol. 332). Policy on Arab representation in UN Secretariat approved (Resol. 286). Policy toward Spain confirmed (Resol. 288). Revised collective security pact signed (without Jordan). Egyptian Government charged with necessary action to secure independence for Libya.

Session: 14
Date: March, 1951
Place: Damascus
Chairman: Jordan

Summary of Activities

Developments in Libya, Morocco discussed and notes dispatched to UN, French (Resol. 342, 343). Policy established governing attendance of Arab states at international conferences attended by Israel (Resol. 356). Proposed eastern Economic Conference approved (Resol. 359). Boycott Office established under Secretary General (Resol. 357).

Session: 15
Date: October, 1951
Place: Alexandria
Chairman: Yemen

Summary of Activities

Session addressed by John Blandford, UNRWA. Council approved proposal to make Arabic an official language of the FAO. Policy on Arab representation in UN Secretariat discussed (Resol. 383). Invitation to League Secretary General to attend 6th session UN General Assembly approved. Continued support for Egypt against British declared (Resol. 390). Policies on Libya and French N. Africa confirmed; steps to be taken to put Morocco case on UN General Assembly agenda (Resol. 387). Cooperation with UNWRA reaffirmed (Resol. 389).

Session: 16
Date: March, 1952
Place: Cairo
Chairman: Egypt

Summary of Activities

Session adjourned immediately after convening.

Session: 17
Date: October, 1952
Place: Cairo
Chairman: Egypt

Summary of Activities

Invitation to Secretary General to attend 7th UN General Assembly approved (Resol. 425). Question of Arab representation in UN Secretariat to be raised in 5th Comm., General Assembly (Resol. 428). Arab UN delegations to unify efforts; Arab representatives on General Assembly to forward reports to League (Resol. 464); Council approved £E 10,000 for "propaganda" at UN (Resol. 470). Council drafted message of support to Bey of Tunis; Arab delegates at UN urged to facilitate hearing for Tunisian delegation (Resol. 469). Palestine Department established in Secretariat, given supervision of Boycott Office (Resol. 471). Boycott extended to foreign companies with branches in Israel (Resol. 482); Arab Governments urged to continue diplomatic efforts to prevent transfer of Israeli foreign ministry to Jerusalem (Resol. 427); policy of Arab refugees based on eventual return (Resol. 462); policy on attendance at conferences in which Israel participates is extended to NGO's (Resol. 463). Lebanon nominated for Security Council. Lebanon raised question of public meetings of League Council. Formal proposal for Arab Court of Justice discussed. Question of W. German reparations to Israel discussed. Secretary General 'Azzam resigned.

Session: 18-ɪ
Date: March, 1953
Place: Cairo
Chairman: Syria

Summary of Activities

Council convened at level of Arab diplomatic representatives in Cairo. Membership application for Libya approved. Support for Egypt reaffirmed in dispute with British over Suez Canal Base. Discussions included question of West German reparations to Israel, visit of Secretary of State Dulles to Middle East. Lebanon proposed public meetings of League Council; approved in principle but shelved. Boycott activities extended to Cyprus.

Session: 18-II
Date: May, 1953
Place: Cairo
Chairman: Syria

Summary of Activities

Representatives of N. African Arab areas in attendance. League Council resolved to contribute full share to peace and security based on justice, freedom, sovereignty, in accordance with commitments under covenants of Arab League and United Nations (Resol. 571). General statement covered support of Egypt *vs.* British; Palestine; implementation of the Arab Collective Security Pact; support of Algeria, Morocco, Tunisia for inclusion in General Assembly agenda; relief of suffering Arab refugees. Budget for information activities of £E 90,000.

Session: 19
Date: September, 1953
Place: Cairo
Chairman: Syria

Summary of Activities

Council protested exile of Mohammed ben Yusuf (Morocco), supported Moroccan political aims; continued efforts to submit Tunisian and Moroccan questions to the General Assembly (Resol. 584). Reviewed agenda of 8th General Assembly; Arab states to unify stands, cooperate with other Afro-Asian states; support candidates to UN posts nominated by Arab governments (Iraq for Security Council); joint discussion with Afro-Asian delegates at UN to back one candidate for General Assembly presidency (Resol. 589). Continuation of UN Commission on Libya recommended (Resol. 592). Attempts to place Moroccan and Tunisian questions before UN to continue.

£E 1.0 million voted in support of Jordan against Israeli border attacks. Resolutions of Economic Conference at Beirut approved. Trade agreements treaty and payments treaty approved.

Session: 20
Date: January, 1954
Place: Cairo
Chairman: Iraq

Summary of Activities
Stronger diplomatic ties, exchanges of political delegations with Afro-Asian bloc approved (Resol. 603). Same type of approach with Latin American bloc, including cultural ties. Relief fund approved for N. African refugee children (Resol. 599). Yemen, Egypt supported in disputes with British. Proposed alliance of Turkey, Iraq, Pakistan discussed. UN Secretary General's invitation to Jordan to meet with Israeli representatives at the UN disapproved. Jordan River development project discussed. Cooperation with the West tied to a solution of the Anglo-Egyptian question (Resol. 595).

Session: 21-ɪ
Date: March, 1954
Place: Cairo
Chairman: Saudi Arabia

Summary of Activities
Council supported Political Committee recommendations for candidates to Executive Boards of WHO, ILO; Syria supported for membership in WHO regional group (Resol. 762, 788). Council offers assistance to Pakistan to diffuse Arab culture and language (Resol. 770). £E 15,-000 appropriated for relief of N. African refugees; harsh sentences against Tunisian, Moroccan nationalist leaders protested, UN Secretary General asked to intervene (Resol. 755, 774). Negotiations with W. German govern-

ment on matter of reparations to Israel to be continued (Resol. 758). Protest made to U.S. Government on aid to Israel (Resol. 757). Council approved Arab military action to prevent Israeli aggression in demilitarized zones (Resol. 785). Jordan Valley scheme discussed. Mission to Yemen thanked; Council pledged support to Imam (Resol. 753). Policy on UNRWA project for Arab refugee education discussed (Resol. 759). Council approved plan for new Secretariat building.

Session: 22-ɪ
Date: October, 1954
Place: Cairo
Chairman: Jordan

Summary of Activities
Arab UN delegations authorized to decide on best candidates for UN committees; UN delegations urged to press issues of Morocco, Algeria, Tunisia by all possible means; request for transfer of UNRWA functions to Arab states rejected; Saudi Arabia, Yemen, Jordan urged to seek membership in ILO; proposal for translation of UN documents into Arabic discussed. Member states to use good offices in Cyprus dispute. Support given Indonesia in dispute with Dutch over New Guinea. Proposed Afro-Asian conference in Jakarta approved. Council reaffirmed decision to seek peaceful settlement of dispute between Aden and Yemen.

Session: 22-ɪɪ
Date: December, 1954
Place: Cairo
Chairman: Jordan

Summary of Activities
Council discussed extension of Arab Collective Security Pact to defend Arab states from "foreign aggression." N. Africa question discussed. Israeli diversion of Jordan River

studied. Question of smuggling oil into Israel examined. Taha Hussein approved as chairman of League Cultural Committee.

Session: 23
Date: March, 1955
Place: Cairo
Chairman: Libya

Summary of Activities
Discussion included Oman's application for membership in the League, question of national status of political refugees, request from Libya for economic assistance, dispute between Yemen and Great Britain. The question of Arabs in Israel was to be raised at the United Nations General Assembly.

Session: 24-ɪ
Date: October, 1955
Place: Cairo
Chairman: Yemen

Summary of Activities
The Council studied the General Assembly agenda and made nominations for vacant UN posts. The question of Palestine refugees was postponed. The Council reaffirmed its support of Egypt, the N. African Arab territories, Yemen, etc. In the case of Algeria, the Council decided to urge NATO powers to insure that France did not use NATO resources to crush the rebellion. Support was advanced for Greece in the Cyprus dispute. The Jordan River plans were referred to a technical committee. An Arab League flag was adopted. Information offices were approved for Latin America and the Far East.

Session: 24-ɪɪ
Date: January, 1956
Place: Cairo
Chairman: Yemen

Summary of Activities
Sudan elected to membership in the Arab League, January 19th.

Session: 25
Date: April, 1956
Place: Cairo
Chairman: Yemen

Summary of Activities
Abd el-Krim, Rif leader, appeared before the Council to urge a boycott of France. A decision was taken to establish annual celebrations of Bandung Day on April 18th. Decisions were made on UN nominations and joint action in UN with other Afro-Asian bloc nations. Action was taken to strengthen the boycott of Israel; Iraq requested inquiry into Israeli aggression by the Military Commission, under the 1950 Security Pact. Establishment of information offices in Brazil, Geneva, and Argentina approved; representatives to be sent to Karachi and New Delhi by the League. Hammarskjold mission discussed.

Session: 26
Date: October, 1956
Place: Cairo
Chairman: Jordan

Summary of Activities
No firm reports. This was the period of the Suez War, following the nationalization of the Suez Canal. The League formally supported the Egyptian move in August 1956. In October, the heads of state met in Beirut and pledged support to Egypt under the terms of the 1950 Collective Security Pact in the event the UN failed to act.

Session: 27
Date: March, 1957
Place: Cairo

Chairman: Sudan

Summary of Activities

Algerian nationalist leaders appeared before the Council, received continued support of League. Council also re-affirmed support of Egypt's Suez policy (restriction of Israeli shipping) and policy governing navigation on the Gulf of Aqaba. Mission sent to Yemen, including Egyptian, Saudi, and Yemeni representatives, with reference to Anglo-Yemeni dispute over border with Aden area. Council reasserted right of Arab refugees to return to homes in Palestine; rejected proposal for resettlement.

Session: 28
Date: October, 1957
Place: Cairo
Chairman: Syria

Summary of Activities

Jordan was absent from the meeting. Arab UN representatives instructed to support Greek Cypriots in their demand for independence and self-determination. Oman Question to be referred to UN Security Council. Approval was given for a committee of experts to attend conference on International Law of the Sea, Geneva, 1958. Arab diplomatic representative in W. Germany reported on German-Israeli relations. Council pledged support and assistance to Algerian refugees. Plan for Arab economic union studied.

Session: 29-ı
Date: March, 1958
Place: Cairo
Chairman: Iraq

Summary of Activities

Funds voted to support Algerian provisional government; partition of Algeria opposed. Council recommended action in UN in support of independence for the Cameroons. Alleged Israeli border violations studied. Sheikh of Bahrein supported against Iran's claims to island. Discussions to be initiated with UN Secretary General concerning distribution of Arab staff members.

Session: 29-ii
Date: June, 1958
Place: Benghazi
Chairman: Iraq

Summary of Activities
Special session called on complaint of Lebanon against the UAR. Session adjourned without decision.

Session: 30
Date: October, 1958
Place: Cairo
Chairman: Saudi Arabia

Summary of Activities
Tunisia and Morocco admitted to League membership. Tunisia delegation walked out, after accusing UAR of dominating League for own purposes. Council voted to assess members $34,000,000 for support of provisional Algerian government. Plan for Arab Common Market studied.

Session: 31-i
Date: March, 1959
Place: Cairo
Chairman: Egypt

Summary of Activities
Council approved nominations for UN bodies; urged consolidation of Afro-Asian ties; approved sending League mission to African countries. Danger of Israeli expansion studied, with problem of immigration of E. European Jews. Protest drafted regarding Italian trade with Israel.

Plans made for coordination of Palestine policy. Refugee problems examined. Aid pledged to Oman against British. Report on the Resolutions of the Geneva Conference on Laws of the Seas approved. Plans studied for increased number of League offices in world capitals.

Session: 31-ɪɪ
Date: July, 1959
Place: Cairo
Chairman: Egypt

Summary of Activities
Iraq, Jordan, Tunisia absent. Approved recommendations of meeting of Arab experts at Sofar, Lebanon, held August 8-18. Casablanca conference agenda approved.

Session: 32-ɪ
Date: September, 1959
Place: Casablanca
Chairman: Lebanon

Summary of Activities
Tunisia and Iraq absent. Council called for international UN commission to study refugee situation in Algeria; NATO powers urged to cease support of France; diplomatic representations to be made to Afro-Asian states to urge recognition of rebel Algerian government; League voted additional $34.4 million to support Algerian government. Proposals to modernize League Charter studied. Questions of Oman and Yemen discussed. Protest of French A-bomb tests in Sahara drafted. 12-mile limit approved for Arab states. Lebanon supported for presidency of FAO. Little progress on coordinated Palestine policy.

Session: 32-ɪɪ
Date: February, 1960
Place: Cairo
Chairman: Lebanon

Summary of Activities
Tunisia and Iraq still absent. Major issues were Syrian-Israeli border clashes, proposed diversion of Jordan River by Israel. Provisional Algerian Government authorized to send representatives to all League conferences; previously restricted to observer at Council meetings. Conflict loomed between Jordan and UAR on project of autonomous Palestinian state. Iraq and Tunisia threatened with expulsion for boycotting League. A commission of 5 experts, presided over by Secretary General, was established to develop program of unified action on Palestine. Most business postponed.

Session: 33
Date: March, 1960
Place: Cairo
Chairman: Libya

Summary of Activities
Council debated organization of proposed Palestine government. French A-bomb tests in Sahara denounced; sanctions threatened against France. Situation in southern Yemen, on border of British protectorates, studied. Council called for Arab volunteers to fight in Algeria. Arab cultural program examined.

Session: 34-I
Date: September, 1960
Place: Shtura, Lebanon
Chairman: Yemen

Summary of Activities
Iraq rejoined Council; Tunisia still absent because of dispute with the UAR. Council approved project to help Arab volunteers join Algerian forces; efforts in General Assembly to end Algerian war to be renewed. NATO nations urged to cease support of French in Algeria. Arab

League members urged to call off press and radio campaigns, work for greater Arab solidarity, Economic Council resolution supporting stand of Arab government on unannounced crude oil price reductions approved. Validity of *laissez passer* for refugees extended 2 years. Lebanon supported as candidate to Human Rights Commission. Iraq nominated to International Atomic Energy Agency executive board. Draft agreement between League and Arab Postal Union approved.

Session: 34-ɪɪ
Date: February, 1961
Place: Baghdad
Chairman: Yemen

Summary of Activities
Tunisia rejoined Council; all Arab League members present for first time since 1958. Secret plan for Arab League action to prevent Israel from diverting Jordan River waters to Negev adopted; reported policy of forceful action regarded as drastic reversal of former League policy. Arab efforts to counter Israeli influence in Africa to be strengthened; Israel's relations with Iran and Cyprus to be reviewed in light of joint Arab interests. Official League delegation to President Kennedy will explain Arab policy. Pressures in and out of the UN to be increased for a settlement in Algeria; Arab states to oppose French atomic tests and French nuclear science aid to Israel. In the United Nations, Mongi Slim (Tunisia) to be endorsed as president, 16th UNGA; questions of Oman and Palestine refugees to be raised at 15th UNGA; Arab states to continue to oppose UN membership for Mauretania. Nomination of Dr. Mustafa Kamil Yasin to UN International Law Committee approved; Fuad Amoun (Lebanon) to be supported for judgeship in World Court. Iraq and Tunisia supported for seats on WHO Executive Council; joint Arab League-UNESCO training center for senior

education officials approved for Beirut. Proposed amendments to Arab League Charter discussed without action.

Session: 35
Date: March, 1961
Place: Cairo
Chairman: Morocco

Summary of Activities
All members represented; Algerian delegation attended. Discussion centered on Algeria, diversion of Jordan waters, Israeli activities in Africa, relations between Cyprus and Israel, opposition to UN membership for Mauretania. Council approved program and budget for 3rd Arab Games, Casablanca; proposal for an Arab encyclopedia; a proposed Arab League-sponsored conference on narcotics. Decisions made on nomination of Arab officers in UN organs and committees; Morocco supported for executive body of IAEA.

Session: 35-Extra
Date: July, 1961
Place: Cairo
Chairman: Morocco

Summary of Activities
Special meeting to consider Iraq's threat to annex Kuwait. Kuwait admitted to membership, July 20, by majority vote; Iraq walked out of Council in protest. League Council approved three point resolution on Kuwait crisis: (1) Kuwait to requested withdrawal of British troops, (2) Arab League to support Kuwait for membership in the United Nations, (3) Arab League to take necessary steps to safeguard Kuwait's independence. (Kuwait also adhered to Collective Security Pact and League economic schemes.)

Session: 36-ɪ
Date: September, 1961

Place: Cairo
Chairman: Jordan

Summary of Activities
Iraq absent; meeting held at ambassadorial level. Council approved secret plan to counter "Zionist aggressive activities," called for closer ties with Africa to counter Israeli activities there, and referred economic problems to forthcoming meeting of the Economic Council. Council recommended member states review relations with the Union of South Africa because of its racist policies. Supported UAR for post in UN Administrative Tribunal, Lebanon for re-election to FAO executive council, Lebanon for executive council of ICAO. Approved recommendations of 4th session of Permanent Information Committee. Supported formation of Arab Federation of War Veterans (proposed by Secretariat) and encouraged establishment of national veterans' organizations.

Session: 36-Extra
Date: October, 1961
Place: New York
Chairman: Jordan

Summary of Activities
Council met at foreign ministers' level in New York during UNGA session to unify policy on the Palestine question. No report available.

Session: 36-Extra
Date: October, 1961
Place: Cairo
Chairman: Jordan

Summary of Activities
Council met to consider Syria's withdrawal from the United Arab Republic and certain UAR allegations of bad faith and fraudulent activities by Syria. Syria read-

mitted to Arab League membership on October 29, 1961. League Council rejected UAR note and assigned Secretary General Hassouna to mediate outstanding problems between Egypt and Syria.

Session: 36-ɪɪ
Date: February, 1962
Place: Cairo
Chairman: Jordan

Summary of Activities
Iraq absent. Council met at ambassadorial level to discuss Israel's plans regarding Jordan River waters; emergency session of Joint Defense Council to be called.

Session: 37-ɪ
Date: March-April, 1962
Place: Riyadh
Chairman: Tunisia

Summary of Activities
Iraq and Kuwait absent; Oman and Algeria represented. Major attention given to Jordan River diversion, problems along Arab-Israeli frontiers, Israel's bid to join the European Community, Arab ties with Africa. Arab League aid to Algeria confirmed, efforts to speed final settlement to be increased. Oman question to be raised at next session of the UN General Assembly. Arab League offices approved for Jerusalem and Lagos. Morocco approved for seat in Security Council, UAR and Lebanon for reelection to executive council of ICAO, Tunisia for reelection to WHO executive council, Sudan to executive committee of UNICEF, Jordan for seat on UN Budget and Administrative Affairs Consultative Committee.

Session: 37-Extra
Date: June, 1962
Place: Cairo
Chairman: Tunisia

Summary of Activities
Emergency session of Arab League Council promised Algerian Provisional Government "continuous and unlimited support."

Session: 37-Extra
Date: August, 1962
Place: Cairo
Chairman: Tunisia

Summary of Activities
Iraq absent. Algeria admitted to membership on August 16, 1962.

Session: 37-Extra
Date: August, 1962
Place: Shtura (Lebanon)
Chairman: Tunisia

Summary of Activities
Iraq absent. Council convened to hear Syria's complaint of UAR meddling in its internal affairs. UAR delegation walkout of Council, August 28, following Syria's accusation that UAR worked covertly with the United States to liquidate the Palestine refugee problem; UAR threatened to withdraw from Arab League. Council session adjourned on August 31, since UAR not present to defend itself, but session to remain legally open. (NOTE: In 1963, the League decided to remove the minutes of the Shtura meeting from its official records.)

Session: 38-I
Date: September, 1962
Place: Cairo
Chairman: Algeria

Summary of Activities
Iraq and UAR absent. Council meeting at ambassadorial

level confirmed appointment of Abdel Khalek Hassouna to a third five-year term as Secretary General, September 15. Agenda items included question of the Palestine issue at the UNGA, nominations for UN posts, approval of recommendations of Israeli boycott conference. Session to remain open, reconvening in New York during the General Assembly session.

Session: 38-II
Date: March, 1963
Place: Cairo
Chairman: Algeria

Summary of Activities
UAR ended boycott of League; new governments in Syria and Iraq announced support of League; Jordan absent. Council denounced Israeli campaign against German scientists in the UAR and (1) called upon member states and Secretary General to make diplomatic representations to West German government, (2) called for special meeting of Joint Defense Council to deal with subject. Syria withdrew its complaint against the UAR, and Council resolved to expunge from its official records all mention of the Shtura session of August 1962. Council reaffirmed support of Yemeni republicans, approved nomination of permanent Yemeni and UAR delegates to League Council. French nuclear tests in Algeria protested. League financial situation discussed.

Session: 39
Date: April, 1963
Place: Cairo
Chairman: Sudan

Summary of Activities
Jordan rejoined League Council and session attended by representatives of all member states for first time in several years. Meetings overshadowed by excitement over

Arab unity talks (Iraq, Syria, UAR, Algeria). Major effort devoted to improving financial status of League, but no public report available.

Session: 40
Date: September, 1963
Place: Cairo
Chairman: Iraq

Summary of Activities
Council urged all member states to work for "Arab solidarity"; it decided Palestine was a problem for the Palestinians, and confirmed Ahmed Shukairi (former League Assistant Secretary) as Palestine's delegate to the Council. Resolutions of Boycott Conference approved. Support for Yemeni republican regime reaffirmed, "British aggression in occupied South Yemen" (Aden protectorate) denounced (copy of resolution passed to the UN Secretary General); support for Imamate of Oman reaffirmed. Council called for expanded information program; it approved cooperation between the Arab League and the Federation of Arab Veterans. Council adopted position on 18th UNGA session, approved Iraq as a candidate for the vacant seat in ECOSOC, agreed to refer the question of support for non-Arab candidates to UN posts to the permanent delegations in New York. UAR supported for election to IAEA executive; support of UNESCO's drive to salvage Abu Simbal and other Nubian monuments confirmed.

Session: 40-Extra
Date: January, 1964
Place: Cairo
Chairman: Iraq

Summary of Activities
League Council convened at request of President Nasser as "Arab summit meeting," most heads of states being in

attendance. Emphasis was on League plans to counter Israel's plans to divert Jordan River water to the Negev. The Council approved a technical plan calling for "counter diversion" of Jordan River headwaters, a permanently constituted Joint Arab Command, and a high-level coordinating committee to supervise the plan. Special funds were established for defense and technical activities, but use of force except in self-defense was rejected. The atmosphere of Arab brotherhood was applauded, and a decision was made to amend the League Charter to make the "summit conference" an annual affair. The proposal for an independent "Palestine entity" was approved. The Council also reaffirmed its faith in the United Nations, in the peaceful settlement of disputes under the UN Charter, and in non-alignment and co-existence. Particular efforts were to be made in 1964 for a positive Arab contribution to the UN-sponsored development and trade conference.

Session: 40-ɪɪ
Date: March, 1964
Place: Cairo
Chairman: Iraq

Summary of Activities
Ambassadorial level meeting included on its agenda discussion of the recommendations of the Palestine offices conference, Israel's claims to unclaimed deposits in Swiss banks, a UAR proposal that Arab ambassadors in key capitals meet periodically, and a report on the boycott of Israel. Sessions supported nomination of UAR Minister of Economy to be chairman of the UN Conference in Trade and Development; Tunisia for election to Executive Committee of the Universal Postal Union; UAR to UN Social Committee.

Session: 41-1
Date: March, 1964
Place: Cairo
Chairman: Saudi Arabia

Summary of Activities
Session opened to hear charges against British attack on Harib (Yemen) and remained open to deal with other facets of the Yemeni-British conflict. Declared British aggression against Yemen is aggression against all Arab states; appealed to Red Cross for intervention; asked member states to review relations with UK; and demanded liquidation of British bases in Arab world. Also discussed establishment of ARESCO, location of boycott offices in Geneva and Bahrain, and assistance to the Yemeni postal service. Approved a special mission to investigate conditions in the Persian Gulf sheikhdoms. Approved establishment of a regional housing center in Cairo. Supported Sudan's nominee for president of UNGA; UAR nominee for chairman of UNGA Legal Committee; Algeria for Vice President of WHO conference.

Session: 41-Extra
Date: May, 1964
Place: Cairo
Chairman: Saudi Arabia

Summary of Activities
Extraordinary closed meeting met at level of permanent delegates in Cairo to discuss British military operations in the Arab South. Demanded UK cease "massacres," resolved to extend all possible aid for the liberation of the "occupied Yemeni South" and to enlist support of the Afro-Asian nations, and proposed Red Cross mission investigate British treatment of prisoners. Other topics on agenda included apportionment of League budget, decisions of the Arab Ministers of Information conference,

the Economic Union Agreement, and the boycott of the 18th Olympic Games in behalf of Indonesia.

Session: 41-X
Date: September, 1964
Place: Alexandria, UAR
Chairman: Saudi Arabia

Summary of Activities
The second Arab Summit convened in secret session at the heads of state level except for King Hassan of Morocco; President-Elect Charles Helou substituted for Lebanon's President Shihab. Sessions were devoted largely to discussions of secret reports by the Secretary General (on the proposals to divert Jordan River headwaters) and by the Chief of Staff of the Joint Arab Command. Press reports commented on extended debates over the jurisdiction of the JAC, plans to station foreign troops in League member countries, and the functions of the Joint Defense Council. All remaining nonsignatory Arab states (Algeria, Tunisia, Libya, and Sudan) adhered to the 1950 Collective Security Pact.

The final communiqué announced a decision to hold annual Arab summit meetings: the next was scheduled for Casablanca, September 1965. Meanwhile, the "follow up" committee was to meet every four months at the Prime Ministers' level to supervise the implementation of key "summit" decisions. The session also approved the establishment of the Palestine Liberation Army (16,000 to 30,000 troops) in the Sinai Peninsula under the command of the Joint Arab Command, which would also provide logistic and administrative support. Other resolutions supported the "Arab struggle" in Aden and the Arab South; denounced foreign intervention in the Congo; deplored the tendency for "imperialists" to settle international disputes by force; urged the liquidation of foreign military bases in Aden and Cyprus; endorsed the establishment of the Arab Court of Justice; and recommended the establishment of a Joint Arab Atomic Energy Council devoted to peaceful uses of the atom.

Session: 41-II
Date: September, 1964
Place: Cairo
Chairman: Saudi Arabia

Summary of Activities
Meeting at the ambassadorial level, the League Council heard Secretary General Hassouna read a report on the recent Arab summit meeting, administered the oath of office to the newly appointed Military Assistant Secretary General, Mohammed Fawzi (chief of staff of the UAR armed forces), and listened to a speech by the retiring chairman before it declared itself closed. (The opening session of the 42nd League Council was inaugurated immediately thereafter by having the Saudi Arabia chairman of the 41st League Council hand over the chair to the Syrian chairman of the 42nd League Council.)

Session: 42-I
Date: September, 1964
Place: Cairo
Chairman: Syria

Summary of Activities
The regular session of the League Council, at the ambassadorial level, was somewhat overshadowed by the earlier Arab summit meeting and by the nonaligned conference scheduled for the following week. The council ratified the recommendations of the 20th Arab Boycott Conference and the resolutions of the Arab delegates of the Arab-Israeli mixed armistice commissions, discussed the Palestine Liberation Organization, moved to support

the "national liberation movement" in the Arab South, and considered a draft of an Arab civil aviation agreement (including the establishment of an Arab Civil Aviation Council in Cairo).

The Council established a special committee on the Arab South (members: Saudi Arabia, Yemen, the UAR, and Tunisia) to study the "Arab struggle" in that area. Other matters reported discussed during the session included: the Arab Court of Justice (the Council split on this question); "Arab-African solidarity"; and support for the resolutions of the African summit meetings.

The United Nations figured prominently in the League sessions: the Council supported the USSR "in practicing its rights at the United Nations" (a reference to non-payment of special assessments for UNEF and other peacekeeping operations), approved a proposed UN regional training center for the Arab states, discussed the agenda for the forthcoming UN General Assembly, and announced nominations to UN posts (Sudan for the presidency of the UN General Assembly, Kuwait and Tunisia for the Financial and Administrative Committee, Jordan for the Security Council, the UAR for the Legal Committee, and Iraq for UNESCO).

SELECTED BIBLIOGRAPHY AND INDEX

SELECTED BIBLIOGRAPHY

I. BIBLIOGRAPHICAL NOTE

A large body of literature has accumulated on regionalism since 1945, but it is diffuse and limited, in most instances, to the scholarly journals. Some of the more pertinent material is cited in the works below, but much of the rest is in danger of being superseded by the school stemming from such students of international organization as Kaplan.

As for the Arab League, its literature is also largely that of the scholarly journals and other periodicals, many of which are not regularly perused by Americans. Because the literature is so diffuse, recourse has been necessary to chronologies in such journals as *Oriente Moderno* (Rome), *The Middle East Journal, Middle Eastern Affairs, International Organization,* and *Middle East Forum.* Reports of the activities of the Arab League Council and other Arab League organs are generally available in these chronologies.

League Council resolutions, however, are more difficult to locate. For the English reader, the most valuable source is the study by the Egyptian Society of International Law which contains summaries (or texts) of important League Council resolutions to 1954. A few more are available in Khalil's excellent collection of Arab documentary materials. For the Arabic reader, League Council resolutions between 1945 and 1957 have been collected and published by the Arab League Secretariat in the volume *Majma'at Qararat Majlis Jami'at ad-Duwal al-Arabiyya* (Collection of the Resolutions of the Council of the League of Arab States, June 4, 1945-Nov. 17, 1957).

II. DOCUMENTS

League of Arab States. *L'Activité de la Ligue des Etats Arabes.* Geneva: Centre d'information arabe, 1950.

———. *Aperçu General de l'Activité Culturelle de la Ligue des Etats Arabes, 1946-56,* Cairo: no date.

———. *The Arab Financial Institution for Economic Development* (Document Collection No. 3). New York: 1958.

——. *A Brief Report on the Work of the Cultural Department of the League of Arab States during the Period from 1953-58.* Cairo: no date.

——. *The Cultural Activities of the Arab League.* Cairo: 1948.

——. *The First Asian-African Conference Held at Bandung, April 18-24, 1955: Report submitted by Mohamed Abdel Khalek Hassouna, Secretary-General of the League of Arab States, to the League Council.* Cairo: Imprimerie Misr SAE, 1955.

——. *The League of Arab States: Its Origins, Purposes, Structure, and Activities.* Cairo: 1960.

——. *Message du Secretaire General de la Ligue des Etats Arabes à l'occasion du 15 me anniversaire de la Ligue, le 22, Mar. 1960.* Geneva: Centre d'information arabe, 1960.

——. *Treaty Series.* Cairo: no date.

United Nations. *United Nations Conference on International Organization.* Vol. XII. New York: 1945.

——. *Economic Developments in the Middle East: 1959-1961.* New York: 1962.

——. *Geographical Distribution of the Staff of the Secretariat: Report of the Secretary General to the Fifth Committee.* Document A/C.5/987, 11 October 1963. New York: 1963.

——. *Repertory of Practice of the United Nations Organs.* Vol. II. New York: 1955.

——. *United Nations at Work: Survey of the Activities of United Nations and UN Specialized Agencies Represented in the United Arab Republic.* Cairo: UN Information Center, October 1960.

——. *United Nations Seminar for the Arab States on Social Welfare Administration and Training.* Document LS/13 (Eng.), Revised. (Notes on Social Affairs Department of the Arab League presented to the Seminar, Denmark, August 15-September 15, 1960).

——. *United Nations Yearbook, 1961.* New York: 1963.

U.S. Department of State. *The United Nations' Conference on International Organization: Selected Documents.* Washington: U.S. Government Printing Office, 1946.

III. Books

Almond, Gabriel A., and Coleman, James S. (eds.). *The Politics of the Developing Areas*. Princeton, N. J.: Princeton University Press, 1960.

Beling, Willard A. *Pan-Arabism and Labor*. Cambridge, Mass.: Harvard University Press, 1961.

Campbell, John C. *Defense of the Middle East*. New York: Harper and Brothers, 1960.

Claude, Inis L. *Swords into Plowshares*. New York: Random House, 1960.

Dib, G. Moussa. *The Arab Bloc in the United Nations*. Amsterdam: Djambatan, 1956.

Egyptian Society of International Law. *Egypt and the United Nations*. New York: Manhattan Publishing Co., 1957.

Foda, Ezzeldin. *The Projected Arab Court of Justice*. The Hague: Martinus Nijhoff, 1957.

Ghali, Kamal. *Mithaq Jāmi'at al-Duwal al-'Arabīya Dirāsah Tahlīlīyah Muqārinah fī al-Qānūn al-Duwalī* (The Charter of the Arab League: A Comparative Study in International Law). Cairo: Dār al-Fikr al-'Arabi, 1948.

Goodrich, Leland M., and Hambro, Edvard. *The Charter of the United Nations: Commentary and Documents*. 2d edn. Boston: World Peace Foundation, 1949.

Hovet, Thomas, Jr. *Bloc Politics in the United Nations*. Cambridge, Mass.: Harvard University Press, 1960.

Hull, Cordell. *Memoirs*. Vol. II. New York: Macmillan Co., 1948.

Institute on World Organization. *Regionalism and World Organization: Postwar Aspects of Europe's Global Relationships*. Washington: American Council on Public Affairs, 1944.

Izzedin, Nejla. *The Arab World: Past, Present, Future*. Chicago: Henry Regnery Co., 1953.

Kaplan, Morton. *System and Process in International Politics*. New York: Wiley and Sons, 1957.

Kelsen, Hans. *The Law of the United Nations*. New York: Frederick A. Praeger, 1951.

Khalil, Muhammad. *The Arab States and the Arab League:*

A Documentary Record. Vol. ii. Beirut: Khayat's, 1962.

el-Khatib, Muhammad Fathallah. *The Status of the League of Arab States in the International Community.* New York: Arab Information Office, 1958.

Kirk, George. *The Middle East in the War: Survey of International Affairs, 1939-45.* London: Oxford University Press, 1954.

Mūsa, Ahmad. *Mithāq Jāmi'at al-Duwal al-'Arabīya: Bayān wa Ta'līq* (The Charter of the League of Arab States: Explanation and Commentary). Cairo: Matba'at Misr, 1948.

Panikkar, K. M., *et al. Regionalism and Security.* London: Oxford University Press, 1948.

Rostow, W. W. *The Stages of Economic Growth.* Cambridge: Cambridge University Press, 1960.

Sanson-Teran, José. *Universalismo y Regionalismo en la Sociedad Interstatal Contemporanea.* Barcelona: Editorial Hispano Europea, 1960.

Sayegh, Fayez A. *Arab Unity: Hope and Fulfillment.* New York: Devin-Adair, 1958.

Sharp, Walter R. *Field Administration in the United Nations' System.* London: Stevens and Sons, Ltd., 1961.

Stone, Julius. *Legal Control of International Conflict.* Revised edn. New York: Rinehart and Co., 1959.

Vandenberg, Arthur H., Jr. *The Private Papers of Senator Vandenberg.* Boston: Houghton Mifflin and Co., 1952.

Welles, Sumner. *The Time for Decision.* New York: Harper and Brothers, 1944.

IV. ARTICLES

Badr, Mohammed Abdel Aziz. "La Ligue des Etats Arabes," *Oriente Moderno* [Rome], xxxii (May-June 1952), 109-119.

Beber, G. "Regional Organizations: A United Nations Problem," *American Journal of International Law,* xlix (1955), 166-184.

Bell, Margaret. "Bloc Voting in the General Assembly," *International Organization,* v (February 1951), 3-31.

Binder, Leonard. "The Middle East as a Subordinate International System," *World Politics,* x (April 1958), 408-429.

Brecht, Arnold. "Limited Purpose Federations," *Social Research*, x (February 1943), 135-152.

Burns, Norman. "Planning Economic Development in the Arab World," *Department of State Bulletin*, xxxix (September 22, 1958).

Bustani, Emile. "The Arab World and Britain," *International Affairs*, xxxv (October 1959), 427-437.

———. "Sharing Oil Profits," *Middle East Forum*, xxxiii (January 1958), 9-13.

Butros-Ghali, B. Y. "The Arab League," *International Conciliation*, 498 (May 1954), 387-448.

Cattan, Selim. "La Lega Araba nel suo primo quinquennio," *Oriente Moderno* [Rome], xxx (July-September 1950), 105-109.

Chejne, Anwar. "Egyptian Attitudes Toward Pan Arabism," *Middle East Journal*, xi (1957), 253-268.

Cleland, Wendell. "The League of Arab States After Fifteen Years," *World Affairs* [Washington], cxxii (Summer 1960), 49-52.

Dajani, Burhan. "The Arab Economic Council," *Middle East Forum*, xxxiv (March 1959), 11.

———. "Deadlock in Economic Union," *Middle East Forum*, xxxvi (July-Aug.-Sept. 1961), 11,59.

Deighton, H. S. "The Arab Middle East and the Modern World," *International Affairs*, xxii (October 1946), 511-520.

"Egyptian—Syrian Mutual Defense Pact" (text), *Middle East Journal*, x (Winter 1956), 77-79.

"First Arab Petroleum Congress," *The Arab World*, v (May-June 1959), 4-7.

"Founding of the Arab Development Bank," *Lands East*, iv (January 1959), 4-6.

Haas, Ernst B. "The Challenge of Regionalism," *International Organization*, xii (1958), 440-458.

———. "International Integration: The European and the Universal Process," *International Organization*, xv (1961), 366-392.

———. "Regional Integration and National Policy," *International Conciliation*, 513 (May 1957), 381, 442.

Hall, Harvey P. "The Arab League States," *Current History*, xxix (August 1955), 91-102.

Hourani, Cecil. "The Arab League in Perspective," *Middle East Journal*, i (1947), 125-36.

Howard, H. N. "The Arab-Asian States in the United Nations," *Middle East Journal*, vii (1953), 279-292.

———. "Middle East Regional Organization: Problems and Prospects," *Proceedings of the Academy of Political Science*, xxiv (January 1952), 541-551.

Ireland, Phillip. "The Pact of the League of Arab States," *American Journal of International Law*, xxxix (October 1945), 797-800.

Khadduri, Majid. "The Arab League as a Regional Arrangement," *American Journal of International Law*, xl (1946), 756-777.

———. "The Problem of Regional Security in the Middle East," *Middle East Journal*, xi (1957), 12-22.

———. "Toward Arab Union: The League of Arab States," *American Political Science Review*, xl (February 1946), 90-100.

Lijphart, Arend. "The Analysis of Bloc Voting in the General Assembly: A Critique and a Proposal," *American Political Science Review*, lvii (December 1963), 902-917.

Little, T. R. "The Arab League: A Reassessment," *Middle East Journal*, x (Spring 1956), 138-150.

"Middle East Defense Command" (text), *Middle Eastern Affairs*, ii (November 1951), 267-368.

Mustapha, Hassan. "Arab Military Cooperation," *Middle East Forum*, xxxvii (1961), 21-23.

"Report of the Resolutions of the Thirty-Second Session of the Arab League Council," *Middle Eastern Affairs*, xi (1960), 123-124.

Schwadran, Benjamin. "The Kuwait Incident," *Middle Eastern Affairs*, xiii, Nos. 1 & 2 (January-February 1962), 2-13, 43-53.

Seabury, Paul. "The League of Arab States; Debacle of a Regional Organization," *International Organization*, iii (November 1949), 633-642.

Sharp, Walter. "The United Nations System in Egypt," *International Organization*, x (1956), 235-260.

"Sixth Committee Endorses Invitation to Arab League," *United Nations Bulletin*, ix (November 1, 1950), 487.

Spain, James W. "Middle East Defense: A New Approach," *Middle East Journal*, viii (Summer 1954), 251-266.

"Statement by Arab League Heads," *Middle Eastern Affairs*, viii (1957), 60-61.

"Status of the League of Arab States in the United Nations," *Arab World*, iv (April 1949), 7-9.

Sweetser, Arthur. "The Non-Political Achievements of the League," *Foreign Affairs*, xix (October 1940), 179-192.

Van Kleffans, E. N. "Regionalism and Political Pacts," *American Journal of International Law*, xliii (October 1949), 666-677.

IV.   PERIODICALS AND NEWSPAPERS

Arab News and Views [Arab Information Office, New York], 1958-1964.

The Arab World [Arab Information Office, New York], 1958-1964.

International Organization, 1947-1964.

Middle Eastern Affairs, 1950-1963.

Middle East Forum [Beirut, Lebanon], 1958-1964.

Middle East Journal, 1947-1964.

Oriente Moderno [Rome], 1945-1962.

United Nations Bulletin, 1946-1954.

United Nations Review, 1954-1961.

Washington Post, 1958-1964.

V.   OTHER

"Arab League: A Step in the Fulfillment of the Ideals of Arab Nationalism," address by H. E. Ambassador Abdel Khalek Hassouna, October 25, 1960. (Mimeo.)

"Arab Nationalism: The Drive toward Political and Economic Freedom," address by Abdel Khalek Hassouna, November 17, 1959. (Mimeo.)

BIBLIOGRAPHY

"Excerpts from the Press Conference held by H. E. Ambassador Abdel Khalek Hassouna, Secretary-General of the League of Arab States at the end of the Summit Meeting of the Arab States in Cairo, January 18, 1964." (Mimeo. memorandum released by Arab Information Center, New York.)